Strategic Partnering

Other Books by A. David Silver

The Radical New Road to Wealth

Upfront Financing, Revised Edition

Who's Who in Venture Capital, 3/e

Successful Entrepreneurship

Venture Capital

When the Bottom Drops

The Business Bible of Survival

The Middle-Market Leveraged Financing Directory

The Middle-Market Business Acquisition Directory

The Bankruptcy, Workout and Turnaround Market

The Turnaround Survival Guide

Strategic Partnering

A. David Silver

McGraw-Hill, Inc.
New York San Francisco Washington, D.C. Auckland Bogotá
Caracas Lisbon London Madrid Mexico City Milan
Montreal New Delhi San Juan Singapore
Sydney Tokyo Toronto

STRATEGIC PARTNERING
International Editions 1993

Exclusive rights by McGraw-Hill Book Co. - Singapore for manufacture and export. This book cannot be re-exported from the country to which it is consigned by McGraw-Hill.

Copyright © 1993 by McGraw-Hill, Inc. All rights reserved. Except as permitted under the United States Copyright Act of 1976, no part of this publication may be reproduced or distributed in any form or by any means, or stored in a data base or retrieval system, without the prior written permission of the publisher.

2 3 4 5 6 7 8 9 0 KHL UPE 9 8 7 6 5 4

The sponsoring editor for this book was Caroline Carney, the editing supervisor was Fred Dahl, and the production supervisor was Pamela A. Pelton. It was set in Baskerville by Inkwell Publishing Services.

Library of Congress Cataloging-in-Publication Data

Silver, A. David (Aaron David), date.
    Strategic partnering / A. David Silver.
       p.   cm.
    ISBN 0-07-057612-2
    1. Strategic alliances (Business) - United States.   2. Venture capital - United States.   3. Capitalists and financiers - United States - Directories.   4. Corporations - United States - Directories.
    I. Title.
HD69.S8S56   1993   93-16621
658'.044-dc20   CIP

When ordering this title, use ISBN 0-07-113680-0

This publication is designed to provide accurate and authoritative information in regard to the subject matter covered. It is sold with the understanding that the publisher is not engaged in rendering legal, accounting, or other professional service. If legal advice or other expert assistance is required, the services of a competent professional person should be sought.
    —From a declaration of principles jointly adopted by a committee of the American Bar Association and a committee of publishers

---

Printed in Singapore

Steve Mariotti
Founder, National Foundation for Teaching
Entrepreneurship to Handicapped and
Disadvantaged Youth, Inc.

Contents

Preface xi

Introduction 1

Who Are These Strategic Partners? 2
Multiple Strategic Alliances 3
Associational Thinking 4
The Reasons for Strategic Partnering 6
Positioning Your Company 7
More Capital; Less Give-Up 8

1. The Elements of a Strategic Alliance 13

Cooperation 13
Points of Alliance 14
Cooperation at the Research and Development Stage 15
   Who Is the Entrepreneur? 16
   The Effect of the Entrepreneur's Emotional Background 21
   A Typical Picture of Personal Entrepreneurial Guilt 25
   The Entrepreneur and His Spouse 28
   The Entrepreneurial Approach to Problem Solving 29
The Production Stage 34
   Production-Oriented Strategic Alliances 36
   Just Ask 36

Marketing-Oriented Strategic Alliances 51
    Virgin Airlines 52
    ChemTrak States Its Mission 53
Strategic Alliances at the Growth Stage 57
Strategic Alliances at the Exit Stage 58

2. Why Corporations Make Venture Capital Investments   59

1. To Incubate and Reduce the Cost of Acquisitions 59
2. Exposure to Possible New Markets 60
3. To Add New Products to Existing Distribution Channels 61
4. A Less Expensive Form of Research and Development 62
5. To Expose Middle Management to Entrepreneurship 62
6. Training for Junior Management 63
7. Utilize Excess Plant Space, Time, and People 64
8. To Mesh the Activities of Several Departments 66
9. To Generate Capital Gains 67
10. Investigative: Develop Antennae for New Technologies 68
11. Income Generating 69
12. Excellent Group Therapy for Senior Management 69
13. Good Public Relations 70
14. The Competition May Be Doing It 71
15. The "ITEK" Reason 72
16. Encourage New Company Formation in the Community 74
Summary 74

3. Matching Your Company to the Most Likely Strategic Partners   75

The DEJ Factor Test 76
    Super DEJs 76
    Majority DEJs 77
    The "Unlikely" Ventures 77
    The DEJ Factors Up Close 78
    Summary 79
Solution Delivery Methods 80
1. Facilities Management 82
2. Franchising 82
3. Party Plan 83
4. The Consumer Products Start-Up 84
5. Celebrity-Endorsed Consumer Products 85

Contents

    6. High-Technology Start-Up   89
    7. The Cookie Cutter   91
    8. Prepaid Subscription Method   92
    9. Capital Equipment   93
  10. Highway Tollgate   96
        Lessons from a Successful Licensor   97
  11. Newsletter/Seminar Launch   98
  12. Franchise on OPA   100

4. Writing a Business Plan for the Strategic Investor   103

The Five Questions of Financial Investors   103
The Launch Plan   106
    1. Formulate the Plan   107
    2. Develop the Solution to the Problem   107
    3. Select the Solution Delivery Method   108
    4. Create a PERT Chart   108
    5. Write a Business Plan   109
    6. Create and Protect Your Prototype   115
    7. Beta-Test Your Solution   115
    8. Debug the Solution and Modify Your Business Plan   116
    9. Begin Production in Small Volumes   117
  10. Hire a Corporate Achiever   117
  11. Raise the Necessary Capital from a Strategic Partner   118
  12. Begin Full Production and Marketing   118

5. Closing the Strategic Partner   121

Six Steps to a Successful Closing   121
    Step 1: Find the DEP Factor   122
    Step 2: Collect Data on Your Potential Strategic Partner   124
    Step 3: Find the Gatekeepers and Go Around Them   126
    Step 4: Leverage Others to Help Close   129
    Step 5: Just Ask   130
    Step 6: Use a Third-Party Endorsement   131

Appendix A. Sample of Confidential Disclosure Agreement   133

Appendix B. Sample Licensing Agreement   137

Appendix C. Directory of Strategic Partners   141

Index   197

Preface

There have been more than 600 strategic alliances in the United States' entrepreneurial community in the past five years, and the number will double in the next two years because of their high rate of success. These alliances generally involve an entrepreneurial company's licensing a large corporation (in the same or in a related field) the right to make, use, and sell an innovative product through its established marketing channels in a proscribed geographic region or in predetermined vertical markets.

If that were all there was to it, these alliances would be nothing more than licensing agreements. (Yawn.) But the entrepreneurial companies are demanding—and getting—venture capital investments concomitant with signing the licensing agreements. Moreover, the venture capital investments are being made at eye-popping valuations—on the order of $1 million for ownership of 10 percent, or less, of the entrepreneurial company's common stock.

From the corporation's point of view, the reasons for the corporate venture capital investment are as follows:

1. We want you to be financially sound so that you can focus on new product development and upgrades.
2. We appreciate that you are able to innovate new and useful products, and bring them to market more efficiently, less expensively, and faster than we can by an order of magnitude.

3. We want to be kept informed, just as any stockholder is entitled to, about your financial health, budgets, plans—and if any of our competitors have gotten their noses under your tent.
4. We do not want you talking to any of our competitors about your innovative products or your plans. We want your complete attentiveness.
5. We may want to acquire you some day, and, by paying a little bit for some of your stock today, we could lower our overall acquisition price later on.

The corporate venture capital investment is separate and apart from *payments* made by the large corporation to the entrepreneurial company under the terms of the licensing agreement. Note the emphasis on the word *payments*. If you are receiving only one form of payment from the licensee, you may be leaving some money on the table.

From the point of view of the entrepreneurial company, some key elements of the licensing agreement are the following:

1. Proscribe the geographic market or vertical industry in which the licensee can sell the product.
2. Is the license to make, use, and sell, or just to sell (with the entrepreneurial company keeping the right to make the product and sell it to the licensee)? Try to hold onto the right to produce, and to sell the product to the licensee for an additional cash flow channel.
3. Set a precise time period for the term of the license, such as five years.
4. Set exact minimum annual royalties.
5. Demand and receive a right to audit the licensee's books and records to make sure the royalties paid to you are accurate.
6. Demand an up-front payment equal to one-half of the licensee's estimated first-year royalty payments to the entrepreneurial company. The logic for this is that it is awfully expensive to audit the licensee. So, to avoid disputes at the back-end, you need a show of good faith up-front.
7. Set precise minimum sales targets on which royalties are based, and have the licensee agree to pay the entrepreneurial company

the minimum each year (or half-year or quarter-year), whether the licensee actually makes the sales or not.

8. Clearly delineate events of default. Set these out in writing, and take back the license if the licensee defaults.

9. As consideration, the entrepreneurial company may have to give a right of first refusal to the licensee on any and all new or related products, share related R&D data, and agree to other restrictions on freedom of movement. You may be able to charge for some of these add-ons, especially if they restrict your freedom to deal with others.

If large corporations could innovate with the speed and efficiency, and pinpoint their markets' needs, as well as entrepreneurial companies, there would be no need for their entering into strategic alliances. But they cannot bring new products to market as well as entrepreneurial companies can. On the other hand, entrepreneurial companies need marketing channels, computer facilities, production capabilities, foreign markets, laboratories, warehouse space, and capital. Large corporations have all these facilities. The innovation arena is ripe for *cooperation.*

Whereas large corporations used to ignore the activities of entrepreneurial companies, they now pay up for rights to get into the sandbox with them. There is a brand new ball game, and it is called the *entrepreneurial company wins.* For example, Microsoft's market value now exceeds IBM's. Think about that for a moment. It was only a dozen years ago that a start-up company called Microsoft licensed IBM its operating systems. Sure, there's a time to compete with the big guys. But the new game stresses *cooperation.*

Want to play ball? You've got to know how the game is played. I think that *Strategic Partnering* will bring you up to speed quickly.

That is why I wrote the book.

A. David Silver
February, 1993

Introduction

When R. Douglas Kahn, president of Interactive Images, Inc., a small developer of graphical image interfaces, told his board that he planned to forge a strategic alliance with IBM Corp., his directors told him he was crazy. "They said, 'Don't waste your time. You'll spend three or four years thinking you've got something going, and you won't,'" Kahn recalls.* But he persisted. Six months later, IBM invested $15 million for 10 percent of Interactive's stock, and signed an exclusive marketing license for a version of its graphics software.

Interactive Imaging is not the only software developer that IBM has invested in. In 1988-1992, there were at least 15 strategic alliances, aggregating over $100 million for equity slices ranging from 2 percent to 40 percent. These agreements also created cooperative relationships ranging from IBM's paying for research and development expenses to IBM's training its sales force to sell the investee's products and paying for sales seminars.

In May 1992, IBM reached across the Atlantic Ocean to invest $2 million in 1.8 percent of the common stock of a start-up software development company in the Netherlands. Sapiens International Corporation N.V. is developing a software development tool used for building and maintaining a wide range of business applications. In addition to its investment, IBM is providing technical assistance and documentation to Sapiens.

*"Suddenly Software Houses Have a Big Blue Buddy," *Business Week*, August 7, 1989, p. 68.

Is your company developing unique software that would help IBM sell more computers? Have the traditional venture capitalists turned you down? Why not give IBM's manager of strategic alliances a call. You may locate your investor, R&D collaborator, or marketing partner all in the same place.

Why do large corporations drop their lines into entrepreneurial waters? Their logic is compelling. Innovation means change. Change means new solutions. New solutions mean filling consumer needs more effectively.

IBM would not need these strategic relationships if it could turn out successful software programs on its own. But it apparently cannot. As computers become commodity products, IBM must rely more on software to maintain satisfactory gross profit margins. To meet that challenge, IBM has become one of the largest venture capitalists in the world. But it is far from being alone in this quest.

Large corporations in the United States and abroad have become, in the late 1980s and early 1990s, one of the primary sources of venture capital for entrepreneurial companies. This new force is called strategic partnering. There are differences between a *strategic* partner and a *financial* investor, such as a venture capital fund. Compared with a financial investor, a strategic partner will invest more money for less ownership, leave its money in for a longer period of time, and invest for many more reasons, only one of which—and not the most important—is capital gains. Moreover, a strategic partner will bring more things to the entrepreneurial company than just money: research and development assistance, beta-testing a new product before it goes to market, providing manufacturing services, and selling the product through its time-tested channels. The entrepreneurial company, simply put, gets more bang from the strategic partner's buck.

Who Are These Strategic Partners?

Electric utilities have put start-up capital into local telecommunications companies in Seattle and St. Paul, and in waste management, real estate development, electronics manufacturers, and medical diagnostics manufacturers in New Mexico, New England, and the

Carolinas. The Tribune Company, publisher of *The Chicago Tribune*, invested in a start-up provider of information transmitted on-line to personal computer users. Contact lens manufacturer, Bausch & Lomb, made 27 strategic investments in 1991, bringing its total to 145 over the prior 10 years, in start-ups as diverse as biotechnology, opthalmic pharmaceuticals, oral care products, and hearing aids. Dow Jones, publisher of the *Wall Street Journal*, formed a $6-million venture capital fund in 1992 to invest in promising companies in the information industry. Dun & Bradstreet funded Information Partners, L.P. with $60 million to do the same. Masco Industries, Alcoa, Nippon Steel, Brown Bovari, BHP (Australia's largest steel company), Neste (Finland's largest oil company), and other heavy industry giants make venture capital investments. American Home Products, Monsanto, Merck, American Cyanamid, Eli Lilly, and Hoffman LaRoche put money into entrepreneurial companies exploring new pharmaceuticals and medical diagnostic devices. Lubrizol, an oil additive manufacturer, invests in biotechnology start-ups. 3M sprinkles its venture funds among several venture capital funds and coinvests with them on a direct basis from time to time. Ameritech, formerly Illinois Bell, made six venture capital investments in 1991 in start-up telecommunications software and hardware producers. Advent International, a venture capital management company, directs the strategic investments of 13 international corporations.

Multiple Strategic Alliances

Tiny Research Frontiers, Inc. of Woodbury, Long Island, New York, a start-up company with no revenues for four years, entered into four separate strategic alliances and leveraged these relationships into an initial public offering in December 1991 that netted the company $4.3 million. Research Frontiers is developing "light valves." These devices use fluid suspensions of microscopic particles that are enclosed between two plates, at least one of which is transparent. When an electrical voltage is applied to the suspension, the microscopic particles align, enabling the operator to rapidly vary and control the amount of light transmitted through or reflected from the device. Research Frontier's light valve technology, when developed commercially, will compete with LEDs, LCDs, and other display technologies and "smart windows."

Very wisely, Robert L. Saxe, Research Frontier's CEO and a Harvard Cum Laude in Physics with an MBA degree, licensed four different marketing partners:

Licensee	Market
Japan Steel Works	Windows—Japan
Hankuk Glass Industries	Windows—Korea
Northern Engraving Co. and National Decorated Products	Display Panels—Automotive Industry
Litton Industries	Eyewear, Windows, and Display Panels—Military and Avionics Industries

Rather than sell its corporate partners common stock, Saxe demanded up-front payments, tight sales royalties, and minimum annual royalty payments whether or not sales minimums were achieved. Japan Steel Works paid $225,000 up front upon the granting of the license. Hankuk Glass Industries paid the company a nonrefundable fee of $209,687 for disclosing its technical information and for providing technical assistance. Between 1986 and 1991, Research Frontiers earned $1.55 million in license fee income. The stock market valued this track record at more than $20 million, or 15 times six years of gross income. This valuation demonstrates, among other things, the public's respect for the endorsement value of strategic alliances.

There are hundreds of strategic investors including the companies that Research Frontiers lined up for start-up capital. They are described in detail in the Directory at the back of this book. To tap into their checkbooks, the entrepreneur must think *associationally*.

Associational Thinking

Linear thinking is following the shortest distance between two points, such as from your address to the closest venture capital fund. Associational thinking means asking "Where can we cooperate?" or "How do we relate?" It means thinking in a branching manner, such as discerning which large corporations could best use your products or services to push through their distribution channels, supplant a dying product, or provide new technologies to penetrate certain markets. Strategic investors would not be involved in the high-risk game of venture capital if they did not firmly believe that entrepreneurs can get new products and services to market better, faster, and cheaper than they can. Going to them for venture capital is not as it was 10 years ago, when an entrepreneur would despair over telling Jonah about a big whale, having their message ignored, then competing with and struggling to sell to the corporations' customers while searching for venture capital to pay marketing expenses. Today, many managers of large corporations know that entrepreneurs beat them all the time, and it is through associational thinking that entrepreneurs can discover which corporations need their products or services very badly. The "Yellow Pages" of strategic investors are for the first time assembled in this book. It is your task to select the most likely strategic partners from the Directory or from a direct competitor of a strategic investor listed in the Directory. As you read this book, practice associational thinking by repeatedly asking yourself these questions:

1. Which corporations address a problem for which my company has a superior solution?
2. Which corporation needs a product licensing relationship with me?
3. Which corporation's channels do I want to ship products through?

These are the gut questions that will lead you to find the best strategic partner for your company.

The third question bears some amplification. Nothing eats capital like marketing costs. If a large corporation has made the investment in creating a sales force and responsive marketing channels, the entrepreneurial company can save buckets of dollars and equity by leveraging the corporate partner's marketing power.

Start-up Marsam Pharmaceuticals, Inc. (Cherry Hill, New Jersey) struck such a deal with pharmaceutical giant CIBA-GEIGY Corporation. Marsam Pharmaceuticals, Inc., founded in 1985, develops and manufactures generic injectable prescription drugs. Generic drugs, the chemical and therapeutic equivalents of brand name drugs, are sold after the patents on the related brand name drugs have expired. The company currently manufactures or markets 22 generic injectable drug products. The products are distributed by Geneva Pharmaceuticals, Inc., a wholly owned subsidiary of CIBA-GEIGY, to hospitals and other health care institutions in the United States. CIBA-GEIGY purchased 794,116 shares or 10.6 percent of the company's common stock in June 1990 for approximately $9 million, and Geneva dedicated 18 of its sales personnel to sell the company's products. Geneva pays the company cost plus 10 percent, with some variances. The agreement runs through July 2000, but may be extended for an additional five years.

If in studying the Directory you ask yourself, "Which of these corporations would like to invest in my company?" you are thinking linearly, and wasting your time. Remember that these corporations have certain *strategies* that brought them into the venture capital business in the first place. It is your task to discover these strategies and sell into them.

The Reasons for Strategic Partnering

Whereas institutional venture capital funds invest for the purpose of achieving significantly higher-than-conventional returns for taking significantly greater-than-typical investment risks, strategic partners invest in entrepreneurial companies for the following reasons:

1. To incubate and reduce the cost of acquisitions.
2. To gain exposure to possible new markets.
3. To add new products to existing distribution channels.
4. To reduce the cost of research and development through strategic partnering.
5. To expose middle management to entrepreneurship.
6. To obtain a management training area for bright young trainees in need of experience.
7. To utilize excess manufacturing capacity, space, or computer time.

8. To mesh the activities of several departments in joint efforts.
9. To generate capital gains.
10. To "look out the window"—to develop antennae for breakthrough technologies.
11. To generate income through strategic partnering (if it is competently managed).
12. To provide excellent group therapy for senior management.
13. To create good public relations by reflecting forward-looking management.
14. To keep pace with their competition, who are probably doing it.
15. The "ITEK" reason.
16. To encourage new company formation in the community.

These reasons, given to me by corporate officials, are not all-inclusive, but they are the ones most often cited in descending order by the most active strategic partners. In Chap. 2, we will examine in depth the reasons behind strategic partnering and review numerous actual case histories so that you can position your company to raise strategic capital.

Positioning Your Company

For now, I strongly urge you to resist the temptation to turn to the Directory and begin contacting the strategic investors listed there. That is a linear approach, and it will lead to dozens of turndowns and frustrations. The correct method of utilizing the Directory is to:

- Think in terms of which industries your new product or service may take market share from.
- Circle the companies in the Directory that could market your product or service through their channels or prop up their sagging product or service sales with your next generation innovations.
- Order their annual reports, 10-Ks, securities analysts' reports, and articles about those companies. Arm yourself with a backpack of data about the most likely strategic partners.

- *Then* contact the corporate officers at the chosen targets.

This process is explained in more detail in Chap. 3.

More Capital; Less Give-Up

Strategic investors generally seek meaningfully smaller ownership positions in entrepreneurial companies than do financial investors. This situation exists because strategic investors become involved in entrepreneurial companies for reasons other than pure capital gain, while financial investors are interested solely and completely in capital gain.

A *venture capital return* is a compound rate of return of 30 percent per annum. This translates into three times the investor's initial investment returned to him in five years. For example, if the investor

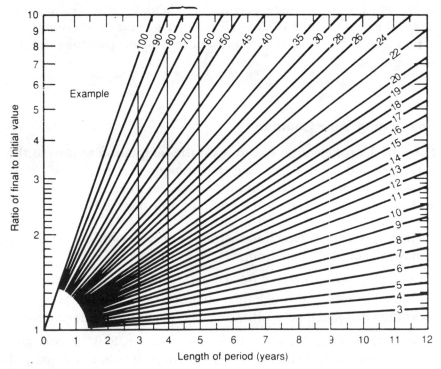

Figure I.1. Target rates of return for a typical venture capital fund.

invests $1 million in January 1993, he or she seeks $4 million back in January 1996—the money back plus $3 million. The relationship of compound annual rate of return, or yield on investment, to "times return," is demonstrated in Figure I.1.

The 30-percent compound annual rate of return target could translate into a hefty equity give-up to the entrepreneur. As an example, pretend you are starting a new company and that you have calculated a need for $1.5 million in venture capital. You prepare a business plan that describes the problem your company intends to solve, the solution that you have conceived, and the management team that you have assembled to carry out the plan. Your operating statement projections suggest that your company might earn $1 million after taxes in the fifth year, as shown in Table I.1.

With $1 million in after-tax earnings in the fifth year, the venture capitalist investigates the possible exit strategies for the investment. These usually consist of the acquisition of the company by a larger, usually publicly held company, by taking the company public, or by selling the investment back to the company. The exit strategy most preferred is acquisition because it pays out cash or salable common stock to you and to the venture capital investor. The second most preferable option is to take the company public. Most underwriters of initial public offerings will not permit insiders to sell their stock at the first offering; the investment cannot be converted into cash, but into "near cash." You and your backers, as insiders are limited as such by Rule 144 of the Securities and Exchange Commission to dribbling out a small fraction of your ownership until a two-year time period passes. But if the price paid for your company's stock is more than the price paid by the venture capitalists, they can mark up the value of the investment on their books, which means a higher management fee for the partners of the fund. Their fees—salaries and money to operate with—are generally $3\frac{1}{2}$ percent of the net asset

Table I.1. Newco's Projected Earnings in Its First Years of Operation

Year	Net profit (loss) after taxes ($000)
Year 1	(1000)
Year 2	(200)
Year 3	275
Year 4	835
Year 5	1000

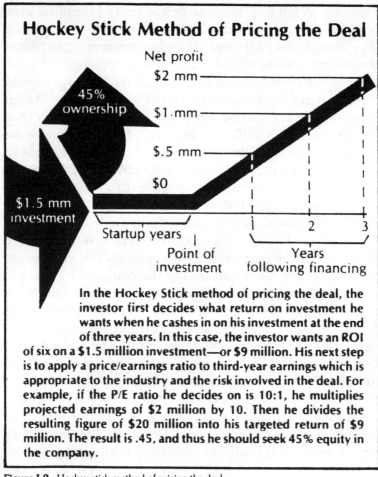

Figure I.2. Hockey stick method of pricing the deal.

value of their investments. Thus, even if you and the venture capitalists are unable to liquidify—that is, convert into cash—the investment in your company, the consolation prize, is higher salaries.

Many venture capital investors will estimate that they will be able to sell the stock in your company at a price/earnings (P/E) ratio of 12× fifth-year earnings. They multiply the P/E ratio of 12 times your projection of $1 million in fifth-year after-tax earnings—if they believe that the company can achieve its projections—and assume a valuation for the company in five years of $12 million. The investor then multiplies the investment by 3× ($1.5 million × 3 = $4.5 million), and estimates the need for ownership to be 37.5 percent: $4.5 million/$12 million = 37.5 percent.

This formula for calculating equity give-up to the traditional venture capital investor is known as the hockey stick formula, and it derives its name from an article I wrote for *Venture* magazine in 1981, which incorporated the diagram in Figure I.2.

Thirty-seven and one-half percent is a hefty equity give-up. Most entrepreneurs would prefer to use the company's common stock to reward valuable employees and key personnel who have stuck by them during the difficult start-up years. An equity give-up of 37.5 percent robs the entrepreneur of the opportunity to reward loyalty, missed paychecks, and around-the-clock laboring to launch the company. A give-up of 15 to 20 percent is more like what you had in mind, and that is why you look for an alternative to venture capital.

The best alternative is strategic partnering.

1
The Elements of a Strategic Alliance

If you have been thinking that your new company's mission is to compete with the giants of your industry for market share, you may be placing a ladder against the wall and climbing it step by excruciating step only to find out that it is the wrong wall. The essence of business—the only reason a company is in business and the object of every business—can be summarized as follows:

> To make your product or service a substitute for all other products or services and to make their products or services no substitute for yours.

This axiom implies that if you cannot develop your product or service, if you cannot produce your product or service, or if you cannot get it into the marketplace, then you cannot tell whether it will be a substitute for all others. Therefore, you must *cooperate* with partners who can help you pass these milestones.

Cooperation

There are times when you should cooperate rather than compete with perceived competitors. Also, once you begin assigning the title "potential strategically" to companies that used to fall under the heading "perceived competitor," you will see that there are more potential partners in your industry than you ever realized. By cooperating with an established company, you can materially reduce the costs of developing, producing, testing, building a sales force, and getting a product into the marketplace. You also eliminate the need to raise capital from a financial investor who questions your ability to accomplish the five steps of a start-up company, since you have never accomplished these steps in a prior business.

Points of Alliance

There are five steps in a start-up (see Fig. 1.1). At each of these steps, there is an opportunity to strike an alliance with a large corporation that is in (or that is waiting to get into) your industry, that needs access to your new product, and that has the scientists, stamping machines, chain saws, customer lists or sales force you need. The five stages are:

1. Development.
2. Production.
3. Marketing.
4. Growth.
5. Exit.

The possible points of alliance between your company and a strategic partner are:

1. Joint development, sharing of research costs, investment.
2. Manufacturing contract, alpha site testing, investment.
3. Beta site testing, marketing license, agreement to sponsor marketing seminars, publish and mail marketing pieces, telemarket to existing customer base, and make investment.
4. Joint research and development of new products, facilities management contracts, investment.
5. Sell investment or acquire the company.

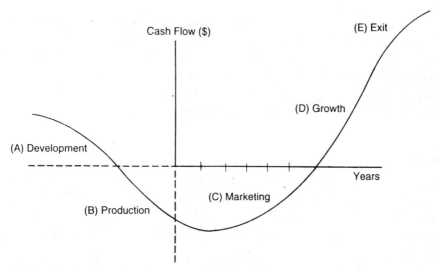

Figure 1.1. The five stages in the life of an entrepreneurial company.

Cooperation at the Research and Development Stage

An example of a strategic alliance at the research and development stage is that between the pharmaceutical giant Glaxo, Inc. and a start-up pharmaceutical company Amylin Pharmaceuticals, Inc. In October 1991, Glaxo paid Amylin $1 million and loaned it an additional $2 million to develop and commercialize Amylin's blockage therapy which is intended to block the production, secretion, or action of a pancreatic hormone to provide a treatment for adult onset diabetes. Glaxo also agreed to put 35 of its scientists to work on the research and development team and invested $200,000 in Amylin's common stock. If Amylin can develop the product, Glaxo will have the right to sell it and pay Amylin a sales royalty.

The Glaxo/Amylin strategic alliance is fairly typical in the pharmaceutical industry, where approximately 300 such R&D-based arrangements have been crafted in the last four or five years. It has become apparent to the managements of large pharmaceutical companies that entrepreneurial teams can bring new products from inception to market faster and less expensively than they can. Having studied the entrepreneur, I believe I know why the entrepreneur can out-innovate the corporate new product developer. Entrepreneurs find their identity and their redemption through the process of defining a new product, raising seed money, scrambling for parts, organizing the manufacturing, and launching the firm. Corporate employees have nothing at risk in the process. They know who they are. They are not searching for themselves.

Who Is the Entrepreneur?

The entrepreneur is someone who is dissatisfied with his or her career path (though not with his or her chosen field), and who decides to make a mark on the world by developing and selling a product or service that will make life easier for a large number of people.

Entrepreneurs are energetic and single-minded, and have a mission and clear vision. Out of their vision they intend to create a product or service in a field that many have determined is important—to improve the lives of millions. Consider the number of successful entrepreneurial ventures undertaken over the last 15 years in the computer, biomedical, and communications industries. The entrepreneur will probably make a lot of money and knows it. When? Who knows and who cares?

What drives this kind of person? Why will he or she forego the conventional career path, ignore all warnings about the likelihood of failure, take on enormous financial burdens, assume responsibilities such as management decisions or marketing plans for which he or she is poorly trained, toss aside the tranquility of home and marriage as if possessed by this single goal?

At what point does the entrepreneur jump into action? What is the personal history behind such determination? And what does he or she say are the driving forces?

Typically, the entrepreneur is between 27 and 34, and is male. Because only men responded to my questionnaires, and because for most of my 25 years working with entrepreneurs, over 90 percent have been male, I would like the reader to allow me to refer to the entrepreneurs as "he." This is not to be interpreted as a reflection on the capabilities of women to be entrepreneurial or to become entrepreneurs. In fact, an increasing number of dynamic young women are becoming dissatisfied with their corporate roles and leaving to start more personally rewarding businesses. There is no difference from my point of view between men and women entrepreneurs.

The archetypal entrepreneur represents—to some—a contradiction. Until the time he conceived of his entrepreneurial (ad)venture, he worked fully within the scope of traditional societal values, perhaps for a corporation, a laboratory, a medical school, or a research center. He had been hired, he believed, for his creative potential and was rewarded, he believed, for his creative contributions. He was well satisfied.

Lurking in the wings, however, was a foil. Initially he believed that the organization valued him and rewarded him principally for his creative potential and output, and he had joined the organization in part because of its prestige. Then he became more energetic and needed increasing latitude and funding for invention. But the organization's commitment to creative output and its willingness to invest in his personal research and development efforts turned out to be less than he wanted, less than he expected. At first surprised, he became increasingly dissatisfied, though for a time he did nothing and said nothing.

At the same time, as trust in the workplace faded, a strong commitment to his own capabilities was unfolding. More and more, he experienced a sense of directedness; an inner voice was asking him questions about his personal values, self-worth, and self-sufficiency. He was not necessarily asking the abstract, philosophical, stock-taking questions that, according to observers and analysts of midlife change, are raised so frequently by people in their mid-thirties and forties: What have I accomplished in my life? What have I sacrificed? What will I do with the rest of my life? Those questions are as likely to come to the entrepreneur as to anyone else. At this point in his life, the Big Question for the entrepreneur was, What will I do with my creativity?

He was intensely, deadly serious about homesteading somewhere and so being able to exercise his confidence in himself. So, before he even knew it had started, the entrepreneurial race was on. For a time, he continued to do his job for his employer, but his dissatisfaction increased. Gradually, the idea for the one product or service would develop—one that would take the marketplace by storm—was putting down roots in his mind. The first growth might be a primary shoot that withers, but the root system was secure, come sunny weather or violent storm. And, as I will discuss in more detail, he will be protected by an enormous potential to replenish psychic energy, by intense pleasure at his activity, and, if he is to be successful, by excellent communication skills and exquisite judgment.

At this point, he comes to me.

I have the enormous pleasure, then, of meeting complex, intense, determined, imaginative people who have faith in themselves, and whose energy isn't sapped by pervasive anger, bitterness, or disappointment. The workplace has not been satisfying, and hasn't rewarded what he most respects in himself; the not-yet-active entrepreneur has put in a lot of time and has tried to contribute his best. He has become dissatisfied and to some extent disillusioned. And he is not politically adept. So pure commitment to human potential irritates rather than inspires management, making it impossible for him to maneuver budgets and other forms of influence the way others can make the organizational dynamics work for, not against, them.

Nevertheless, though he resents the system, he proceeds in the disillusion and goes on to create his own reality; thus, *the true entrepreneur does not feel victimized.* He doesn't plot and plan retaliation. Rather, he accepts that the organization will not provide a place to do what he wants to do and believes should be done, and he decides to create such an organization on his own.

Acceptance of reality brings determination—not depression, not distraction, and not diffuse, flailing attempts to get even or to "show them." He has others to "show," as does the archetypal hero of the great American adventure novels that we read from childhood. We see him in Twain, Melville, Faulkner, Hemingway. They are typically cast in the role of an outcast, a ragged woodsman, a despised sailor ("Call me Ishmael!"), or an unregenerate boy. Huck Finn, before the prospect of being "sivilized," cries out, "I been there before."

Stephen Jobs, the founder of Apple Computer Company,

> had reached his eminence after a long period of searching in the wilderness for gurus and genetic forebears, sampling vegetarianism and primal scream therapy, and slouching through the seventies in jeans and sandals. But in the repeated pattern of entrepreneurs, the anxieties of his early years became the energies of upward mobility. All the emotional turmoil and restless energy of his youth—the

rebellion, the failure, the guilt, the betrayal, the identity maw—suddenly fuse into an irrepressible force of creation.*

Accepting reality also brings dedication to building on his own strengths rather than to demonstrating the weakness of the organization (and thereby deluding himself that it would change anything with respect to his position). He knows he cannot reduce its power; so he decides to establish his own.

And, since personal goals and needs have been emerging as the strongest forces, they take over to govern his behavior. He directs his psychic and creative energy into building on the emotional self-sufficiency that has been slowly, steadily taking hold. He does this with an ease that astounds people who know or hear about him.

The creative intelligence he brought to his employer's business is now directed toward designing a product or service and positioning it for the marketplace. He examines opportunities, perhaps for licensing, but sees none he likes. He may work for a short time as an independent consultant or for a consulting firm, but he continues to see the need he himself identified, and finally decides to create his own opportunity.

He is getting ready to make preparations for building his place in the sun. Note that building a place in the sun is not building an empire, for empire building is not what he is about. Rather, he is planning for, and is after, self-reliance, a quality-controlled provision for creative output. He talks about building an organization where people will not get lost, where creativity will be rewarded, where salaries and benefits will be just, where participative management (though he doesn't call it by that name) will be the rule, not the exception.

And to the amazement of people who are not able to turn anger, energy, disappointment, and dissatisfaction into focused personal directedness, he begins to experience intense pleasure. The undercurrent of basic optimism and trust in his professional power, given momentum by the ever present certainty that his expertise in his field is unequalled, flows toward a clear decision to be on his own and succeed. He has no fear of failure, though he makes careful, detailed plans to avoid it. With confidence, optimism, courage, focus, and

---

*George Gilder, *The Spirit of Enterprise* (New York: Simon & Schuster, 1984), p. 161.

determination, the would-be entrepreneur sets out to look for money.

Statistics of new business and small business failure offered to him by well-meaning friends and family are dismissed as irrelevant. "Sure, lots of people fail, but since I'm going to succeed, why are you telling me about these numbers?" he demands. Then he goes on with his phone calls to bankers, brokers, friends of friends, making presentations end to end. Failure is simply not a possibility. He has spotted an opportunity and is leaping forward to take advantage of it as rapidly as possible.

What happens then depends on whether he carries two other attributes, and seems well to correlate with several factors in his childhood home life. The inability to give up the chase in the face of seemingly insurmountable odds appears to be related to the entrepreneurs having been deprived in childhood by physical handicaps, confinement by a foreign dictatorial regime or social barriers, plus the level of guilt that the entrepreneur feels for having disappointed a parent by going into business rather than the arts or sciences. (Here we must assume that the product or service is, in fact, one for which a market exists.)

Next come second-stage predictions of success. To succeed not only in finding venture capital but also in building a successful business, the would-be entrepreneur must be able to lead his team by exercising good judgment—by knowing the right thing to do at the right time. But since he may not have a clue about *how* to do the right things, he will eventually become entangled in the snare of trying to plan a business. Without knowing word one about functional areas like strategic planning, sales projections, market research, or even simple accounting practices, he will at this point select a manager who does, someone who can at the same time allow the entrepreneur chieftain to maintain leadership.

The higher the entrepreneur reaches for a manager, the more likely is his business to succeed. Entrepreneurs exhibit the keen judgment they are known for when they ask an achiever to join them, someone who has demonstrated first-class management ability in a growth situation.

To tie up the venture capital package, the entrepreneur must be able not only to make and keep the process simple, but also to convince others that it is so.

What might make others topple into confusion and frantic despair nourishes his spirit and his animated intellect. Out of the complexity he pulls the necessary interim funding—usually the day the telephones are to be shut off—from the most unlikely sources: a first-rate impressive venture group presentation, a corps of dedicated partners or colleagues, determination and confidence enough to refuse equity-hungry vulture capitalists.

Simply put, would-be entrepreneurs who have the product or service and the character prerequisites will become wealthy; those who don't will be wiped out in the marketplace.

The Effect of the Entrepreneur's Emotional Background

The successful entrepreneur brings his well-known brand of emotional baggage to the work. His parents desired and worked for a place in the status hierarchy. They valued a traditional, socially acceptable, orderly life . . . a position vis-á-vis others. The future entrepreneur's father either died early or was absent from family life often, due to divorce or business or due to dissatisfaction with himself, his marriage, or his perceived place in the family. So all was held together by a devoted, attentive mother, apparently well-intentioned but very ambitious for her children.

Doing double duty, his mother pushed for achievements, competence, and public recognition of her son's accomplishments. It's no surprise that the successful entrepreneur starts his professional life seeking to work in a well-regarded "establishment" organization, and then, when he leaves, he has the motivation to succeed at all costs.

Kemmons H. Wilson is a case in point. In 1951, he put his wife and five children into their station wagon for a family vacation in Washington, D.C. The motels there charged the Wilsons' kids $2 a head even though they were sleeping in the same room as their parents. Wilson's Scottish blood boiled, and he pledged that when he got back to Memphis he would build a chain of motels that would never charge extra for children. One year later, Wilson opened the first Holiday Inn, named for the Bing Crosby movie of that title. Within 18 months, he had built three more, covering all four main approaches to Memphis. Wilson built his motels with swimming pools, air conditioning, 24-hour telephone service, televisions in every room, ice and soft drink machines in the halls, and babysitters, dentists, and clergymen on call. These features reflected Wilson's preferences.

Wilson was an entrepreneur by the time he was 12 years old. He bought a $50 popcorn machine with nothing down and payments of $1 a week, installed it in a Memphis theater, and took in $30 a week. This was done out of necessity. Wilson's father died when he was nine months old, and he was raised an only child by his mother, Ruby (called "Doll" because she was less than five feet tall). Doll supported the family with a variety of low-paying jobs, but when she got sick, Wilson dropped out of high school and began an early career in the vending equipment business (pinball machines, jukeboxes, and cigarette machines). Wilson once bought 250 cigarette machines with six postdated checks of $10,000 each, and pulled the quarters out of each machine three or four times a day to cover the checks.

To expand Holiday Inns, Wilson teamed up with Wallace Johnson, an experienced builder who had the contacts and the financial expertise to build a franchised network. Holiday Inns changed the lodging industry, crushed the competition, and grew to 1750 establishments, the world's largest lodging chain.

As another illustration, W. Clement Stone's father died when he was very young, and his mother worked as a seamstress in their native Detroit to support the family. She was a deeply religious woman who talked to God as if He were a provider of customers and capital. She invested her savings in an insurance agency. The first day that she owned the agency, she sold no policies. That night she and young Clement, still a teenager, prayed that she would do better the next day. In the morning, she marched into a bank and sold policies to bank employees. She came home and told Clement to go to an office building the next day and sell insurance policies to everyone he saw. He sold 12 policies in his first three days.

Stone moved to Chicago three years later and started his own agency at age 20. He was unusually successful, achieving a personal high of 122 sales one day in Joliet, Illinois. Ten years later, with over 1000 employees, Stone sought an insurance company to purchase. He bought Pennsylvania Casualty Co. from Commercial Credit Corp., on a fully leveraged basis, for $1.6 million. It became the foundation of Combined Insurance Co., which had revenues of $869 million in 1981 and earnings of $100 million. As a venture capitalist,

Stone has done nearly as well, obtaining one-fourth of the ownership of Alberto-Culver Corp. for a loan guarantee of $450,000 in the mid-1950s.

Like his mother, the son does double duty in the loneliness arena. For one thing, the future entrepreneur must be a boy on his own longing for a much absent father. Typically, he feels lonely among his peers because he has a relatively minor handicap, which to him, in his youth, is very powerful with regard to society's idealized picture of the American male. Many entrepreneurs are of shorter-than-average stature. Many were very poor (although the mother's drive denied that the poverty could keep any of *her* sons down). Perhaps excessively poor eyesight or a worst-case acne condition imposed a hurdle to the social approval that the family—and adolescents—needed so much. So our boy grew up longing to be more "like other boys," but not being seen, or necessarily seeing himself, as such. Early approval from the traditional sources wasn't available, and he carried a deep longing for it into his adult life.

An entrepreneur whose childhood was one of bone-chilling deprivation would be wise to obtain a partner to offer guidance and support so that the options can be expanded in difficult times. Astute venture capitalists are quick to measure the length of the hill that the entrepreneur has climbed. Vertical movement through extraordinary deprivation does not make for successful entrepreneurship. The pain is often borne forever, making the entrepreneur excessively bitter and too much of a street fighter.

On the other hand, those who don't suffer during the formative and adolescent years simply are not likely to become successful entrepreneurs. Entrepreneurs do not come from pampered childhoods, where life has been full and abundant. Perhaps they don't have the staunch determination or the need to reverse things that leads to extreme transformations.

To satisfy my curiosity about deprivation, I have asked applicants for venture capital over the last 15 years to describe their childhood history and their feelings about it. The most successful seem to have endured one or more of the following conditions:

- Small physical stature
- Physical illness that prevented athletic or social participation

- Skin conflagration (acne, eczema) that prevented social aggressiveness
- Relatively less wealth than others in the peer group
- Arrested educational development

Charles Revson, the dynamic founder of Revlon, was less than 5½ feet tall. He was not above walking on top of the conference table during management staff meetings. Gino Paulucci, the founder of Chun King, is slightly over 5 feet tall. He too paced on top of the conference room table during management staff meetings. Tom Kelly, who founded TIE/communications, is a bantam weight as well. Among other successful entrepreneurs who are shorter than the average adult male are:

Meshulam Riklis	Rapid-American Corp.
Charles Bluhdorn	Gulf & Western Corp.
H. Ross Perot	Electronic Data Systems Corp.
Erroll Beker	Beker Industries Corp.
Ronald Perelman	MacAndrews & Forbes
Joseph H. Hirshhorn	Rio Tinto Mines
J. Paul Getty	Getty Oil Co.
Henry Kravis	Kohlberg, Kravis, Roberts & Co.

The great merchant bankers who wheeled and dealed with the railroads in the first two decades of the twentieth century—Jacob H. Schiff, J. Pierpont Morgan, Jay Gould—were all short men. One 5-foot-tall entrepreneur once told me, "I'm really 6 feet 2, but wound up real tight."

Other common threads in entrepreneurs' backgrounds are childhood physical illnesses that prevented active participation in sports or social activities. Francis Copolla was bedridden with polio for a year. Among the infirmities most frequently listed are:

- Vision impairments.
- Asthma or hay fever.
- Skin eruptions, acne.
- Motor impairments.

It bears pointing out that, regardless of the physical impairments of youth, adult entrepreneurs are almost never sick. There are two explanations for this: (1) They are having too much fun to miss a day of work, or (2) entrepreneurs do not know how to delegate responsibility and cannot afford to be absent.

The successful entrepreneurs who dropped out of school are too numerous to list. There are substantially more entrepreneurs who never finished college than there are entrepreneurs who graduated from the 50 most highly regarded universities in the country. The better schools turn out professional managers and highly paid consultants.

A Typical Picture of Personal Entrepreneurial Guilt

Possibly the most potent generator for entrepreneurial drive and ultimate success is fixed and pervasive guilt. "Guilt" is a psychiatrist's term as well as one we all use in our day-to-day experience to a greater or lesser degree. And it is a slippery subject with which highly trained professionals wrestle. I don't pretend to know what it is exactly. So I am not attempting to offer any explanations about the psychosocial or psychosexual ramifications or manifestations of psychological guilt. I am describing only feelings of guilt that entrepreneurs have reported to me. And they all did, which is why I bring it up here.

The entrepreneur reports a continual sense of guilt in merely existing as an entrepreneur. Brought up to meet traditional expectations and gain approval from society (in the absence of approval from parents, peers, or self), he strikes out on his own. As he does, society tugs at him, pokes fun, queries him endlessly, questions his sanity, patronizes him, reminds him he has not done what was expected of him.

This guilt manifests itself profoundly on a personal level, and to a much lesser extent as a minor recurring annoyance when society tells him he has not done well.

Picture the room behind a Chinese laundry where the father has been on his feet washing shirts for 12 hours, the mother has been standing just as long over a steam iron, and the eldest daughter, a 12-year-old, is teaching the abacus to the eldest son, an 8-year-old. As the son grows older, the parents encourage him to pursue his study of mathematics and pay for the best books, schools, and so forth with the only capital they have: longer hours. Their hard work is not lost on the son, who applies himself diligently in school and is accepted at a major university, where his achievements in mathematics gain for him high marks and a doctorate in record time. The parents attend all his commencements, so proud are they to have produced a professional, a scientist, a professor. The American dream has been achieved.

One year later, the son leaves academia to start a computer manufacturing company. Thinking they will be pleased, he is thunderstruck by the sorrow his news causes them. He returns to his small office in great sadness. His drives are entrepreneurial, but he has done something very bad to his parents. The guilt that he now carries with him will become an agency of great force and energy to make his parents very proud of him once again.

Society seems either to envy or to be disdainful of the entrepreneur, and he is an easy target because the process, grueling as it is, is a very enjoyable process for the entrepreneur. He is happy virtually all of the time. Until recently, the entrepreneur has not been viewed kindly. Even now he is truly accepted only in certain entrepreneur enclaves such as Silicon Valley, Route 128 west of Boston, the Raleigh-Durham area, and a few others. At best, entrepreneurs in postwar America have been considered promoters, because they are either packaging a plan, planning a program, programming a package, planning a pilot, piloting a program, or packaging a programmed pilot for a plan. Journalists have approached entrepreneur thrashing with about the same relish and exuberance as they have enjoyed politician bashing.

As recently as 1970, one did not admit to being an entrepreneur in the company of gentlemen. Entrepreneurs become bored with the same old questions: Yes, but what do you *do*? Who are your people? Whom are you with? More recently, entrepreneurs have been hoisted higher by the pulley-and-lever combination of money and publicity. Yet entrepreneurs are not revered, as are heart surgeons; not trusted, as are bankers; not looked to for wisdom, as are college professors. To the public, they are still opportunity hunters, somewhat more colorful or more amusing than the average Joe due to their inexhaustible enthusiasm or their penchant for risk taking. Ultimately, however, they are dismissed as people who could not cut it professionally and took the last resort—going into business for themselves, something akin to being a consultant, I guess.

The entrepreneur sees his role very differently, of course. It's all a matter of connotation, nuance, inference; it has to do with his perception of self and his place in the world as he views the world. His decision to go on his own was conscious, positive, and affirmative. He was not fired; rather, he became dissatisfied and left with some ideas to test in the marketplace. He sees himself not as an opportunist but as a creator of a solution for one or more of the country's tangled sets of problems. He sees himself not as a promoter, but as a builder. He and other entrepreneurs are warmed by the fact that their ideas and energies—and not smokestack America—create jobs. While the audience places the entrepreneur somewhere between Charles Keating and P. T. Barnum, the entrepreneur regards himself as excellent dinner company for Albert Schweitzer and Enrico Fermi. He is proud, believing himself to be a social asset. Furthermore, he would like to be given recognition for the social goods that his company provides—problem solving, job creation, a more efficient product or service—than for any entrepreneurial wealth that he might create. Why must the audience use money as the entrepreneur's scorecard? Scientists are awarded Nobels. Artists' works are hung in museums. Writers are awarded Pulitzers. Entrepreneurs are discussed in a handful of magazines in terms of the wealth they have achieved.

Hence the irony that, although the happy entrepreneur may create more new jobs in three years with an investment of $100,000 than the entire automobile industry could in the last 10 years, he endures the circumspect view of him held by family, friends, corporate America, professionals, and the media. Dr. Schweitzer versus Charles Keating.

Practically every entrepreneur with whom I have discussed this subject has three reactions, usually in the following sequence. He:

- Admits to being guilt-driven.
- Is delighted to be able to discuss a shared experience.
- Is able to tell me what he thinks makes the guilt.

The Entrepreneur and His Spouse

The stony silence maintained by most entrepreneurs, which in the man's eyes is a survival mechanism, often leads to misunderstandings between the entrepreneur and his wife. His wife wants equal time with the new business, of course, which is an impossibility. Recognizing the unlikelihood of achieving anywhere near equilibrium in the entrepreneur's world, she strives to become an advisor or confidante. In most circumstances, an entrepreneur does not select another entrepreneur for a spouse. Thus, she cannot provide a sounding board for the entrepreneur. If the entrepreneur is alert to having his wife achieve a sense of fulfillment of the kind that he does, he will locate an area of his business where she can contribute meaningfully.

Many entrepreneurs utilize their spouses to interview potential managers. This is done unobtrusively at dinner or the equivalent, and the wife's judgment is taken seriously. Frequently, a spouse can zero in on things that the entrepreneur cannot because she is not distracted by extraneous bits of information. The entrepreneur who relies on his spouse to contribute in a meaningful way is often rewarded with a tenacious, enthusiastic supporter.

Unfortunately, just the opposite happens more frequently. The spouse is frozen out of the entrepreneur's thoughts, actions, and conversation. He does not seek her advice, does not welcome it when it is given, and, in a moment of business stress, launches a verbal tirade of invectives at her for "butting in." A few shocks like these, a lonely bed due to several weeks of the entrepreneur's extensive travel, and brain rot due to long stretches at the sandbox with the kids, and the marriage crashes.

But the end of a marriage only strengthens the entrepreneurial drive. Venture capitalists have long known that a postdivorce entrepreneur is a missile carrying a neutron bomb, releasing an order of magnitude more energy than when the marriage was intact. So demanding is the entrepreneur's lifestyle that, if they remain married, it is because the wife possesses equal doses of courage, pride, and drive. She wants to make the marriage work.

The guilt of the divorced entrepreneur is turned inside and energizes the entrepreneur to "show her that I can make it without her." Departing for just a moment from my aim to avoid Freud, I'll share with you the fact that the divorced entrepreneur describes guilt as the fear of losing love. Without the spouse available when needed for companionship, romance, or having and rearing children, the divorced entrepreneur lives a lonely existence—one too similar to that of his childhood. He may feel he has failed, as he did as a child when (he believed) he caused his father to stay away. To erase the flaw in his otherwise noble character, the entrepreneur plunges more earnestly into his business to show his exspouse that she made a tragic error in terminating the marriage; it wasn't *his* fault. The energy that a divorce releases in an entrepreneur is titanic. It is not always well-directed, but so many shots are taken that a few are bound to reach targets.

Note: Venture capitalists are high on divorced entrepreneurs and the "guilty marrieds," but they are loath to back the never married bachelor. A married entrepreneur feels guilty because his parents put in for a doctor or other professional but got an entrepreneur, and he also bears the constantly-out-of-town guilt. A divorced entrepreneur has these two guilts plus the "I'll-show-the-wife" guilt. But the bachelor, never having committed himself to either a wife or children, has much lighter guilt baggage to carry around. Low guilt transfers into low drive.

The biggest strike against the bachelor is that he has not made and may not be able to make commitments. There may be no meaningful relationships in his life. He may not have even one close personal friend; he may not intend to marry any of the girls he dates; he may never become involved. Bachelors tend to be, or become, narcissistic. They are happy with this existence. But those who work for them and with them, as well as those who loan to them, invest in them, or provide services to them, sometimes walk away disgusted and discouraged at the insensitivity of the bachelor entrepreneur.

Although it is a known fact that a handful of committed bachelor entrepreneurs have succeeded, they are the exceptions rather than the rule. This is not a condemnation of bachelors; rather, it is a statement that the condition of bachelorhood does not appear to blend well with the other ingredients in the entrepreneurship recipe.

The Entrepreneurial Approach to Problem Solving

Entrepreneurs see options. Many of us know brilliant people who have creative solutions to myriad problems, but who are unable to implement them. They are not entrepreneurial. If you have spent any time in or around New York City, you have undoubtedly heard countless solutions to that city's commutation problems. The problem, in a nutshell, is how to move eight million people into and out of Manhattan twice a day with some semblance of speed, safety, and comfort. It is not insoluble. The roadbeds for high-speed electric trains exist, should someone want to fix them. This would permit the trains to run at speeds in excess of 120 miles an hour, as fast as the trains of Tokyo and Osaka, and cut the present commutation time in half. The commuter business could be sold to entrepreneurs. They could raise venture capital to pay for the capital investment in roadbed reconstruction and in new trains. Passenger revenues would increase as more cars were left at home.

An acceptable alternative solution is the hovercraft. Port cities such as Hong Kong and Honolulu ferry their commuters on these high-speed boats that float on top of the water. They have stewardesses who serve coffee, rolls, and the morning newspaper. There was a hovercraft experiment in New York City in the mid-1970s; the acceptance rate was fairly high, but a couple of icy days on the East River stopped service and the project folded.

There are other alternatives, such as time-sharing STOL (short-takeoff-and-land) aircraft and large helicopters, ferryboats operating on the Hudson River, and double-decker buses operating in bus-only lanes, but these projects have not been initiated.

It is possible to flip through the pages of large city newspapers that index the world's problems and discover tough problems in search of solutions. The New York City commutation problem is one of many that seem too difficult to conquer.

Fortunately, that is not so. This particular problem, like others of long standing, has not been addressed entrepreneurially. It remains in the political arena. Few problems are solved here, but quite a bit of patronage is generated to enlarge and define the problem. In the case of New York City's commutation problem, the politicians address the issue by spending taxpayers' money to tear up and rebuild the roads, usually at rush hour, and nationalizing the railroads to crush workers' incentive.

Why could this problem be solved entrepreneurially? The principal reason is that an entrepreneur stays with a problem from beginning to end. He selects a problem that he likes. He does not attack a problem because his seniors assign it to him. Rather, he commits himself to one in a very personal, almost religious way. He becomes strongly identified with its solution. Not one thought is ever given to the possibility of walking away willfully from a problem before it has been solved. He will solve the problem, and the marketplace will reward him.

The greater the problem, the larger the reward. The stock market has said this for years by maintaining extraordinarily high prices on the shares of companies that lose money continually in pursuit of solutions to large problems. The best example in recent years is Genentech Corp., an early stage biotechnology company that is attempting, among other things, to develop a cure for cancer. Possessing all the major risks that a company can bear—the research risk (can a product be found?), the manufacturing risk (can a product be produced?), the marketing risk (can a product be sold?), and the management risk (can the company make a profit in this business?)—Genentech's common stock was offered to the public in mid-1981 at a price of $35 in order to raise capital. The public bid the price up to $88 by the afternoon of the day of the offering. Remember, Genentech had no products, no production facility, no marketing plan, and a management team headed by a scientist and a former venture capitalist. That spells no track record. At a price of $88 per share, Genentech was worth more than either Control Data Corp. or the Chase Manhattan Bank.

If the Genentech story is not sufficient proof that problems are worth millions of dollars, Cetus Corp., another biotechnology company, went public on the heels of Genentech and raised $120 million. This offering represented the largest new issue of all time—more than Ford Motor Co., Coors, *The New York Times*, or any of the large new issue public offerings of the last 25 years. In 1992, more than fifty biotechnology start-ups achieved initial public offerings of their common stocks raising over $1.2 billion in the process to head out on the trail of cancer, heart attack, AIDS, or diabetes cures or to find solutions to some other problems involving pesticides and fertilizer.

Although Genentech and Cetus are examples from the biotechnology field, there are companies with targets other than cancer cures with high market values and no product on the market. They abound in the fields of medicine, telecommunications, defense, and urban development, among others. For examples, MCI Telecommunications, an early challenger of AT&T, was forced to go public to raise capital to install microwave links long before it had revenues of any meaningful amount. The Rouse Co., rebuilder of downtown Baltimore, Boston (Faneuil Hall), and New York (South Street Seaport), has a price/earnings ratio greater than 10 times that of any other comparably sized real estate development company because it tackles the huge problem of rebuilding America's inner cities, rather than the replacement of farmlands with tract homes.

Thus, if the problem is large enough, the capital will flow to the entrepreneur to spend for developing the solution. Look at the billions of dollars that have flowed into leveraged buyouts to help smokestack industries deconglomerate and downsize themselves into more efficient companies. Further, the federal government has become increasingly liberal about solving problems with its money. Corporations have recognized that the best new products are developed by entrepreneurs, and hundreds of them now invest in entrepreneurial companies in order to capture new and important technologies. Entrepreneurs are attracted to areas where capital is easier to obtain. With capital more abundant in areas of greater problems, solutions tend to be addressed entrepreneurially.

The result, then, is that the entrepreneur picks a problem that he likes, likes the problem that he picks, and finds ample funds to spend on its solution. In this situation, the entrepreneur is able to focus intensively for long periods of time until a solution is found. It would be difficult to accomplish this if the problem were not chosen personally or if the resources of time and capital did not permit it. Fortunately, the marketplace produces problems, time, and capital for its entrepreneurs.

This intensity of focus means hours, days, and frequently weeks and months spent on one or two problems to the exclusion of all other things. The entrepreneur's mind envelopes the issues at hand, blocks out all others, and wrestles with the issues until they are solved. Returning to the New York commutation problem, the initial problem that an entrepreneur would have to address would be obtaining the rights to operate the trains and all related equipment. This would require negotiating with the Department of Transportation and other branches of the federal government. Although this might take months to accomplish, an entrepreneur who adopted the New York

City commutation problem would be prepared to lobby, negotiate, and arm-twist in Washington until he obtained a satisfactory result.

Washington is a tough sell. The Wright Brothers asked the U.S. Department of War for over five years to watch a demonstration of their airplane. The British and French were placing orders while Washington was still saying the airplane would not work.

Some industries that were not begun by, or peopled with, entrepreneurs are forever losing ground to politicians, because the members of these industries are not prepared to live in Washington for 90 to 120 days to talk to legislators and regulators. The venture capital industry is certainly a case in point. The Reagan and Bush Administrations attempted to kill most government guarantee loan programs plus the Small Business Investment Company program without a concerted opposition. But entrepreneurs understand that if they get into the ring with a problem and stay on their feet for a full 15 rounds, they have a good chance of winning. However, they must never take their eyes off their opponent, and they must keep sticking him with the jab and countering with the hook.

The entrepreneur's intensity of focus is a trait common to successful scientists. Charles Darwin, for example, in 1837, at the age of 28, was a confirmed evolutionist. "Acquainted by his education and readings with the controversial evolutionary thinking of others, he had been impressed by symptoms of evolution observed during his five-year voyage of geological and biological inquiry on the *Beagle*—symptoms such as the variations in species on islands isolated from the mainland."* He then set out to *prove* that evolution was a reality. It was 15 months later that he discovered the principle to explain evolution. And 20 years after the discovery, on July 1, 1858, when all his data had been painstakingly gathered, collected, and assembled, Darwin went public with his landmark book, *On the Origin of Species by Means of Natural Selection, or the Preservation of Favored Races in the Struggle for Life*. This quality—intensity of focus—is shared with scientists by artists and entrepreneurs.

Speaking of Darwin, precursors of today's entrepreneur were the fifteenth- and sixteenth-century explorers. The length of time they were able to focus intensively on a problem was frequently measured

---

*D.N. Perkins, *The Mind's Best Work* (Cambridge, Mass.: Harvard University Press, 1981).

in years. One of America's most famous explorers, Christopher Columbus, is a perfect case in point. Once Columbus had convinced himself that he could sail to India by going west, he had to raise the capital and obtain the ships necessary to produce the proof. He moved to Spain from Italy and devoted six years to getting an audience with King Ferdinand and Queen Isabella (who were preoccupied with the Inquisition) and then convincing them to invest. Once, when his fortunes were at their lowest, Columbus went to England to try to raise the capital there. When the king and queen of Spain got wind of this, they called Columbus in for a meeting. Two years later, he was on his way. Not everyone is prepared to focus on a single issue for six lean years.

The Production Stage

The trend among industrial corporations is to slash costs. One of their strategies for doing this is to spin off entrepreneurial departments and factories via management buyouts and facilities management contracts, thereby eliminating the overhead that accompanies these operations. One might consider this a *reverse strategic alliance* because the skills vested in the department or factory employees are the key to achieving lower costs and high quality. When these skills are nucleated in the combustible enthusiasm of an entrepreneurial shop, where the workers own a piece of the action, the former sole parent can benefit from:

- The capital gain from selling a substantial part of the division.
- Having a subcontract manufacturer with known managers and employees.
- And a second capital gain when the spun-off division achieves a public offering or is acquired.

Express Scripts, Inc. was partially spun out of New York Life Insurance Company. In June 1992, approximately 27.5 percent of its shares were sold to the public for $26 million, valuing New York Life's investment at more than $75 million, a significant increase from the $4.2 million that New York Life was carrying it on its books. Express Scripts offers pharmacy benefit management services including integrated mail order and local retail pharmacy network services. Originally, the company developed these services for 653,000 members of SANUS, a health maintenance organization owned by New York Life. It has since expanded its services to more than 1150 health benefit plan sponsors covering over 1.5 million eligible employees, retirees, members, and their dependents. Sales in 1991 were $47 million, on which the company earned $2.9 million.

Ford Motor Company formed an alliance with Excel Industries, Inc. in 1986. Excel, founded in 1928, is the leading independent designer, manufacturer, and supplier of window systems to the automotive, van, recreational vehicle, and truck industries. Ford purchased 40 percent of Excel's common stock in 1986 for $19.3 million and transferred its modular window manufacturing subsidiary to the company. Ford also agreed to purchase from Excel 70 percent of its modular window requirements through 1998.

In January 1992, Sears, Roebuck & Co. spun off part of its renamed subsidiary, SPS Transaction Services, Inc., which processes point-of-sale credit card transactions. In February 1992, it achieved an initial public offering, selling 23 percent of its common stock to the public for $44.6 million. The value of Sears' remaining shares became $208 million, substantially greater than the SPS' net worth of $14.9 million. Part of the incentive for Sears to spin off its credit card processing subsidiary was that SPS had accumulated liabilities of $275 million. Sears continues to provide SPS access to its facilities, computers, and telecommunications networks under lease agreements.

Thermo Electron Corp., a manufacturer of environmental and analytic instruments, industrial process equipment, and drug detection devices with $800 million in revenues, has adopted a strategy of selling a minority interest in subsidiary companies. It has created to date Thermedics, Inc., Thermo Instrument Systems, Inc., Thermo Process Systems, Inc., Thermo Electron Technologies Corp. and Tecogen, Inc., all publicly held subsidiaries of Thermo Electron. The prospectus for the parents newest spin-off, Thermo Cardiosystems, Inc., states that one of Thermo Electron's reasons for the spin-off strategy is its belief that it has "enhanced the entrepreneurial environment for employees of the company." The parent leases facilities and provides a sharing of resources among its subsidiaries, along with centralized administrative, banking, and credit services under a five-year renewable blanket charter.

Production-Oriented Strategic Alliances

More conventional production-oriented strategic alliances are entered into by cash-conscious entrepreneurial companies that would rather concentrate their energies on product development and have more experienced manufacturing companies produce their products. These deals are typically straight supplier relationships, but when the entrepreneur is unable to pay the supplier on conventional terms, strategic partnership agreements are struck. At first blush one might think a supplier would be out of its corporate mind to manufacture products for a company that has no visible or tangible means of paying for them. But it happens all the time, every hour of every day. And it happens because the entrepreneur is the master of two of the most important words in the business lexicon: *just ask*.

Just Ask

The entrepreneur questions everything. He has been in the wilderness. Now he sees the light—not clearly, because it is at the end of a long, dark tunnel. But he *knows* it is there. He is allied to the chase, in love with the chase, and bonded to it in a manner not dissimilar to the romantic young heroes of the great American novels. The entrepreneur plunges forward, always forward in a childlike ignorance as if a fall to the bottom of the dark tunnel and humiliation and ruin are impossible. And the entrepreneur's allies are the all-encompassing questions: Will you do this for me? Will you help me? Will you join me in my chase? Will you wait to be paid until I raise some money?

And suppliers agree to do it. Employees sign on. Landlords go along. Printers extend credit.

Why? Because of the myth of the entrepreneur. If his dream is realized, then the supplier, the employee, the landlord, the printer will have been part of the dream—will have for a moment in their hard, reality-intrusive lives, lived the myth of the frontiersman ingrained in them from childhood.

They cooperate as well because it may be good for business. They deliver a key component or product to the entrepreneur *without an invoice*. They supply analytical instruments on extended terms. They send in technicians to help install their products. They permit the entrepreneurial team to develop software on their computers.

Are these strategic alliances? They are more in the genre of cooperative arrangements. Let me describe a handful of them for you, all of which are the result of the two words, *just ask*.

K. Philip Hwang Asked a Korean Supplier. Hwang, 52, founder of TeleVideo Systems, Inc., introduced the first low-cost video display terminal for the personal computer industry, driving the established players—NCR Corporation, Lear-Siegler, and Hazeltine—out of the marketplace. "Oh, those guys are just trying to buy the market," says Hwang. "They thought we would last three months, maybe six months. Our competitors thought we were losing money from the beginning. That was good for us. They didn't challenge us because they thought we would be out of business before long."* TVS shipped 7500 terminals in its first year, at prices 30 to 40 percent below its competitors for twice the performance; 27,500 in its second year; and 120,000 in its fifth year, 1983. TeleVideo Systems became the dominant supplier of smart terminals without an injection of equity capital.

Philip Hwang was born in Hungnam, North Korea, and developed a survival instinct when he escaped the Korean Conflict to Pusan, South Korea, at age 14. When the war ended, Hwang quit his $5-a-month job as an errand boy for the U.S. Tenth Army to attend school in Seoul. He sold pencils and pads, kept up his studies during rigorous 18- to 20-hour days, and repeatedly took examinations to qualify for overseas study. Eleven years later, in 1964, he enrolled in Utah State University with a scholarship and $50 to his name. He would have starved in his first year except for a Christmas basket of damaged cans of pumpkin pie filling given him by a kindly Presbyterian minister.

He married a friend from Seoul in 1966, Gemma, and they worked in Lake Tahoe restaurants in the summers. After graduation, Hwang

---

*Gene Bylinsky, "The All-American Success Story of K. P. Hwang," *Fortune* (May 18, 1981), p. 86.

worked for several big companies—Ford Motor Company, Burroughs Corporation, NCR Corporation—but his entrepreneurial urge made him restless. He jumped to a small Silicon Valley electronics company, and in that fertile nursery of innovation, it did not take long for Hwang to begin thinking of his own business.

To generate some business experience, he and Gemma acquired a 7-Eleven franchise, at which she and he worked day and evening shifts. With $9000 pulled out of the sale of the 7-Eleven, Hwang and two partners set up shop in a garage to manufacture video game monitors. When they could not raise venture capital, the two partners left.

Hwang had the idea of going to his homeland, where he made the rounds asking seven Korean television companies to make monitors for him. Six turned him down; *the seventh was conditionally interested* if Hwang could order several thousand monitors per month.

He returned to California and approached Atari and other game manufacturers. They were interested because of Hwang's low price. He went back to Korea and struck a deal for 5000 monitors per month, raising the capital with letters of credit backed by orders. When Hwang needed more capital, he pledged his house, furniture, and car to a bank for $25,000 and then went back to Atari. In exchange for cutting the price by 5 percent, Atari provided Hwang with additional credit, and he was off to Korea with a firm order for 6000 monitors. Although Hwang's operation was profitable in its first few years, the video game business was becoming very crowded and he decided to switch to video display terminals for computers.

Steven P. Jobs and Steven Wozniak Asked Motorola for Chips. Jobs and Wozniak, two self-taught engineers and dropouts, introduced the typewriter-sized, $1350 Apple II in 1977, the state-of-the-art home and small business computer for the next five years. Notwithstanding the onslaught of practically every mainframe and minicomputer behemoth in the United States and Japan, Apple Computer has held its ground. It is one of the greatest entrepreneurial success stories in the history of the American economy.

An adopted orphan, Steven Jobs wandered through the wilderness of Oregon apple orchards after leaving Reed College in his freshman year. Then he cavorted with gurus and primal scream therapists while searching in sandals for his identity until he became reacquainted with a high school friend, Steve Wozniak. Jobs found in Wozniak's engineering brilliance an opportunity to channel the energies of his search into a frenzied five years of scrambling for components, raising money, and selecting business partners that created the mystique and the reality that was and is Apple Computer, Inc.

Jobs and Wozniak met in 1975 when Jobs was a video game designer at Atari, where founder Nolan Bushnell wanted to reduce the number of chips in his Pong game from 150–170 to less than 40. Wozniak, then an engineer at Hewlett-Packard Company, had designed a version of Pong that used about 30 chips. Bushnell told Jobs and Wozniak that he would give them $700 if they could design "Breakout," a Pong upgrade, with less than 50 chips, and $1000 if it was under 40 chips. Wozniak and Jobs delivered a breadboard model in four days with 44 chips.

After that chance encounter, Wozniak began designing a personal computer at his bench at Hewlett-Packard Company because he wanted one for his personal use. Wozniak tells the following story:

> One day I mentioned to Steve that I had noticed something interesting in the video addressing. I could make a little change by adding two chips, and then I could just shift each byte out onto the screen and we'd have hi-res graphics. I wasn't sure it was worth the two chips. ... But Steve was pushing for all the features we could get, so eventually we put it in. At the time we had no idea that people were going to be able to write games with animation and little characters bouncing all around the screen.... I would take it into Hewlett-Packard to show the engineers. Sometimes they would sit down and say, "This is the most incredible product I've ever seen in my life."*

His first computer was slow and its timing was off because Wozniak was using the oldest, cheapest surplus parts he could find, plus a home television set. Wozniak says,

> Steve got intrigued with all these ideas and one day he asked me, "Why don't you use these new 16-pin dynamic RAM's from Motorola?" I had looked at them in my work at Hewlett-Packard, but they were new and I couldn't afford any parts that didn't come my

---

*Gregg Williams & Rob Moore, "The Apple Story," *Byte*, (December 1984), pp. A67–A71.

way almost free. I'm a little bit shy, and I didn't know any of the reps, but Steve just called them up and talked them into giving us samples.*

The two Steves had become members of the Homebrew Computer Club, a meeting place for high school students and Silicon Valley engineers to discuss microcomputers and to show one another their designs. Jobs came up with the idea of building a few of Wozniak's computers and selling them to club members. As Wozniak tells it:

> We had about 500 members in the club, and I thought that maybe 50 people would buy it. It would cost us about $1,000 to have the board laid out, and each board would cost us about $20. So if we sold them for $40 and 50 people bought them, we'd get our $1,000 back. It seemed pretty doubtful. But Steve said, "Well, yes, but at least for once in our lives we'll have a company." So Steve sold his van and I sold my HP calculator to raise money to make the PC boards.†

Soon thereafter, Wozniak and Jobs received an order from a local computer dealer to supply completely built computers. He ordered 100 units at $500 each, a $50,000 order. To obtain parts, the supplier approved the credit of the dealer, and provided Apple Computer with $20,000 of parts on 30 days' credit. A friend, Alan Baum, loaned $5000 and Wozniak was able to build the computers and deliver them in 10 days.

To build the Apple II, Wozniak and Jobs needed to raise $250,000. Nolan Bushnell, Jobs' boss at Atari, put Jobs in touch with Don Valentine, a venture capitalist, who had been involved in Atari. Valentine introduced Apple Computer to Mike Markulla, a former marketing manager with Intel Corporation. Markulla wrote a business plan and invested $91,000. He attracted $1 million in venture capital plus a line of credit from the Bank of America. Within three years from the time Markulla joined the company, Apple's sales exceeded $100 million, and four years after that, the company's sales reached approximately $1.5 billion.

*Ibid., p. A68.
†Ibid., p. A69.

Raphael Klein Asked Ebauches. Raphael Klein, 46, is the entrepreneur of whom the Silicon Valley venture capitalists like least to be reminded. He built the kind of company that venture capitalists like most to finance—productivity-improving, electronics-based, capital goods—without a dime of their money. He was trained at National Semiconductor Corporation and Fairchild Semiconductor Corporation, from which came the brilliant triumvirate who founded Intel Corporation, as well as Jerry Sanders, who launched Advanced Micro Devices Corporation. Klein's entrepreneurial team includes experienced semiconductor engineers and executives from Intel, Fairchild, Texas Instruments, National Semiconductor, Data General, and Honeywell. Klein is a physics graduate from Technion, Israel's equivalent of the Massachusetts Institute of Technology (MIT), and his team graduated from California Institute of Technology, University of Chicago, University of California, and so forth. Klein and his cofounders, to top it off, invested over $160,000 of their personal savings in Xicor. Notwithstanding, Klein could not generate any interest from the professional venture capital community. The alternative, a public offering, was the route taken, and D. H. Blair & Company, one of the best at judging which new issues to back, did its usual admirable job.

Klein and his wife came to the United States in 1974 with one suitcase and a ticket to fly to San Jose, California to begin working for Monolithic Memories, Inc. The Kleins had no money. But he had a job offer.

Soon after joining Monolithic, Klein left for National Semiconductor, continuing to learn about semiconductors. The reputation of Fairchild Semiconductor as the "university" that graduated Noyce, Grove, and Moore (the founders of Intel) was too great a magnet. Thus, he joined Fairchild where, from 1975 to 1976, Klein was manager of technology and manufacturing engineering for charge-coupled memory devices. He moved on to Intel in August 1976, and remained there until August 1978 as program manager for research and development of an advanced memory device. For his unique contribution to Intel's product line, Klein received a cash award of $70,000. He was launched.

Xicor's initial offices were in Klein's home and subsequently the home of a cofounder, where the NOVRAM memory device was developed. The need for a facility to test design concepts became apparent in late 1978, and Klein convinced Ebauches in Marin, Switzerland, to undertake a cooperative development effort in exchange for a minority equity interest. Ebauches received one board seat as well. The founders kept Xicor alive with personal investments and loans and with two private placements: $476,300 in June 1979 at $1.18 per share and $2,487,100 in April 1980 at $3.80 per share (most of it purchased by Ebauches).

In October 1980, D. H. Blair took Xicor public. It sold 1.98 million shares of common stock at $6.50 per share. In December 1980, CIN Industrial Investments, Ltd., a subsidiary of the British coal miners' pension fund, invested $2 million and committed another $4 million. Another D. H. Blair offering at $7.15 per share in May 1982 brought in $10 million.

The financial history bears pointing out because it shows that major amounts of money can be raised for a high-technology company, even when the traditional and most likely investors turn thumbs down. Xicor is today considered a leader in the EEPROM niche. How big is this niche and how fast is it growing? EEPROM sales exceeded $1.1 billion in 1990, and over half of all design engineers use EEPROMs at their workbenches. Each microcomputer includes $6 of nonvolatile memory, most of that EEPROMs.

Raymond A. Kroc Asked for the Franchise Rights. Raymond A. Kroc, who died in 1984 at the age of 82, was raised by his mother after his father "worried himself to death." He attended public school with Ernest Hemingway and dropped out of high school to become a musician. Later he served in World War I with Walt Disney, enlisting at the age of 16. While in his early twenties, Kroc got a job as a musical director of a Chicago radio station and discovered the singing comedy team of Sam and Henry, later to be known as Amos 'n' Andy.

In the 1920s, he drove to Florida to try to make a fortune in real estate. He drove back "stone broke." He was a failure by his thirtieth birthday. He bounced around, finally becoming a milkshake machine salesperson. Orders frequently came from a drive-in restaurant in San Bernardino, California, owned by the McDonald brothers. Like so many crazes, the drive-in began in California. The McDonald brothers had so many hungry adolescents clamoring for their 15-cent burgers stuffed into paper bags, that the day Kroc visited the restaurant, security guards were needed to quell the mob. Kroc saw an opportunity to sell franchises, so he asked for the job. Kroc gave the brothers 0.5 percent of the gross receipts of franchise fees and royalties. After six years of paying the brothers, and 300 franchises later, Kroc found the brothers "were beginning to get on my nerves." He bought them out for $2.7 million in cash.

Kroc was a self-taught businessperson with numerous one-line prescriptions for success. For example, to select sites, he recommended flying over neighborhoods to count church steeples and schools. Service personnel who dealt with customers could not have long hair, sideburns, moustaches, bad teeth, severe skin blemishes, or tatoos. A vicious competitor, Kroc is remembered as having said, "It's dog-eat-dog and if anyone tries to get me I'll get them first. It's the American way of survival of the fittest."

Sandra L. Kurtzig Asked Hewlett-Packard. Sandra L. Kurtzig founded ASK Computer Systems, Inc. in 1974. The company designs, develops, and produces MRP turnkey systems. This is software that is marketed along with minicomputers to industrial corporations to assist them in improving manufacturing productivity through optimizing inventories, reducing operating expenses, and improving customer service. Kurtzig designed software modules for the factory and warehouse, integrated them into a well-known minicomputer, the Hewlett-Packard 3000 series, and began selling and installing software with the customer's needs in mind. With customer input, the modules became a complete manufacturing information system called MANMAN, and further refinements have included a network and microcomputer system for smaller users.

Kurtzig, 43, was trained in math, engineering, and computer systems marketing but in 1972 wanted to start a family, so she quit her job at General Electric Company. Feeling the need to work part time, she took $2000 of her savings and started a contract programming business in a spare bedroom of her California apartment. "My part-time job was taking up to 20 hours a day. I had the other 4 to start my family."* Her first program was one that let weekly newspapers keep track of their newspaper carriers.

*"A Most Successful Part-Time Job," *Forbes* (Fall 1983), p. 198.

She recruited several bright computer and engineering graduates and directed them to write applications to solve problems of local manufacturers. Manufacturers' needs were well-known to Kurtzig. She says,

> When you spend a fortune buying expensive equipment and end up following some manufacturer's programming book one-two-three-four, it gets frustrating. You want someone to come up with easy answers, and the big companies are not aggressive or creative enough to supply them. The big companies put in the computers and open the doors for the new, aggressive companies to nibble away at the business. In general, the small companies are better at this business because the employees feel they can make a difference.*

Kurtzig has always been cash-conscious. Initially, she stashed all her business funds in a shoe box in her closet. If there was more money in the shoe box at the end of the month than at the beginning, her company made a profit. The Silicon Valley venture capitalists would not contribute to her shoe box, so Kurtzig had to launch ASK on retained earnings alone.

Friendly executives at a nearby Hewlett-Packard Company plant permitted Kurtzig and her programmers to use one of the company's 3000 series minicomputers at night to try to develop a manufacturing inventory control program. The group slept in sleeping bags at the company, and by 1978 it had a salable product. The breakthrough was the result of putting useful, easy-to-use software on a well-known, highly reliable computer. ASK's sales soared. From $1.9 million in 1980, the company achieved revenues of approximately $150 million in 1991 with profits of $30 million.

Unable to interest many investors in her stock when ASK was privately owned, Kurtzig is one of the wealthiest self-made women in America. Stories like this one surely help the shoe box producers.

George Lucas Asked Francis Coppola. George Lucas founded Lucasfilms, Inc. in 1975. The company is the leading producer of optical effects and science fiction "chase" movies, including the *Star Wars* saga. Lucas discovered a subject matter that appealed to the greatest

---

*Joel Kotkin, "New Money," *TWA Ambassador* (April 1982), p. 48.

number of moviegoers: chase films (bright young boy and girl armed with a magical force attempting to rid the world of evil) that blended high tech (computer-controlled space ships) with high touch (warm, fuzzy animal creatures and humorous robots). Lucasfilms has attracted some of the most technologically competent cinematographers and optical technicians in the world, and it exploits the most advanced computer-aided design (CAD) and computer-aided engineering (CAE) technology to make movies.

Lucas, 47, has brought many innovations to the movie industry:

- Blockbusters.
- High-tech chase scenes with high-touch characters battling machinelike, Nazi-type enemies.
- The summer spectacular (all *Star Wars* movies were released as schools let out).
- The use of CAD and CAE to lower the cost of producing movies.
- The multiplier effect (generating 10 to 20 revenue sources from a single movie).

Lucas began like movie producers always begin, with a screenplay and lots of desire. This one was *American Graffiti*, a story about teenagers growing up in a small town in the 1960s: cars, music, a gang fight, love affairs ended by college and the draft. To get a studio to finance the low-budget movie, Lucas asked Francis Ford Coppola, of *The Godfather* fame, to coproduce. *American Graffiti* was a hit and gave Lucas the credibility to launch *Star Wars*.

Like all the successful entrepreneurs who fill these pages, Lucas watched every detail. He equipped his partner Gary Kurtz with a microphone and announcer, and sent him into a sewer with actor James Earl Jones to obtain the unique voice of Darth Vader. He shot most of the scenes in England to avoid higher unionized costs of labor in the United States. Snow scenes were shot on location. Bullets slashing through the air were digital signals generated by CAD/CAE.

Lucas bought an old egg factory near United Airlines and pulled together a movie production company that licensed everything "except the squeal." The CAD/CAE engineers remained in San Raphael, California, in an inconspicuous building near a strip center called Industrial Light and Magic. Lucas' desire for anonymity is towering; many employees wear beards and glasses like his (and Coppola's) so that visitors who do not know Lucas cannot identify him.

Twentieth Century Fox reluctantly agreed to put up some of the capital for *Star Wars*, after a prolonged negotiation on dividing the net profit (after the exhibitors' 50 percent). They did not share Lucas' belief in the *Star Wars* saga. On the next film, *The Empire Strikes Back*, Lucas did not have to find financial partners; Lucasfilms' income was in the range of $10 to $12 million per month for the year that *Star Wars* was being shown. Thus, Lucas had the distributors begging for the sequel. He also kept all the rights—no need to sell VCR, cable, network, and so forth to raise capital. And he kept the rights to toys, books, clothing, calendars, masks, and the other paraphernalia, selling off licenses whenever he felt the price was right.

Jack R. Simplot Asked How to Make Onion Powder. Simplot founded J. R. Simplot Corporation in 1927 in Boise, Idaho. It is the largest potato processor in the country with a patent on frozen French fries. Simplot has consistently jumped into opportunities, justifying it with the message on a small metal plaque that has been on his desk for the last 25 years: "Nothing will ever be attempted if all possible objections must first be overcome." This spirit got him into producing dried onion powder and flakes, freezing French fried potatoes, and investing venture capital in Micron Technology. Simplot learned the principles of investment while still a teenager. When the farmers feared a pork surplus and slaughtered their hogs, 16-year-old Simplot collected and fed hogs and waited out the period until hogs were in short supply. He made a profit that financed his first potato processing plant.

Jack R. Simplot, now 83, was born in a one-room cabin in Declo, Idaho, where he was raised by a stern father and loving mother. Except for hunting to put food on his family's table, young Simplot's life was one of work on his family's 120-acre farm, where he pulled out rocks and sagebrush by hand. In town, Simplot was variously a paper boy, scrap collector, and caddy. Driven by an intense desire to succeed, he dropped out of school in the eighth grade and left the father he feared and the mother he loved.

He learned to live on his entrepreneurial instincts at 14, when he made $7800 in a year on his pork "corner." For the next three years, he went into farming, trading animals, and learning how to survive on sparse land and in hard times. He heard of an electric potato sorter in 1928, bought it for $345 and began sorting and storing potatoes for other farmers. The Great Depression increased the demand for potatoes and Simplot's business expanded. By 1940, he employed about 1000 workers at 30 potato and onion warehouses, each of which had three electric sorters.

He got into the onion powder and flake business in a classically entrepreneurial manner, cleverly described by George Gilder in *The Spirit of Enterprise*:

> Then in the spring of 1940, Jack Simplot decided to drive to Berkeley, California, to find out why an onion exporter there had run up a bill of $8,400 for cull (or reject) onions without paying.... The girl in the office said the boss wasn't in. Fine, said J.R., he would wait until the man arrived. Two hours later, at ten o'clock, a bearded old man walked in. Assuming this was the debtor, Simplot accosted him. But he turned out to be a man named Sokol, inquiring why he was not getting his due deliveries of onion flakes and powder. They sat together until noon, but still the exporter failed to arrive.
>
> As the noon hour passed, Simplot was suddenly struck with an idea. He asked the bewhiskered old trader to a fateful lunch at the Berkeley Hotel. "You want onion powder and flakes," said J.R. "I've got onions. I'll dry 'em and make powder and flakes in Idaho."
>
> The two men shook hands on the deal and returned to the exporter's office. Mr. J.R. Simplot had entered the food processing business, without any clear notion of how to produce dried onion powder or flakes. Once again he followed his lifelong precept of entrepreneurship: "When the time is right, you got to do it." The objections to signing a contract for delivery of 500,000 pounds of dried, powdered or flaked onions—without drier, pulverizer, or flaker or any clue of how to build them—seemed altogether prohibitive. But J.R. Simplot struck when the time was right.
>
> Finally, the owner returned to his office and surprised Simplot by agreeing to pay off the debt, albeit on a slow schedule. Simplot then casually asked him where he performed the processing. The man avoided the question, thus heightening the Idahoan's curiosity. Leaving the office, Simplot noticed one of the exporter's trucks pulling out of the driveway. He followed it out to the plant, where he identified the equipment as Nipchild Prune driers from St. Helena, California. Simplot then rushed to his car and drove out through the Napa Valley to St. Helena, arriving just before dark. Before he left Nipchild Prune, he had made a down payment on six tunnel driers,

and he had learned from Nipchild how to manufacture a vertical hammer mill and shaker to produce the powder and flakes. It had been a good day's work, Simplot thought as he returned to his car.*

Simplot quickly learned that other foods could be dried as well, and that the process reduced the storage requirement to one-seventh the warehouse space required prior to drying. When America entered World War II, Simplot's dried potatoes were in enormous demand as field rations. To get more potatoes, he bought and cleared more land for farming. To dispose of the endless skins, he bought a feedlot for 3500 hogs. To get more fertilizer, he bought mineral rights to 2500 acres of phosphate-rich Indian land. Each production obstacle was met with vertical integration. Although he worked day and night to increase productive capacity to feed the Army, the IRS sued him for tax evasion and war profiteering in the late 1940s. In addition, labor unions closed a plant, and Simplot was hit with unfair labor practice suits. Fearing the worst was to come, Simplot's partners, including his father, demanded to be bought out in cash on the spot. He bought them out.

In 1946, a Simplot chemist came up with a process to freeze dry French fries. Frozen French fries did not catch the attention of consumers or restaurants until 1960, making the intervening 14 years very tough at J.R. Simplot Corporation. But the entrepreneur's patience and belief in this innovation paid off fully in the mid-1960s when Ray Kroc, head of McDonald's, ordered the frozen French fries to be tested in a few stores. The customers kept coming back for more. McDonald's soon accounted for 40 percent of Simplot's revenues.

Robert A. Swanson Asked Herbert W. Boyer. Swanson founded Genentech, Inc. in 1976. The company is a leader in the development, manufacture, and marketing of pharmaceuticals produced by recombinant DNA technology. Principal products include human growth hormone, gamma interferon, tissue-type plasminogen activator, and bovine interferon. Swanson, a venture capitalist, wanted to run a science-based company that solved some of society's major problems. He met Herbert W. Boyer, one of the first scientists to synthesize life:

---

*George Gilder, *The Spirit of Enterprise* (New York, Simon & Schuster, 1984), p. 30.

He had taken DNA strands from two different living organisms and glued them together, creating a bit of life that had never existed before. Boyer convinced Swanson that this scientific achievement could be commercialized, and the two became partners to create solutions to various medical problems utilizing recombinant DNA methods.

Robert A. Swanson, 43, and Herbert W. Boyer, 54, have formed the most potent entrepreneurial team in biotechnology acceptable to investors, the scientific community, and the large pharmaceutical companies. When the chase is to conquer life-threatening diseases, the ingredients are capital, great scientists, and outstanding marketing companies, such as Eli Lilly & Company. Genentech has won the hearts, minds, and pocketbooks of all three. It has raised over $1 billion—much more capital than its revenues—and licensed Eli Lilly & Company, Hewlett-Packard Company, Boehringer Mannheim Corporation, Miles Laboratories (subsidiary of Bayer, A.G.), and others to market its products or to codevelop new ones. How did Swanson, who left Kleiner & Perkins at 28, and Boyer, a scientist, pull off this miracle, where so many others have failed?

Boyer had agreed to leave academia, a difficult step for a distinguished scientist to take. Swanson had telephoned him out of the blue, but Swanson had a record of impetuousness. When he completed his undergraduate work at Massachusetts Institute of Technology (MIT) in chemical engineering in three years rather than four, Swanson had convinced the Sloan School of Management to let him begin graduate school early. Later, Citicorp Venture Capital hired him, and although he was just 25, sent him to San Francisco to open an office for them. A year later, Kleiner & Perkins hired him. Swanson was an entrepreneur, however, not a venture capitalist; so his next step was to find a problem that he could be happy solving.

After learning about Cetus Corporation, a 1971 biotechnology start-up, Swanson focused his investigations at the local library on the infant science of bioengineering. He compiled lists of authors and started telephoning the scientists one by one for their opinions on commercializing gene splicing. Each call would give Swanson more and more data, but none of the scientists believed that recombinant DNA could be bottled and sold as a remedy. Then he called Boyer to find out if this technology could be commercialized. Boyer replied that it could.

The two repaired to a local saloon and, several beers later, agreed to invest $1000 to exploit recombinant DNA technology through a new company called "Genentech," for genetic engineering technology. Their strategy violated several implicit rules of high-tech entrepreneurship, as promulgated in Silicon Valley during the 1970s. Instead of raising millions of dollars through an offering, plowing it all into huge expenditures for plant and equipment, and going on a hiring binge, Swanson and Boyer acted on Tom Perkins' advice and contracted out their early research to university labs. Rather than attempting to bring a product to market immediately (which was, after all, the goal), they opted simply to demonstrate that the technology would actually work—that through genetic engineering a microorganism could be made to produce a substance that it ordinarily does not make. In the original experiments by Boyer and Stanley N. Cohen, an artificially created gene had simply been replicated or cloned. Now they were trying not only to create and clone a gene in a laboratory, but also to place it inside bacteria and cause the bacteria, in turn, to manufacture a useful protein. This had never before been accomplished. This certification of the technology, the principals believed, would generate the excitement and money necessary to finance a continuing operation.

For their experiments, Boyer selected somatostatin, a hormone found in the brain. It has no market to speak of, but Boyer felt certain it could be synthesized. Its structure is simple, consisting of four amino acids. They would synthesize the DNA fragments at City of Hope National Medical Center, recombine the DNA, insert it in a bacterium (in this case *E. coli*, a fast reproducing bacterium found in the human intestine), and then assay the "molecular soup" back at City of Hope to detect somatostatin.

The first test, which took seven months, was unsuccessful. Swanson was worried. Then one of the scientists thought of protecting somatostatin from some proteins in *E. coli* that might be attacking it. Says Robert Crea, a chemist at City of Hope, "We found that by playing this genetic trick of protection, there is really that thing in the soup."*

---

*Randall Rothenberg, "Robert A. Swanson, Chief Genetic Officer," *Esquire* (December 1984), p. 372.

Swanson and Boyer had the beginnings of a new pharmaceutical company: recombinant DNA was a replicable technology. They then decided on a first product: synthetic human insulin. For this they needed to raise capital and recruit scientists. Swanson went after the best molecular biologists, protein chemists, and fermentation experts he could find. The accomplishment was similar to compressing at least 10 years of new product development at a major pharmaceutical company, because Genentech was only two people.

Manufacturing synthetic insulin was integral to Swanson's business strategy. Immediately after the somatostatin synthesis, Swanson informed Eli Lilly & Company, the $5-billion pharmaceutical giant, of their insulin plan. Eli Lilly & Company had begun marketing insulin in 1923; by 1979, it held 85 percent of the American insulin market. Swanson had no intention of competing with Eli Lilly & Company; it would have been futile, perhaps suicidal, to challenge its advanced sales and marketing staff.

But Swanson knew that the mere existence of synthetic human insulin would seem a threat to the giant. To raise capital, Swanson sought to license Lilly to market insulin, which he did.

In early summer of 1978, the final breakthrough occurred—the recombination and the expression of the insulin gene. Genentech was at last a company. It had the credibility to attract major financing and to find scientists to join it. Like Luke Skywalker hiring Han Solo to join in attacking the Empire, Swanson and Boyer found their own "Force"—interferon—to attack the big problems of cancer, diabetes, and other serious illnesses. The future of entrepreneurship as a mechanism for solving life-threatening diseases owes a large debt to the initiative of Swanson and Boyer.

Marketing-Oriented Strategic Alliances

Some strategic alliances are apparent before they are canonized by the lawyers. A large company controls a highway lined with consumers. A small company can deliver a new product or service that the consumers want to purchase. The company that controls the highway is a tollgate keeper. For a consideration, it will raise the tollgate and allow the smaller company to sell to its customers. For example, supermarkets charge tolls in the form of shelf-facing fees to food processors that want shelf space to test new products.

However, sometimes the small company persuades the gatekeeper to *invest* in its company in order to obtain the small company's allegiance in jointly selling product to the gatekeeper's customers. That type of agreement is the genius of entrepreneurship: the marketing-oriented strategic alliance.

Virgin Airlines

Richard Branson, 42, is just such a genius. To look at Branson one would not think of a towering entrepreneurial giant. He dresses casually—sweaters, open-necked shirts, faded Levi 501 jeans. Although he launched his company, Virgin Group ($2.5 billion revenues) in a houseboat, the company, which comprises a major independent recording company, a record retail chain, and an international airline, now has offices in a three-story, white Victorian villa backing onto London's Holland Park.

Strategic alliances are Branson's fish and chips. In 1986, for example, Branson took the music and retailing business of his Virgin Group public, valuing it at $440 million. Two years later, he took it private again, valuing the company at the same $440 million. But within months, he sold a 25 percent stake in his recording company, Virgin Music Group, to Japan's Fujisankei Communications Group for $170 million—valuing Virgin's recording group alone at $680 million.

Branson has gone on selling. In 1989, he sold 10 percent of his airline, Virgin Atlantic, to the Japanese travel group, Seibu Saison International, for $60 million. Soon after, Branson brought in partners for his retailing operations.

In a tough market, Virgin Atlantic has been more than holding its own. Its load factor (the percentage of seats filled) has been running at a healthy 80 percent; the airline is making money and paying its suppliers on time. Meanwhile, the load factors on the North Atlantic routes of both United and American (at around 55 percent to 60 percent) have been lagging, as Branson's business class to New York, Newark, Los Angeles, and Miami, with free limo service and a bonus economy ticket, has grown to be the market leader.

ChemTrak States Its Mission

When this development stage company went public in February 1992, it set forth its mission statement in its prospectus:

> The company's primary marketing strategy is to form corporate partner alliances with established domestic and international pharmaceutical and consumer products companies with the capital resources, distribution network and advertising and promotion expertise to market ChemTrak's products successfully. To date, the company has entered into corporate partner alliances with American Home Products Corporation, Bristol-Myers Squibb Company, The Boots Company PLC, and A. Menarini SRL for marketing and sale of its AccuMeter Total Cholesterol Test. The company believes that these alliances will enhance its ability to penetrate the point-of-care markets, and, in particular, the consumer retail market.

Corporate Partners. Through its corporate partner alliances, ChemTrak expects to more effectively reach the consumer retail and physician office markets. ChemTrak has entered into contractual relationships with the following corporate partners.

Corporate partner	Market	Country
American Home Products Corp.	Consumer retail	United States Canada Puerto Rico Mexico
Bristol-Myers Squibb Co.	Physician Office	United States
The Boots Company PLC	Consumer retail Physician office	United Kingdom
A. Menarini SRL	Consumer retail Physician office	Italy Spain Portugal Greece

American Home Products Corporation. In December 1991, American Home Products Corporation (AHP), acting through its Whitehall Laboratories Division, entered into license and supply agreements with the company. According to these agreements, the company granted AHP an exclusive right to market and sell, subject to certain performance requirements, the AccuMeter Total Cholesterol and proposed HDL cholesterol tests, and their improvements, in the U.S. consumer retail market and in certain specialty markets under brand names chosen by AHP. Under the license agreement, AHP has also been granted certain rights to future products. In exchange for such rights, AHP paid ChemTrak a one-time licensing fee upon execution of the agreement and is obligated to pay nonrefundable license fees based on certain milestones, including receipt of FDA clearance for the consumer retail market. The supply agreement provides that, in the event the company is unable to meet its supply obligations, AHP will have the right to manufacture products upon specified terms. The term of the license agreement extends to the point at which the last of the patents covered by the license agreement expires, although AHP has reserved the right to terminate the agreement upon 30 days' written notice to the company. AHP is a leading U.S. pharmaceutical and health care products company with other significant consumer retail products. AHP had sales of $7.1 billion in 1991.

Bristol-Myers Squibb Company. In November 1991, the company entered into a one-year agreement with Squibb U.S. Pharmaceutical Division, a division of Bristol-Myers Squibb Company, under which Squibb must purchase a certain minimum number of units of the company's AccuMeter Total Cholesterol Test, which Squibb intends to distribute to physicians in the United States in connection with the promotion of Squibb's cholesterol-lowering product, Pravachol^{tm}. This agreement may be extended for an additional one-year period, under similar terms and conditions. Squibb had sales of $11.2 billion in 1991.

The Boots Company PLC. In December 1991, the Company entered into a multiyear agreement with The Boots Company PLC for the sale of the AccuMeter Total Cholesterol Test under Boots' brand name in the United Kingdom. Boots is a diversified company with revenues of approximately $7 billion for the fiscal year ended March 31, 1991. Boots The Chemists, the 1069-store pharmacy division of Boots, had revenues of approximately $4.5 billion for fiscal year 1991.

A. Menarini SRL. In July 1991, the Company entered into a multiyear agreement with A. Menarini SRL for distribution of the AccuMeter Total Cholesterol Test on an exclusive basis in Italy, and on a nonexclusive basis in Spain, Portugal, and Greece. Under the agreement, Menarini must purchase certain minimum quantities of the product during specified time periods. Menarini is an Italian pharmaceutical company with 1990 sales of approximately $1.0 billion.

Licensee Money. Each of ChemTrak's corporate partners paid up front for marketing rights. This is *profound* leveraging. Here's how it works:

In an ideal marketing licensing situation, you can sell off an exclusive product or territorial right and use the proceeds as capital to finance the development of the major activities of the company. This type of opportunity exists principally with multimarket proprietary products but also, perhaps surprisingly, with commonplace products as well. For example, framed art print offers can be put into credit card stuffers and can be licensed to a catalog, premium, or direct mail firm or to a publisher for inclusion in a book. The computer software industry is another area where licensing is the norm, rather than the exception.

Licensing has myriad ramifications. In terms of raising up-front cash, however, one should think in terms of the following:

1. Is there a submarket for my product willing to pay a premium for it because of a serious problem that my product solves?
2. Is there an entity in that submarket that can manufacture and market my product?
3. Is that entity large enough to pay me a substantial down payment and to guarantee the payment of future minimum royalties?
4. What is the potential size of the submarket in terms of the number of units (dollars) per annum?
5. What is the highest-level contract that I can establish with that entity? (An introduction through an investment or commercial banker is preferred.)

The optimal licensing arrangement involves a substantial down payment by the licensee and relatively high annual minimum sales goals. All arrangements must be carefully drawn up, of course, with the proper legalese to protect the participants' rights and to ensure payment as agreed. If you are a tiny company and your licensee is very large, headquartered very far away, and expensive to visit and audit, you should ask for a substantial up-front nonrefundable payment representing what the licensee believes it would pay you within the first 6 to 12 months. Your argument is that you are too small to afford to audit the licensee's books several times each year.

Developing a Licensing Opportunity. Let us consider a hypothetical licensing situation. Assume you develop an "alcohol breath" sensor that can be implanted on automobile dashboards. If the driver has alcohol on his or her breath, the sensor will automatically lock the ignition and prevent the driver from driving away toward possible murder or maiming. Your manufacturing cost in volumes of 1000 units per month is $7.50 per device. The cost of labor to implant the device on dashboards of existing automobiles is $20 per unit, or 30 minutes of a mechanic's time. Clearly, automobile service stations and muffler shops would love to make $20 to $40 installing the device (markups on mechanics' time are legendary). Further, parents of teenagers would be an excellent market.

But to put 10,000 or 20,000 units into production, you need up-front money of $75,000 to $150,000. To raise this you might license the device to the new car market via a components manufacturer that provides other electronic components to the automobile industry. This would be an exclusive license—new cars only—with a $150,000 down payment against a per-unit royalty, say $1.50 per unit for a defined period of time. You might set minimum royalty payments each year of an increasing amount, say $150,000 in the first year, $300,000 in the second, and $500,000 in the third. After that, the exclusive licensing agreement can be renewed and new prices and terms established for the next three-year period.

As licensor, you will want the right to review the licensee's books and records to make certain that you are receiving a fair accounting. You will also want to make certain that the licensee is going to spend a satisfactory amount of marketing dollars in order to generate continuous cash flow for you to use in developing the retrofit side of your business. In this example, you will receive $950,000 over three years. If the licensee is strong financially, you might be able to borrow up-front money of $600,000 or so by pledging its guaranteed minimum royalty payments.

As mentioned previously, it is important to draw up clear, airtight licensing agreements. For this you will want to hire competent counsel, which means you need another source of up-front money before the licensee money begins to flow in. Licensing is a method that requires forward vision and planning. As a source of start-up funds for the ideally suited new concept or as a way to increase the profitability of a successfully launched company, using licensee money can be a lucrative opportunity.

Strategic Alliances at the Growth Stage

The primary purpose of forming strategic alliances in the growth stage of the "S" curve is to monitor and police the growth of an important division. For instance, Polo Ralph Lauren, an apparel and home furnishings design, manufacturing, and marketing firm struck an arrangement in early 1993 with Perkins Shearer to acquire and manage 29 of Polo's retail stores located in 20 states. As retail is not the strongest strength at Polo, and it is at Perkins Shearer, and because the two firms had worked together for many years, the alliance is a natural fit.

The management of special categories of investments, such as growth stocks or venture capital, is frequently contracted out by pension funds to experienced fund managers. Senior management of Standard Oil Company of Indiana was very impressed by the entrepreneurial ability of Raymond Stata and his teammates who founded and built Analog Devices, Inc. So much so, in fact, that Standard Oil invested $10 million in Analog Devices for the purpose of permitting it to make venture capital investments in emerging high-technology companies. Strategic alliances at the growth stage are frequently characterized as joint ventures, in which two companies, one on a rapid growth track and the other with enormous assets, agree to work cooperatively.

Analog Devices, Inc., founded in 1965 in Norwood, Massachusetts, is the leading producer of precision data acquisition components and subsystems used in measurement and control instruments and in computerized control systems. Stata spotted a very large problem in 1965: The operational amplifiers ("opamps") that were used in electronic test and measurement instruments were of poor quality and marketed without a service component. Analog Devices was launched to manufacture, sell, and service opamps. It subsequently broadened into devices that monitor and control medical instruments, aircraft, automobiles, the temperatures of electrical equipment, and other devices.

Stata and cofounder Matthew Lorber made $100,000 on the sale of their first company to Kollmorgen Corporation. The Kollmorgen stock was used as collateral for a bank loan to start Analog Devices.

It is easier for a manager to fail when he or she tries to be everything to everybody. That is over-commiting and it is a sure bet that many of the functions will be done poorly. Retailers have known this for years and they sell concessions to specialized service providers such as beauty salons, jewelry retailers, and photographic departments. Pension fund managers and retailers are two diverse groups who regularly subcontract to experts, with a license, the management of operations (which they need but do not do well).

Strategic Alliances at the Exit Stage

The ultimate strategic alliance is the sale of the entire company to a strategic acquiror—a company in the same industry that you have been knocking heads with for decades. To consider an acquisition with a like-size look-alike company, it should have some strengths where your company has some weaknesses and your company should fill some holes in its business plan. For example, a pharmaceutical company that sells products through the professional marketing channel would do well to acquire a health and beauty aids producer that sells products through the retail marketing channel. This is a means of spreading the risk and broadening the market, while opening the acquiree's markets to the acquiror's products, and possibly vice versa.

2

Why Corporations Make Venture Capital Investments

In interviews with approximately one hundred people responsible for the strategic investments of their corporations, I asked them to tell me why they made investments in entrepreneurial companies. Some of their reasons could not be divulged, but I was able to make certain assumptions based on the pattern of their investments. The reasons are arranged according to the frequency of their being given, with the most frequent first.

1. To Incubate and Reduce the Cost of Acquisitions

Many strategic partners invest in entrepreneurial companies with an option to acquire a larger percentage of ownership in the future, subject to a number of factors including performance, at a predetermined date and at a predetermined multiple of earnings. The purpose of investing with the option to acquire is to provide the strategic partner with lower-cost acquisitions. In addition to lowering the cost of acquisitions, the entrepreneurial company's close working relationship with various members of the venture company's management provides the would-be acquirer with a better knowledge of the company it is acquiring. The chance of buying a pig in a poke is reduced.

Philips Electronics N.V., a Dutch consumer electronics giant controls the 600-outlet video store chain, Super Clubs, and it recently exercised $66 million of options to become the largest outside investor in the video retail giant, Blockbuster Entertainment, Inc. Philips manufactures a significant number of video and audio cassettes. As another example, a leading manufacturer of fertilizer, Monsanto Company, has made several investments in agricultural genetics companies, with the intent of acquiring the first one that proves its ability to eliminate the farmer's need for fertilizer by nitrogen fixation of the soil. Approximately 40 percent of Monsanto's $4.5 billion in revenues come from fertilizer sales.

Since all investments of the venture capital subsidiary will not result in profitable companies, it may take a number of investments to generate acquirable businesses. However, if the strategic partner's overall loss ratio can be held to a reasonable level, incubating acquisitions through the venture capital operation can be an efficient adjunct to an overall corporate growth plan. This is generally accomplished by the investing corporation's obtaining an option to make a follow-on investment at a predetermined price when it makes its original investment.

2. Exposure to Possible New Markets

The entrepreneurial process often begins in "skunk works" and universities, where the seeds of new ideas can be evolved in an intellectual environment unfettered by practical considerations. In this manner the historic revolutions in communications, transportation, biotechnology, and information processing have been spawned. Following his university experience, the incipient entrepreneur will usually join a large corporation where he develops practical applications for his ideas, as well as the systems for conveying these applications to markets. When he has had sufficient first-hand experience, he will then leave to form a new company.

This process, repeated over and over again, has delivered life-saving drugs and medical instruments, lasers, semiconductors, computers, cable television, xerography, light-emitting diodes, and many other revolutionary products.

From the standpoint of the large corporation, the important point is to be positioned in such a way as to be able to capitalize on change as and when it occurs. Strategic investors call this "window investing," that is, sitting on the window sill and peering into the future. Many large corporations have determined that the best vehicle for exposure to revolutionary changes in the marketplace is a venture capital operation. For it is to venture capitalists that entrepreneurial revolutionaries come in search of the fuel to launch their new companies. Corporations that operate in windowless offices cannot possibly see revolutions in their markets.

3. To Add New Products to Existing Distribution Channels

Most large corporations are unable to bring products to market as rapidly as can entrepreneurs. Entrepreneurs bring products to market in one-fifth the time of large corporations. But large corporations have established distribution channels to move products from the factory to the end users, and the entrepreneurial company desperately needs access to consumers.

In a strategic partnering relationship, in which the entrepreneur needs marketing channels and the large corporation needs innovative products, the basis of the deal is a license.

When a large corporation chooses to license a small company's product, the entrepreneurial company is paid an advance and sells the right to market the product in certain regions or to certain industries. However, there is more. The entrepreneurial company then persuades the strategic partner to make an investment in the entrepreneurial's company's equity, to make sure that the latter is sufficiently capitalized to develop product upgrades and to service end users. Note in Appendix C, "Directory of Strategic Partners," that most of the strategic partnering agreements involving marketing licenses call for the large corporation to invest $1 million and up for *less than 5 percent ownership*. A sample licensing agreement appears in Appendix B.

4. A Less Expensive Form of Research and Development

Imagine the senior management of a large corporation saying this to the scientists and engineers in its R&D Department:

> You, ladies and gentlemen, must invest your own money, or raise it outside this organization in order to bring your new product ideas to a prototype stage. Borrow money if you like. Take out second mortgages on your homes. Ask your spouses to work two jobs. Obtain government grants and SBA loans. We will not put you on salary or pay any expenses until you have a working prototype that we can see. Then, before we invest money to produce the product and market it for you, we reserve the right to have the Production and Marketing Departments analyze the device. That shouldn't take over four to six months. Finally, depending on the whims of our Finance Committee, which meets twice a year, and depending on the state of the economy—we'll have to give the "green eyeshades" a few months at it—not to mention the stock market and other commitments for our capital, we may or may not make an investment in your new product. That's our deal. Take it or leave it.

The effect, of course, would be the wholesale resignation of most of the personnel in the R&D Department. This scenario, as exaggerated and exasperating as it may sound, is in fact the "entrepreneurial process" exactly. Entrepreneurs shoulder the bulk of the risk for product development, and the large corporations obtain *leverage* on their early efforts by investing in the companies after the early-stage risks are taken. Accordingly, the large corporations can reduce their investment in R&D by investing in entrepreneurial companies after the products have been developed and tested. The savings can be significant.

5. To Expose Middle Management to Entrepreneurship

There is a certain amount of cradle-to-grave security in a large corporation that negates or impedes progress and change. Junior management strives to become middle management, and middle management strives to become senior management. This upward progress through the corporate hierarchy more often breeds a reluctance to rock the boat than it does a drive to improve the stockholders' equity. In excess, this level of security is not healthy for growth or change.

Entrepreneurs, on the other hand, are very different from corporate managers. *Security* is simply not in their vocabulary. They are sellers. They are competitors. They are driven men and women. Exposure of entrepreneurs to middle managers and vice versa sends off electricity in both directions: The entrepreneur learns planning and systems, and the middle manager learns to *compete*. Many of the successful venture capital operations utilize the services of corporate middle management to monitor their investments. Strategic partners place their vice presidents on the boards and executive committees of entrepreneurial companies to monitor them and to provide advice and assistance. But in this transfer of electricity, the manager from the strategic investor normally learns how to compete like an entrepreneur.

The terms *competitive* and *competent* have quite similar meanings, particularly when used in the context of describing entrepreneurial characteristics. The *Oxford Entymological Dictionary of the English Language* points out that the words *competent* and *competitive* came into use in the English language at about the time of Shakespeare, and have the same French derivative: *competere*, which means "to be able to fly." Shakespeare used the two words interchangeably to point out a character's overall ability.

If one is competitive, then one is competent. The marketplace will eliminate anyone who is unable to compete. For a seller, the difference between being competent and incompetent will determine survival. As a result, the decision-making ability and business judgment of a seller or an entrepreneur are of critical importance.

A competent entrepreneur, given an equal footing with a middle manager in terms of capital, will outperform the middle manager by a country mile every time. However, by continuous exposure to entrepreneurial strategies, an observant middle manager can begin to draw even over time.

6. Training for Junior Management

It is difficult to attract and hold onto good management trainees. Occasionally, these young $40,000-per-annum, right-out-of-business-school demigods insist on running the entire corporation casebook style before they have drawn their first paycheck. And if they are given an unattractive assignment or two, they bristle and perhaps leave.

Some corporations have a management trainee turnover rate in the first two years of 8 out of 10. If a corporation hires 10 MBAs in a one-year period at $45,000 each, and half of them leave, the corporation has misallocated $225,000 plus benefits and training costs.

A number of corporations move their management trainees through the various line and staff departments to gain exposure to the organization and to the people. Frequently, the department heads, and even more frequently the people working in those departments, are unnerved by the more fortunate trainees who are on a brain-picking assignment. The results can be upsetting to both the picker and the pickee.

A possible solution is for the venture capital operation to actively participate in the management training function by assigning various analytical functions to the trainees; such duties could involve the trainees in learning the corporation's strategic plans. As the venture capital division is usually answerable to the Corporate Planning Department, the various duties for the trainees can be recommended by the manager of the venture capital operation for the approval of the Director of Corporate Planning.

As they complete the analysis stage, the trainees spend time carrying a deal all the way through from beginning to end, thereafter to be reassigned. However, they continue to monitor the investment they helped to originate not withstanding their reassignment.

7. Utilize Excess Plant Space, Time, and People

Leveraging assets is one of the fundamental aspects in maximizing profits. Among a corporation's various assets are its production facilities, space, time, and people. Unlike venture capital funds, which offer only money and advice in consideration for equity, a corporate venture capital operation may offer any of these assets, not only in addition to money, but sometimes *in lieu of* money as well.

The charter given to venture capital operations is fairly broad, that is:

> Invest in companies whose products can be sold through our channels, whose markets exceed $2 billion, whose markets are expected to grow in excess of 30 percent per annum, whose net profits before taxes are in excess of 20 percent per annum, and whose total capital requirement to obtain a representative market share is not more than $5 million.

Now, a number of new markets may fit that category: new drugs, new medical diagnostic devices, interactive television, biotechnology, environmental engineering, ethnic foods, water pollution systems, voice response computers, and undoubtedly more.

Assume that this particular corporation manufactures valves and fittings for water pipes sold to public utilities. Your company has developed an algorithm to enable water companies to route their water supplies less expensively. Your product sells for $200,000 per water company installation plus another $40,000 in installation, training, and monitoring costs. You make a profit of $350,000 on every sale, but gaining credibility with water company managers is not your strongest suit, and it takes you 6 to 9 months to make a sale. The multibillion dollar valve manufacturer knows the CEOs of the companies you want to meet, knows their golf handicaps, and has gone on vacations with them. The tollgates that make your sales so expensive could be lifted with a morning's worth of telephone calls by an executive at the valve manufacturer.

In addition, your software company needs, among other things, production of certain steel components, warehouse space to store parts, regional locations from which to offer service and maintenance, computer time to monitor its customer installations, health insurance for its personnel, and office space. As these cost items have been detailed in your company's financial statements, they are readily ascertainable. Assume they add up to $200,000 of the $1-million capital requirement.

These assets are offered to you at the corporation's cost, say $150,000. The final investment proposal then is:

> In consideration for 30 percent of the common stock of your software company, the corporation will invest:

$1 million, of which $850,000 will be cash and $150,000 will be services and assets.

Thus, the corporation obtains a 30 percent interest in a rapidly growing company with 15 percent less cash than is believed to be required and on better terms than might be obtainable by a purely financial venture capital fund. The corporation's leverage factor is 15 percent, which could be extremely important on a multiple basis, should your software company ever go public or be acquired.

Also, the utilization of bank loans or letter of credit guarantees is an important leverage tool, generally not done by venture capital funds for their portfolio companies. If the deal requires a line of credit as part of the financing, the guarantee could be worth additional equity points to the corporate venture capital investor.

8. To Mesh the Activities of Several Departments

The venture capital business is a lot like cattle raising. New companies, like calves, are bought cheap, are fattened, and then sold at a higher price. The managers of the venture capital operation are the farm hands responsible for the day-to-day chores, but the managers of the other departments are involved in the buying, fattening, and selling functions. Research looks for the right strain of cattle to be buying, Finance examines the financing of the purchases, Production understands the costs of fattening, and Marketing can tell how much they can be sold for and into what markets. Senior management of the corporation makes the final investment decision.

Although this is very oversimplified, the point is that six often disparate functional areas may be brought together through the venture capital subsidiary to work out problems jointly:

1. Senior management
2. Corporate Planning
3. Research
4. Finance
5. Production
6. Marketing

This process of bringing several departments together is healthy and, unfortunately, somewhat idealized. There are personalities and time considerations to contend with. The Director of Research may be frightened by a revolutionary invention, or the Marketing Vice President may feel insecure when an entrepreneur discovers a market that he overlooked. Consequently, a certain amount of rational thinking and planning may get lost in the process, or the process could take so long that the entrepreneur, his or her patience evaporated, goes elsewhere.

An inventor once applied for patents on a system that would enable the television viewer to send messages back to the transmitter in an unused portion of the television signal. This device had the potential of being a unique responsive teaching system, good for playing television quiz games in one's living room, or an excellent accessing system depending on where the transmitter was focused—in a library, office, warehouse, or the like. The television set, with this little black box attached, could become a revolutionary information-handling service. The patent protection was found to be excellent and the invention definitely proprietary and unique. What was missing was the demand curve and a marketing method to create demand.

In this case, there was a potential corporate sponsor whose R&D Department agreed that the black box was novel and proprietary, and whose Production Department agreed that it could be made for less than $40 per unit. But the Marketing Department threw a wrench into the gears with a simple observation: There is no serious demand for the product at the price at which it must be sold, and the markets are too fragmented to launch an inexpensive marketing program. A marvelous intellectual experience over several months involving four or five departments—Research, Production, Marketing, Legal, and Corporate Planning—led to closer ties among the departments through a healthy exchange of differences, even though the investment was eventually turned down.

9. To Generate Capital Gains

For a number of years Exxon Corp. operated one of the most successful and professional venture capital subsidiaries in the United States. Exxon's net profits after taxes are approximately $3 billion.

Clearly, its venture capital subsidiary was not formed to generate capital gains; the combined earnings of 10 of the most successful venture capital deals of the recent past—Digital Equipment, Intel, Apple, Teledyne, Hybritech and Microsoft, to name a mere handful—would be needed to reach Exxon's bottom line.

However, Cummins Engine Corp., with net profits after taxes of approximately $400 million, must certainly have considered capital gains as one of the reasons for creating its venture capital operation. One of the largest capital gains, more than $700 million, was made in Digital Equipment Corp. The company, a successful investment of American Research & Development Corp. (AR&D), was at the time the primary impetus to the enormous venture capital formation of the 1970s. AR&D invested a mere $70,000 to launch Digital Equipment Corp.

The first corporate venture capital investment was made by Allstate Insurance Co. when it invested $500,000 in Control Data Corp. in 1964 and made $50 million on its investment. Allstate, a subsidiary of Sears, Roebuck & Company, continues to be one of the most active venture capital investors in the country. It made gutsy early-stage investments in Federal Express, ActMedia, and the Berlinni's Oven Baked Pizza chain, among many others.

A company does not form a venture capital subsidiary with the anticipation of hitting another Digital Equipment or Control Data home run. But if it is not in the venture arena at all, it cannot even wistfully contemplate a return on the order of Digital Equipment.

10. Investigation: Develop Antennae for New Technologies

With a venture capital shingle on its corporate door, a great number of deals will be mailed, telephoned, carried, and dropped in over the transom to the officers in the venture capital department. If the traditional averages hold up, about one in 20 will be worth serious study, and perhaps one in 50 will be worth investing in. The remainder in many cases will provide useful information regarding new technologies and new markets. Before the shingle is hung, some outright acquisition possibilities may be considered too small to submit, or the large number of deals that come to the corporation in one form or another anyway may go to the wrong place and be either turned down or accepted on the basis of limited information.

The investigative reason for operating a venture capital division is of great importance. A large chemical corporation recently identified the field of oral health care as a new market it would like to have a stake in. A number of oral health care deals are being shown to the corporate venture people, and a very large bank of information is beginning to be formed. Rather than selecting the first gingivitis mitigator deal that looks good, the venture capital division will see, perhaps, a wide variety of ways to prevent gum disease: nutritional means, hormone injection in expectant mothers, laser, gum injection by heat sensors, nuclear medicine, or genetic engineering. The odds of picking the winning horse in an eight-horse race improve exponentially when you are able to observe the statistics on more than one or two of the horses.

11. Income Generating

The competently managed corporate venture capital divisions and investment firms generate ordinary income each year. Although it is not critically important to generate ordinary income, it is important to know that the officers of the venture capital operation are constrained by a budget. One of the means of supplementing their budget is by purchasing equity-linked debentures and notes of entrepreneurial companies and charging them monthly monitoring fees. The debt instrument provides hooks and handles to enable the investor to get inside the company and change things, such as management, or arrange for the sale or disposition of the company if it fails to achieve its projections.

12. Excellent Group Therapy for Senior Management

Members of senior management apply all of their powers of concentration daily to the subject of overcoming a myriad of problems so that the stockholders will continue to be pleased with their investment. Problems at this level are not only difficult to solve, but every year they grow more complex.

One of the reasons that large corporations become involved in venture capital investing is that it is more *fun* than doing what they normally have to do. Senior managements of corporations with venture capital divisions relate to the subsidiaries in two ways:

1. Setting the investment objectives of the venture capital operation.
2. Voting as an Investment Committee on thoroughly analyzed and completely structured deals recommended by the officers of the venture capital division.

By taking an afternoon every two or three months to review and vote on deals, senior managers can take their minds off the various serious problems of the corporation and devote their collective powers of concentration on a single $1-million investment. In addition, thinking through an investment decision for the venture capital subsidiary involves taking positive steps for the corporation. This contrasts favorably with the day-to-day problem solving that involves wrestling with government agencies, lawyers, personnel disputes, and other tar-baby type problems that do not, and cannot by their very nature, result in positive steps forward for the corporation.

A venture capital operation is not formed to provide an encounter group for senior management. However, the time devoted to the subsidiary by senior management will be, for the most part, filled with refreshing projects, forward planning, and positive, goal-oriented decision making.

13. Good Public Relations

The price/earnings ratio of a corporation's common stock is related to the stockholders' opinions about the future growth prospects for earnings. For example, in 1992, the average price/earnings ratio of corporations that operate venture capital divisions was higher than the DJII:

Avg. 1992 P/E Ratio Control Group*	Avg. DJII P/E Ratio 1992
18.5X	15.0X

*Comprised of U.S. corporations that presently own and operate venture capital divisions or that have venture capital investment activities. P/E ratios are for end of year 1992 and first month of 1993.

Note: This is not a one-to-one relationship. A lot of factors other than the existence of a venture capital division are at work to create a price/earnings ratio.

Venture capital investing is investing for a return five years hence. It is investing in the future. By creating a venture capital division, the corporate management is telling its stockholders: "We are looking out for your future. We are exploring revolutionary new technologies, new markets, new products, and a variety of new ideas that could result in a higher level and quality of earnings." As long as only a small portion of the corporation's equity is at risk, the stockholders generally will regard such an activity as good common sense.

First National Bank of Chicago nearly failed in the early 1980s from disastrous oil loans, and it would have were it not for the enormous capital gains that First National's venture capital subsidiary had in Federal Express Corp. A $457 million markup of its venture capital investments produced Citicorp's first earnings in fiscal 1991 in two years. Most corporations with venture capital divisions do not advertise their existence too frequently or loudly. Such broadcasting may produce negative effects if the details of the division are not thoroughly explained. Management may appear to be engaged in excessive risk taking or involved in activities not in the best interests of the stockholders. A line in the annual report, the 10-K report, or a speech before an analysts group is sufficient dissemination.

14. The Competition May Be Doing It

Management on a me-too basis is not generally sound, but when it comes down to protecting your markets from competition, keeping up with the Joneses is a sound policy.

Senior corporate officers of large corporations engaged in producing and distributing products in the areas of medicine, electronics, information processing, computer-related products, chemicals, industrial equipment, and consumer products would be surprised, perhaps astonished, at the types of venture capital investments their competitors were making as well as at the investments of corporations not regarded as direct competitors. Some of the major oil companies have achieved stunning venture capital returns in medicine and information processing.

The total amount of venture capital available for new companies varies from year to year within a range of $10 billion to $40 billion. In 1992, there was more, thanks to the buoyant new issues market, and it was distributed approximately as follows:

Table 2.1. Present Estimated Distribution of Venture Capital in the United States

	Available venture capital
Private venture capital investment companies	$14,000,000,000
Small business investment companies	3,500,000,000
Public stock market new issue investors	25,000,000,000
Institutional investors	1,500,000,000
Investment banks, law firms, family funds	4,500,000,000(*)
Corporate venture capital subsidiaries	10,000,000,000
Estimated total venture capital available for new companies	$58,500,000,000

Source: Primarily Venture Economics, Inc., the Wall Street Journal, Corporate Annual Reports.
*Precise data not available. Estimates only.

Although there are fewer than 200 corporate venture capital operations worldwide, the rate of new formation appears to be ahead of the rate of formations of other forms of venture capital investment companies. Corporations have begun to recognize the extraordinary opportunities in the venture capital area. Also, the formation, staffing, and operation of a subsidiary appears to be a more systematic method of doing something that has been going on inside many large corporations informally for a long time.

15. The ITEK Reason

The initials that make up the corporate name ITEK are rumored to stand for "I took Eastman Kodak." Four employees of Eastman Kodak developed a new optics device in the early 1970s, showed it to their bosses, and were told it would never amount to anything. The employees left and formed ITEK, which became successful and was acquired 10 years later by Raytheon Corp. for $350 million. True or not, the story makes the point: Entrepreneurs launch companies in the labs and around the water coolers of large corporations such as Eastman Kodak; they leave and take their ideas with them, and their ventures cut into the markets of their former employers.

A reason frequently cited for forming a venture capital subsidiary is to enable the large corporation to maintain a partial ownership in a new company being launched by its employees. After all, it is not unlikely that the solution to a problem or the development of a market was initiated, in part, within the corporation or at least shaped with skills learned within the corporation. How, then, can the stockholders of the corporation obtain the benefit of the potential growth of the new company being launched by the employee/entrepreneurs? Some corporations believe the answer is a venture capital subsidiary.

Corporations that lose supercharged employees to the entrepreneurial process are really the most likely sources to have grubstaked those employees for a number of reasons:

1. They know the people best.
2. They know the market best.
3. They know how much money the new company will require.
4. They owe it to their stockholders to keep the potential earnings in-house.

Cobe Laboratories and Bentley Laboratories were launched by entrepreneurs who were formally employees of Abbott Laboratories. The combined market values of Cobe and Bentley was approximately $500 million when they were acquired, or about 20 percent of the market value of Abbott Laboratories. Would Abbott Laboratories' market value have been $500 million greater if it operated a venture capital subsidiary? The answer is "perhaps." Some strategic partners clearly believe the answer is "yes."

16. Encourage New Company Formation in the Community

Corporations are citizens of the communities in which they operate plants, distribution centers, and administrative offices. As such, they are expected to be good citizens, at least to the extent of preventing urban decay or air and water pollution, if the costs are not unreasonable. A number of corporations, principally electric utilities, have formed venture capital subsidiaries in order to invest a portion of their capital in local entrepreneurs. Citizens Utility, Portland, Oregon's provider of electricity, provided $2 million in seed capital to launch Electric LightWave, an alternate access, all-fiber-optic telephone company servicing the Pacific Northwest.

Data processing service bureaus, clinical laboratories, and proprietary mental health/alcohol treatment centers have been strategic investment targets of large corporations that cofound them to serve the community, including employees of the large corporations located in the community. Some of these small service companies that rely on employees of the large corporations for their revenues become preferable small businesses.

Summary

As the owner of an entrepreneurial company, you are aware of the general objectives of strategic partners in potentially investing in your company. You can cite in your business plan several of the reasons why a strategic alliance will work for your company as well as for potential corporate partners.

3

Matching Your Company to the Most Likely Strategic Partners

Imagine yourself in a video game, landing on an enemy-held island with a machine gun in your hand containing 40 rounds of ammunition. The enemy holds 40 positions on the island and each one could cost you if you don't knock it out first. You fire in the direction of the first enemy position you see. You miss. You fire at the next position you see. You miss again. You fire at the third position. It falls and you run in that direction. That's the crisis mentality in which most entrepreneurs operate. And it is the wrong one. In many cases, it leads to accepting capital from a bad partner, in too small an amount, and of the wrong kind.

How does an entrepreneur know the "right" source from which to raise capital? The answer lies in associational thinking. Your company will in all likelihood require launch capital of some amount from one or more sources and, accordingly, your company will have to associate with one or more sources of capital. This is determined by running the characteristics of your company through the DEJ Factor test to estimate how much capital you will need to raise. Then you can focus on where it can be most easily raised with the minimum amount of equity give-up.

The DEJ Factor Test

Entrepreneurs can predict the eventual success or failure of their new company and estimate the amount of capital that will be needed by counting the number of DEJ factors in his or her new company idea. (See Table 3.1.) *DEJ* stands for *Demonstrable Economic Justification* or, if you prefer smaller words, validity, viability, or *raison d'etre*. I prefer DEJ (pronounced dedge) because fundamentals should be new words that serve a single and original purpose. The beauty of the DEJ Factors is their absolute infallibility. A new company is either Super DEJ (having all eight of the DEJ Factors), or Majority DEJ (possessing seven or more DEJ Factors); or Non-DEJ—it possesses too few DEJ Factors to be launched.

Super DEJs

If an entrepreneur can be confident that his or her insight or idea for a new company possesses all eight DEJ Factors, he or she should *run*, not walk, to launch the new company. Super DEJ companies practically guarantee the entrepreneur of solving a problem for a large number of people and creating wealth. Moreover, Super DEJ companies do not require very much start-up capital—usually less

Table 3.1. Eight Demonstrable Economic Justification (DEJ) Factors

1. Large number of buyers
2. Homogeneous buyers
3. Qualified buyers
4. Competent sellers
5. No institutional barriers to entry
6. "Hey! It Really Works!"
7. Invisibility
8. Optimum price/cost relationship

than $500,000. The problem is usually so large and the solution, or its delivery system, so unique that the new company is launched largely with customer financing. With few outside investors, Super DEJ entrepreneurs become wealthy in a short period of time. Examples include Bill Gates, who founded Microsoft, Jean Neditch, founder of Weight Watchers International, and Sol Price, founder of Price Clubs.

Sol Price founded The Price Company in 1976 in San Diego, California. The company operates nationwide Price Club cash-and-carry membership-only wholesale outlets. The outlets sell a variety of goods and services to member businesses that buy for their own use or for resale, and to a selected group of retail customers. Price conceived a novel idea for consumer goods marketing, featuring low prices and convenience, seven days and 61 hours per week, achieved in part by selling prepaid memberships to customers, which obviated the need for venture capital.

Majority DEJs

With seven of the eight DEJ Factors—a Majority DEJ situation—the idea for a new company should be vigorously pursued because it has a very high probability of success. However, it will require a considerable amount of start-up capital, perhaps $2 million or more, and raising that kind of money leads to the questions, From whom? and How? The rate of return on a Majority DEJ company will be less than that on a Super DEJ, and that is the return not only on capital, but on the entrepreneur's time and labor as well. Most computer-related start-ups are members of the Majority DEJ category.

The "Unlikely" Ventures

A new company that possesses six or less of the eight DEJ Factors is likely to be only marginally successful. It should be very carefully considered before it is launched because it will require more than $20 million in venture capital without a very high probability of success. If the entrepreneur can count only five DEJ Factors, or fewer than five, the new venture should be forgotten entirely. It will waste the entrepreneur's time and it will trash everyone's cash.

The DEJ Factors Up Close

Let's see how the eight DEJ Factors operate as the fundamental predictors of success in entrepreneurship.

DEJ 1: Existence of Qualified Buyers. The persons to whom the product must be sold know that they require the product. Buyers do not have to be *educated*, that is, told they have a problem. Buyers know they have a problem and know they must pay for a solution. Buyers are able to pay for a solution. A minimal amount of buyer education is required.

DEJ 2: Homogeneity of Buyers. The problem that the entrepreneurial company solves is essentially the same for all buyers, with minor differences in the degree of severity. The solution does not have to be tailor-made or customized for each buyer. Selling product off the racks is cheaper than selling it custom-made and provides more rapid cash flow.

DEJ 3: Large Number of Buyers. The number of potential buyers sharing essentially the same problem is very large. One test is to multiply the number of potential buyers (sometimes referred to as the *universe of selling sites*) times the price they would pay for the solution. If the number exceeds $1 billion, the business plan should be undertaken.

DEJ 4: Existence of Competent Sellers. The entrepreneurs, and the people they hire to join them, are competent at providing the solution to the problem. The premise or proposition that the product or service can achieve for buyers can be stated succinctly and quickly. PhD's are not required to sell the product, and the period from contact to contract is no more than a few hours at most.

DEJ 5: Lack of Institutional Barriers to Entry. The buyers are not organized. They do not belong to an association. There is no regulatory body to which they are responsible for their activities, such as the Food and Drug Administration, American Medical Association, or Federal Aviation Administration. Scaling institutional barriers to entry can be as difficult as seeking Federal Drug Administration approval for a new drug—requiring several years and over $50 million in costs—or as simple as obtaining a state license to sell a new insurance product by depositing $25,000 with the state insurance commissioner.

DEJ 6: "Hey, It Really Works!" The solution is passed along from buyer to buyer by word-of-mouth advertising. Word of mouth is not only the cheapest form of advertising, but also the most effective. A solution that is passed along from buyer to buyer has far greater credibility than one that must be advertised to attract buyers. The need for advertising, by definition, is the need for venture capital.

DEJ 7: Invisibility of the New Company. The new company operates quietly and without fanfare. It does not advertise or promote heavily. It does not gain attention so that it could be copied by competitors. When a company goes public very early, it risks allowing potential competitors the opportunity to gain information about its business plan and financial statements. Exposing critical operating ratios to a large number of competitors will attract competition.

DEJ 8: Optimum Cost/Price Relationship. The price of the solution is approximately equal to the cost of the problem. The price of the solution cannot be questioned as being excessively high or unwarranted if the buyers are paying the same price for their problem that they are asked to pay to have it solved. Yet to operate with a gross profit margin below 60 percent is a requirement for venture capital.

Possession of all eight DEJ Factors ensures the entrepreneur of a major success without having to raise significant start-up venture capital, unless, of course, the entrepreneur fails to carry the launch through in a competent manner. The launch includes building a skilled management team, designing an intelligent business plan, and remaining market-driven and innovative. There have been instances in which entrepreneurial teams have screwed up perfect DEJ companies, but they are too few to count.

Summary

The eight DEJ Factors represent the fundamentals of entrepreneurship. They are carefully examined before the new company is launched because an entrepreneur cannot play the game successfully unless he or she thoroughly understands these factors.

Possession of all eight DEJ Factors could mean starting your business with a few thousand dollars and creating wealth of more than $100 million. More than 100 entrepreneurs have done just that in the last 20 years. If you are in this lucky category, you need not read further, because your new business can be customer-financed.

Solution Delivery Methods

Once the entrepreneurial opportunity has been weighed to measure its number of DEJ Factors, the next step in the entrepreneurial game is to select one or more Solution Delivery Methods (SDMs) that will be used to convey the solution to the problem and to generate up-front cash. To provide the solution to the greatest number of people, competent entrepreneurs generally select one primary Solution Delivery Method and several ancillary ones. Depending on the SDMs that the entrepreneur selects, the need for strategic alliances is either more or less. Extraordinarily creative (or merely desperate) entrepreneurs have demonstrated their ability to discover numerous subsets of SDMs, which have generated more than 20 separate and distinct channels to the consumers and an equal number of sources of cash flows back to the company. Publishing entrepreneurs seem to be exceptionally good at conceiving revenue-generating subsets of SDMs. In addition to the magazine itself, which has the two primary revenue sources of subscriptions and advertisements, the following revenue-generating subsets frequently are created:

- Rental of subscribers' names.
- Seminars, symposiums.
- Joint venture direct response marketing sales.
- Sales of feature articles to small town newspapers as Sunday features.
- Audio cassettes of important articles.
- Video cassettes of interesting features.
- Books composed of several series.

- Sale of articles in foreign markets.
- Diaries.
- Prepaid membership clubs, such as travel.
- T-shirts, sweatshirts.
- Consulting services.
- Endorsement fees (such as the Good Housekeeping Seal of Approval).
- Trade shows.
- Reprints.

New publishing companies require strategic alliances primarily to access the subscriber lists of existing publishers. In 1991, The Tribune Company entered into an agreement with American On-Line, Inc. by which the parties agreed to produce "local editions" in Illinois and Florida of *America Online*, a subscription news and information service provided online to personal computer users. Material for *America Online* is taken, in part, from the Tribune Company's primary newspaper, the *Chicago Tribune*, and its television station WGN. In consideration, Tribune Company invested $2 million in *America Online's* preferred stock, subsequently converted into 511,921 shares or 9.5 percent of its common stock. The Tribune Company's holding was worth $10.2 million two years later.

What SDMs will your new company employ to deliver its product or service to the marketplace? Here are the 12 SDMs to choose from:

1. Facilities management
2. Franchising
3. Party plan
4. Consumer product start-up
5. Celebrity-endorsed consumer products
6. High-technology start-up
7. The Cookie cutter
8. Prepaid subscriptions

9. Capital equipment
10. Highway tollgate
11. Newsletter/seminar
12. Franchise on OPA (other people's assets)

1. Facilities Management

In this SDM the entrepreneurial company agrees to manage a certain facility for a corporation or government agency at a price equal to what the corporation or agency is currently paying, that is, its budget. The entrepreneur assumes full responsibility for the direct expenses and overhead of the facility. If the company is able to deliver the solution efficiently, the resulting profit is its reward, and the reward is usually substantial.

TriMas Corporation was founded in 1988 via an acquisition of 15 operating businesses from Masco Industries, Inc. including the manufacturing of industrial container closures, pressurized gas cylinders, towing systems products, specialty fasteners, specialty tapes, and precision cutting tools. Masco Industries retained a 51 percent ownership interest, diluted to 36 percent following the company's initial public offering. Under a corporate services agreement, Masco provides the company with the use of its data processing equipment, R&D services, corporate administrative staff, and legal services for an annual base fee of 0.8 percent of the company's annual sales.

2. Franchising

According to the United States Department of Commerce, total retail sales of franchised companies were approximately $2.1 billion in 1991, or roughly 45 percent of all retail sales. The growth rate of franchising has been remarkable: Sales of franchised companies have tripled since 1986.

The principal reasons for the success of franchised retail businesses are:

1. The franchisor formulates the entrepreneurial opportunity, creates the elegant solution, and provides training for the franchisee's management.
2. Franchisors are aware of the need to prepare instructional material for franchisees with great attention to detail. Murphy's Law—everything that can go wrong, will go wrong—applies among franchisees, and providing answers to franchisees' questions, no matter how minute, is of vital importance.
3. Franchising is first and foremost a means of raising cash for the franchisor. Within two to three years from its launch, well-managed franchisors normally go public, and with part of the proceeds they acquire the most profitable franchises. This provides an incentive to all franchisees that there is a capital gain opportunity available to them as well, through acquisition by the franchisor.

3. Party Plan

This SDM has been underutilized. But for those who have adopted it—Tupperware Division of Dart-Kraft, Mary Kay Cosmetics, Discovery Toys, Shaklee Corporation, Amway Corporation, Transart Industries, and others—it has acted as a cash cow. In the party plan SDM (sometimes called *in-home marketing*), salespersons call on private individuals to invite their friends to a party at their homes: a Tupperware party, for instance. The salesperson sets the products out in the living room or dining room, and demonstrates them. Not available in the stores, the products are generally the kind that need touching, feeling, moving around, and playing with, for customers to place orders. Thus, there is quite a bit of demonstrating and conversation at these product parties.

The salesperson writes invoices for each of the customers and promises shipments within three weeks (normally), taking cash, checks, and credit card purchases. The orders are telephoned into the company's warehouse from the party giver's home, as are the credit card orders. Checks are deposited the next day. Thus, the party plan company has the use of its customers' cash for three weeks or so.

The party giver receives a commission of 10 to 15 percent, the salesperson receives a commission of 10 to 15 percent, the district manager and the person who trains and supervises the salesperson receives a smaller commission, and the regional manager receives an override on the sale as well. There is very little product advertising in the party plan SDM, thus permitting these hefty commission structures.

4. The Consumer Products Start-Up

A large number of consumer products are launched every week. The success rate is quite low, however, because the entrepreneurs fail to review the product's DEJ Factors. If the DEJ Factors are not observed and followed, the new consumer products company will probably fail unless it is a "trendcatcher," such as the pet rock or the hula hoop. The most frequently absent DEJ Factor in new consumer products companies is the absence of a large problem in search of a solution. The newsletter is a consumer product designed to solve problems for its readers.

David M. Johnson and Owen Wollum plunged into the publishing business with a great idea applied to a doomed market. In 1985, the pair, then students at Pacific Lutheran University, started publishing a newsletter devoted to the workings of a pioneering database package called O'Hanlon's Sensible Solution. The company selling Sensible Solution got into financial trouble, and Johnson and Wollum found themselves without an audience. But the partners made one more risky bet. This time they created a periodical on the subject of Clipper, a database program from Nantucket Corp. Clipper, which can run programs written in the popular dBase language, took off. And now, Johnson and Wollum, doing business as Pinnacle Publishing in Seattle with seven newsletters, are grossing $4 million a year. With costs low, their pretax profits could be approaching $1 million a year.

The secret to Pinnacle's success is simple: Find software publishers with which to form symbiotic relationships. The software firm wants the mark of acceptance that comes from an independent publication devoted to its product. Pinnacle wants prospects—a list of the people who have registered with the software firm as buyers. Pinnacle gets the lists free, and they generate the kind of response rates (as high as 7 percent) that any ordinary magazine publisher would die for. Pinnacle also stuffs fliers advertising its journals into software boxes.

Pinnacle keeps its cash outlays to a minimum. The firm has almost no editorial staff, instead contracting out for a freelance editor and letting the subscribers fill the pages with their own comments, queries, suggestions, and technical tips. Subscriptions, at up to $100 a year, are paid in advance.

"One of the nicest things about the newsletter business is all the revenue is realized up front," says David Johnson, 29, a 40-percent Pinnacle shareholder and vice president for software products. "With 3,000 subscriptions we get an immediate hit of $300,000, and the expenses are staggered over time."*

Why would the developer of Clipper, DataEase, or R:Base want to share something as valuable as a customer list? It's symbiosis. More subscribers to the newsletter mean more fanatics using the product, and more sales of the software mean more subscribers for Pinnacle.

"Any program that can claim it has a dedicated, independent journal gains a lot of prestige," says Johnson. "We add value to the program, because there is a limit to the number of things that a software developer can envision his product doing. The user's manual is directed only at the operation of the product, not the application of it."†

5. Celebrity-Endorsed Consumer Products

In the celebrity-endorsed SDM, a well-known figure proclaims the virtues of a product or service, and he or she is marketed as a testimonial to the value of the product or service. Frequently, the celebrity is not active in the business, but his or her likeness is ubiquitous. Arthur Murray Dance Studios is an example, and Charles

---

*David Churbuck, "Symbiotic Software," *Forbes* (October 29, 1990).
†*Ibid.*

Goren's highly successful bridge tour and book business are prime examples. Goren's death has not deterred the revenue growth or profitability of the business that he endorses. The late Nathan Pritikin was relatively active in his successful diet and wellness center in Santa Monica, California, and it continues to thrive in his absence.

One of the most successful celebrity-endorsed consumer products companies was the Park-Hines Corporation, launched in 1955 by a young advertising executive, Roy C. Park. Park, 79, was born on a farm in Dobson, North Carolina, but his father could afford to send the four children to college. Park's first job came in 1931, while he was still a student at North Carolina State University in Raleigh.

> "I saw a want ad in *The News and Observer*.... Someone was looking for a young man to do some writing. Those days many ads like that were come-ons, and I wanted to be sure this one was legitimate. The ad said to write Box 731, Raleigh, so I did. But I put the letter in a pink envelope. Then I went to the post office the next morning and waited till I saw someone take that pink envelope out of the box. Then I eased over and found out who was offering the job." It was the North Carolina Cotton Growers Association. Anticipating that he would be interviewed for the job, "I had bought myself a white cotton suit and showed up for the interview wearing it."
>
> The Cotton Growers Association was reluctant to hire him. So Park told his prospective employer, "I had my own typewriter and didn't need an office. If they'd just find me a table in a corner somewhere, I'd work three months for nothing."*

Park was hired and he stayed with the Association for 11 years, editing a magazine and taking care of public relations and sales promotion.

One day out of the blue, Park received an invitation from Dr. H. E. Babcock, head of a farmers' cooperative called GLF, now known as Agway, to come to Ithaca to discuss an opportunity. Park replied that he would move only to have his own business. "Young man," Dr. Babcock said, "you just bought it."

"What business did I buy?" Park asked.

---

*Guy Munger, "Farm Boy to Boss of a Communications Empire," *The (Raleigh, NC) News and Observer* (July 29, 1984), p. 3D.

"Your own ad agency," he replied. "If you need money, we'll lend it to you."*

Park grew the business steadily and wisely, sticking to advertising for farm businesses. He opened branches in five other cities and expanded to 125 employees in six years. Then, "I fell on my face. My mistake was getting into political advertising, where we did several campaigns for Tom Dewey, including appeals for the farm and small town vote in 1948.† When Truman beat Dewey, many clients identified Park's firm as a "loser" and switched to other agencies. Park had to come up with a new idea.

The farm cooperatives had shown the need to Park for a consumer brand name of their own. Extensive market research indicated to Park the enormous consumer appeal of the name Duncan Hines. At that time, Hines was America's most famous restaurant reviewer and the author of guidebooks that rated restaurants. Park felt that a line of Duncan Hines food products would be potent. There were two obstacles, however: (1) Hines had never permitted his name to be used, and (2) Park didn't know how to get to Hines. To prepare for his eventual meeting with Hines, Park read everything he could find on the man. He knew that Hines did not want to license his name for the wealth it might bring him. Park was introduced to Hines by a mutual friend, and Hines asked the young man: "So, you're going to make me a millionaire?" Park said, "No . . . [but] you can help upgrade American eating habits." Knowing also that Hines never endorsed anything, Park came prepared to the meeting with completely finished Duncan Hines labels, in full color, on dummy cans, cartons, and jars so that Hines could see what the concept looked like. They shook hands on a deal.

Park and Hines began product planning and testing immediately. All products underwent blind tests before market introduction to assure consistency from one product to the next. Rigid quality control standards were set by Hines, and he saw that the company's manufacturers met those standards.

---

*Roy H. Park, "Building a Business with no Outside Stockholders," a speech delivered Nov. 2, 1976 at Cornell University Graduate School of Business and Public Administration.

†*Ibid.*

In the meantime, Park's farm cooperative clients backed out of their commitment to pay some of the up-front costs for an interest in the profits. Park had to raise money quickly, which he did by approaching family and friends and by pulling cash out of his advertising agency and letting it slide away. To save production and shipping costs, Park mailed the labels to the packagers rather than the other way around. Soon after its introduction, Duncan Hines cake mix captured a 48-percent market share. Pillsbury, Swanson, Aunt Jemima, and Betty Crocker brands took the hit. As Park says, "We could never outspend those giants—so we out-thought them.*

Duncan Hines was the first cake mix to be advertised on television. In the late 1940s, Mr. Hines acted in the commercials, which was also a first in consumer products advertising. Hines-Parks Foods was also the first company to use four-color ads in newspapers. Park also used outdoor ads to remind the housewife of the commercial she saw the previous evening on television. Park took Hines on the road, talking mayors and governors into declaring Duncan Hines Days and presenting him with keys to the city. The Duncan Hines Days generally ended with a big dinner, to which the governor, the mayor, city bigwigs, and the key chain store buyers were invited, along with their wives. The latter were presented with a corsage and an autographed Duncan Hines Cookbook on arrival. Park instructed his people to sell nothing at the party. "Next day was another story," says Park.

With distribution in 23 states and 120 different cake mixes, the Duncan Hines brand was second in sales among all brands by the mid-1950s.

A buyout offer from Procter & Gamble Company was accepted, for a price never made public. Park stayed at Procter & Gamble Company for seven years under the terms of a noncompete agreement, and in 1962 he left in order to begin his third career—and in a sense a return to his first love—journalism.

Park is a frequent speaker to business school and journalism students. His basic rules include the following:

1. Pay attention to details.
2. Get things done on time.

*Ibid.

3. Delegate to others all that they can handle as well or better.
4. Use showmanship, imagination. Dramatize what you are doing.
5. Take action. If you have the facts and a little common sense, and you *move*, you've got better than a 50-percent chance of being right.
6. Do your business homework.
7. Reinvest the cash flow as it is generated—but always keep a liquid position.*

6. High-Technology Start-Up

Entrepreneurs who select this SDM are well-advised to select a strategic partner because one of the most costly DEJ Factors—no institutional barriers to entry—is missing in spades. The FDA "charges" companies over $50 million for new drug applications and diagnostic devices. For entrepreneurs who seek to solve major medical problems, knowledge of the high-technology start-up method, coupled with an understanding of the DEJ Factors, is critical. This start-up method has been done supremely well by a number of biotechnology companies.

Photronics, Inc., founded in 1969, is a manufacturer of photomasks, which are ultrahigh-precision photographic glass plates containing microscopic images of electronic circuits. Photomasks are a key element in the manufacture of semiconductors, specifically for the transfer of circuit patterns onto semiconductor wafers. In 1987, VLSI agreed to purchase the greater of $2 million of photomasks per year, or 50 percent of its annual photomask requirements. Sales of photomasks to VLSI are at discounted prices. In consideration, Photronics issued VLSI warrants to purchase 120,000 shares or approximately 2 percent of its common stock at $6.80 per share.

Simtek Corporation, a development stage company founded in 1986, develops and produces nonvolatile static random access memories (nvSRAM). These memory products have greater capacity and faster data access speeds, and they retain their information when power is interrupted. Nippon Steel in 1988 obtained nonexclusive,

---

*Ibid.

worldwide marketing rights to Simtek's nvSRAM, the right to manufacture the company's nvSRAM, and the right to use the company's manufacturing process technologies for payments of approximately $5 million, a portion of which may be converted into Simtek common stock. Nippon Steel purchased 633,000 shares, or 10.7 percent of the company's common stock, for $2 million.

The initial steps to be taken in the high-technology start-up company launch are similar to the steps in the consumer product company launch, and include the following:

1. Identify a large problem in search of a solution; determine that the solution is a technological one; determine that the eight DEJ Factors are in existence. Frequently one of them will be absent—no institutional barriers to entry, such as the FDA—which will increase the need for venture capital.
2. Locate a scientific team with demonstrable achievement in the appropriate field to design and develop the solution.
3. PERT chart the events needed to launch the company and plot them against time.
4. Prepare a business plan by placing costs on the events, then project revenues and describe the strategic plan.
5. Produce a prototype of the solution.
6. Beta-test the solution with a prospective initial user and protect it with patents.
7. Debug the solution according to the results of the beta test, and modify the business plan.
8. Hire a corporate achiever from a related industry to manage the company.
9. Raise strategic capital to fund the research and development costs.
10. Begin production and marketing.
11. Take additional steps that are particularly useful in high technology start-ups, such as:
    a. Forming a scientific advisory board to assure high standards of quality in production.
    b. Encouraging the formation of users' groups to gain continuous marketplace feedback.
    c. Forming a board of directors that can help develop a strong management team while opening industry doors.

In the high-technology SDM, you will have to raise significant amounts of strategic capital, in the tens of millions of dollars. But the payoff is frequently higher. Genentech's market value exceeds $4.2 billion, Amgen's $10.4 billion, and MCCaw Cellular's $3.7 billion.

7. The Cookie Cutter

"You can't franchise quality," the axiom says. If you have a solution that is best marketed through multiple retail locations, your initial thought may be to sell franchises. After all, it has that most attractive benefit of up-front cash from the customer. However, if the product requires skill in producing, assembling, or training in its use, or if it has an after-sale service component, you will probably have to consider owning and operating your retail outlets. Wal-Mart Stores, Inc., one of the most successful entrepreneurial companies of the last 25 years, grew to sales of more than $24 billion and produced over $69 billion in wealth for its investors via the Cookie Cutter SDM.

Dr. Thomas F. Frist, Sr. founded Hospital Corp. of America. He gathered a handful of investors in 1960 to build the first investor-owned hospital. The group then went looking for the best doctors, technicians, and administrators they could find. "Quality attracts quality," Frist told a Forbes reporter. "Good people generally have good people as their friends, and I hired them too."* The initial hospital was built, operated and debugged. In 1968, Thomas F. Frist, Jr. left the U.S. Air Force to join HCA and one of this country's most successful expansion plans began.

As of March 31, 1992, HCA owned 170 general hospitals in the United States with 28,225 beds and 25 psychiatric hospitals with 3182 beds, and it managed for others 177 units with 23,297 beds. Overseas, the company owned 24 facilities with 2109 beds and managed two units with 500 beds. Hospital admissions are declining as a result of the growing trend toward ambulatory care centers and the cost-cutting pressures of the Clinton Administration, but HCA has managed to maintain its growth of revenues by a steady program of acquisi-

---

*Paul B. Brown, "Band-Aids by the Boxcar," *Forbes* (August 31, 1981), p. 88.

tions. Earnings have not suffered—they're at $262 million for 1992—primarily because of belt tightening.

HCA's formula is traditional conservative management. It has strict inventory controls, computerized billing, and low-cost purchasing. If certain procedures increase during the period of a month, they are flagged to see if so many were essential.

The publicly owned hospitals have accused the investor-owned hospitals of "skimming," that is, accepting patients covered by insurance carriers who pay more than Medicare or Medicaid. Frist, Jr. has rebutted those charges by showing that HCA owns hospitals where patients stay much longer than they do in not-for-profit hospitals. Humana, a large, investor-owned competitor of HCA, hired Dr. William DeVries, an expert in artificial heart implants, in order to develop an important specialty and leadership role in this critical area. Humana has gained much publicity through Bill Schroeder and other heart implant patients. HCA recently built a 109-bed cancer treatment center in Nashville, Tennessee. The significance of HCA and Humana is that they are living proof that highly visible community institutions serving the needs of people in serious pain can be managed and managed well by for-profit companies. Frist, Jr. says:

> You and I were brought up thinking hospitals shouldn't make a profit. They were there to provide quality health care, period. Well, that was in the days when if you needed a $1 million addition, you could raise half through donations. Today, that addition might cost $20 million, and you probably still couldn't raise more than $500,000 in donations. We have been the stimulus for a cottage industry to reorganize itself.*

If Frist is correct—and HCA's record is testimony to steady, unerring growth of revenues and profits—then there are other institutions that should be managed by entrepreneurial companies in order to deliver quality service. Could investor-owned universities be next?

8. Prepaid Subscription Method

The prepaid subscription method is an SDM that requires very little start-up capital and has one of the highest probabilities of success.

---

*Ibid, p. 89.

Entrepreneurs that use this extraordinarily successful SDM are often in the insurance and publishing fields.

Subscribers pay insurance companies and health maintenance organizations (HMOs), as well as magazine and newspaper publishers, $6 to $600 per month for the privilege of receiving a benefit sometime in the future such as physicians, medication, and hospital care, as long as they are members of the club or group. Insurers and publishers then use the subscribers' prepayments as up-front cash for their operating capital, which reduces their need for venture capital.

The membership concept has been used in industries other than health care. The father of membership merchandising is Sol Price, who, in 1975, formed The Price Company, which sells consumer nondurable merchandise in large warehouses to members of The Price Club. Individuals or businesses may become members of The Price Club by paying annual membership fees of $25; for an additional $10 per person, a member may designate two additional buyers. Price Club members are offered goods at substantial discounts from retail prices. Price has 170,000 members at $25 and 800,000 members at $10 shopping at his 20 stores. That represents $13.5 million in annual prepaid membership fees, or $600,000 per store. A successful entrepreneur can leverage $13.5 million in up-front cash into a fair amount of debt financing to grow his business, and Sol Price has done just that. Other companies have used prepaid subscriptions as a Solution Delivery Method. They include:

1. Franklin Mint (marketing collectibles via direct mail).
2. Book-of-the-Month Club, Inc.
3. Commerce Clearing House Corporation (a daily compilation of court decisions sold to lawyers).
4. Harry & David (fruit-of-the-month club).
5. Jeffrey Norton Publishers, Inc. (Audio Forum).

9. Capital Equipment

This SDM requires buckets of venture capital to get off the ground. A capital-intensive product must be produced, demonstrated to corporate customers, tested, debugged, remanufactured, redemonstrated, and finally sold. The salesperson must be trained to understand the product, which ties up more capital. In selling the product, the time from contact to contract is sometimes as long as three to nine months. This SDM literally screams out for strategic partnering.

"This device will allow you to save 30 percent of your departmental costs, and it will operate 30 percent faster than your current methods, and it is 30 percent more efficient," the salesperson says to the industrial customer. "How can I say no to that?" responds the customer. The rule of 30-30-30 has become the norm among capital equipment start-ups. Because the microprocessor seems to reduce the cost, increase the speed, and enhance the efficiency of practically every device it attaches to, the entrepreneurs in these companies speak of the rule of 30-30-30: a 30-percent improvement in cost, speed, and efficiency.

If a capital equipment company does not make improvements of at least that magnitude when installed in the user's plant or office, the sale will very likely not be made. The reason is that the user must uproot and replace old systems, routines, and equipment at a significant cost—in terms of both dollars and disruption time. The new equipment must justify the cost of changing the way the user has been doing business. Some of the more successful capital equipment entrepreneurial companies of the last 10 years have found strategic partners with deep pockets to fund the launch.

Cable News Network is one of the best examples. Robert Edward (Ted) Turner, III founded Turner Broadcasting Systems, Inc. in 1969. The Company launched the first cable television Superstation, WTBS, and has introduced a 24-hour, all-news service, Cable News Network (CNN), seen in 85 percent of homes that have cable television hookups. Turner saw an opportunity to build a major cable television network. He observed correctly that NBC, CBS, and ABC would not enter the cable market to compete against themselves and that Westinghouse Electric Corporation and other large cable television station owners could not move as rapidly as an entrepreneur.

Turner began with a bankrupt Atlanta television station, WTBS-Atlanta, whose programs he sold to cable TV stations across the country. This not only increased the number of viewers, but also attracted national advertisers to WTBS and increased Turner Broadcasting's cash flow. With the cash, he launched Cable News Network.

Turner, 52, complained about the poor quality of programming on the three major television networks for 10 years. His style was more than brash. It was antagonistic. The rude barbs draw the bears out of their caves and made them say silly things as did ABC program advisor Mike Dann: "The days of Mr. Turner's clear sailing are over."* What Turner knows, of course, is that entrepreneurs *always* beat corporate managers at the same game, and Turner proved it during Operation Desert Storm when more viewers, including the antagonist Saddam Hussein, watched the war on CNN than on the networks.

Turner is used to living on the thin edge. Intense, arrogant, full of braggadocio, combative for the sheer hell of it—all the adjectives have been pulled out to describe this phenomenon and they all miss the mark. They are form. The substance is this: Turner has made a career of taking on apparently impossible challenges and making spectacular successes of them against all odds.

He is also a canny opportunist. Enthusiastic about CNN, he hardly sounds like the man who said in 1974, "As far as our news is concerned, we run the FCC minimum of 40 minutes a day."†

While Turner has decried for years the "crappy programs" the networks have produced, he did not hesitate to run junky sitcom series he could buy for a song. Professional wrestling is junky, too, and Turner embraces it as well.

This ability to rationalize has enabled Turner never to paint himself into a corner. When trapped, he just knocks down the wall. Consider the fortunes of CNN, which created a $24-million working capital deficit at TBS before Turner was able to convince Manufacturers Hanover Trust Company and Citicorp to loan TBS $50 million for three years. No matter that the loan cost him three points over prime and a $3 million fee, tying up TBS' advertising accounts receivable for three years, Turner did not have to give up any equity. Cleverly, TBS borrowed $50 million when its retained earnings deficit was $9 million. How many entrepreneurs have pulled off that pretty a piece of leverage? Not too many would even dare to *ask*.

Turner began with a bankrupt billboard advertising company in 1969, which he forsook to purchase WTBS, a UHF station in Atlanta,

---

*Howard Rudnitsky, "Don't Count Ted Turner Out," *Forbes* (August 31, 1981), p. 31.
†*Ibid*, p. 32.

whose future looked bleak. It was losing half a million dollars a year, it was last in a market dominated by three network stations, and its signal was often weak and distorted. Through purchases of other stations for stock and debt, WTBS improved its stature in the Atlanta marketplace.

Turner bought up old movies on the cheap, including the *Star Trek* series, and ran them against the network stations' newscasts. Then, when the local NBC affiliate refused to take some network programs, Turner picked them up. He also paid to get the Atlanta Braves' telecasts on WTBS. By 1974, Turner Broadcasting was operating in the black and Turner bought out his three largest stockholders for a debenture, Rice Broadcasting, and the billboard business. With 87-percent ownership, Turner became more aggressive. He paid $1.3 million for a Charlotte UHF station that was later sold to Westinghouse Electric Company for $20 million to help Turner finance CNN. He bought the Atlanta Braves and the Atlanta Hawks that same year with financing provided by the sellers.

Meanwhile, Turner had long been interested in cable television as a way to break out of his limited Atlanta market. But building a string across the South to reach cable operators was out of the question. When RCA Corporation launched a commercial communications satellite in late 1975, Turner jumped at this chance to build a $750,000 earth station. That way he could send his signal not just across the South but *everywhere* in North America, and at a fraction of the cost of a ground system. In 18 years' time, Turner has built the fourth major network. In May 1985, he began a campaign to acquire CBS, and many analysts believe he will succeed.

Frequently, an entrepreneur is driven to succeed to overcome the business failures of a father. Turner's father sold his failing billboard business to his son, and then killed himself. This may or may not be Turner's principal driver. But he has accomplished things in an intensely competitive market that men with 100 times the money and corporate treasure have not been able to do. He has moved mountains using verbal skills, financial leverage, and initiative.

10. Highway Tollgate

Some of the most lucrative companies in America are those that extract a fee to enable people to come onto their "highway" (or into

Some of the most lucrative companies in America are those that extract a fee to enable people to come onto their "highway" (or into their market). Microsoft Corp. is the best known and most successful highway tollgate SDM ever conceived (except for the federal government, which licenses everything that entrepreneurs don't think of doing first).

Microsoft developed the most popular and widely used operating systems for personal computers, licensed to IBM Corp., and the dozens of IBM clones that emulate it. The operating system, known as MS-DOS, enables these computers to operate.

For virtually every personal computer sold, Microsoft earns a licensing fee. Microsoft never required venture capital, although Bill Gates, Microsoft's CEO, elected to take in a partner from the venture capital community in order to have a financial market-wise ally on his board. Of Microsoft's $27 billion market value, Gates owns one-fourth.

Lessons from a Successful Licensor

International Water Savings Systems, Inc. (IWSS) was a company founded by the late Walter Heinze who acquired the patents, tooling, and designs for a 1-quart toilet, which operates on 1 quart of water rather than the conventional 5 gallons needed to flush most standard home toilets. (The rights to a companion product for boats were sold outright for $1.6 million, plus a royalty to recoup development costs.)

The water-conservative toilet could be manufactured for less than $200, which, at a retail price of $600 to $700 (the price of commensurate toilets made by American Standard and Crane), would permit sufficient manufacturing and distribution profits. Toilet manufacturing is easy for American Standard and Crane, who have highly skilled product managers and efficient machinery and labor. For IWSS, which had to add a patented mascerating device and some electronics to its toilet, the job was not so simple.

Heinze was an experienced marketing entrepreneur. In addition to this 1-quart toilet, he has brought us the Playtex "Living Bra" and STP, the oil additive successfully commercialized by cofounder Andy Granatelli. Heinze's skill was in product positioning, developing a sales force, and penetrating markets. Naturally, he licensed the manufacture of his newest product, since that was not his bag.

to generate or save water. (The Saudis even tried, futilely, to float an iceberg from Antarctic to their doorstep.) Saudi Arabia needs 36 billion gallons of water per year just for flushing toilets, and it does not have 36 billion gallons of water in a year. Some people must discharge waste without toilets, which leads to epidemics such as typhus and cholera. Countries such as Saudi Arabia were approached by IWSS not just for the granting of manufacturing licenses, but for the exclusive rights to sell the toilets in their markets. The price for this privilege involved a $1-million down payment plus minimum royalties for each of the next 10 years in the range of $1 million a year. Such royalties, at $50 per toilet, represented 20,000 unit sales in the Middle East.

Heinze, who launched IWSS at age 76, died before the license with Saudi Arabia was signed.

11. Newsletter/Seminar Launch

In numerous marketplaces, the buyers and sellers need to come together several times a year to gain information about a problem (as others like themselves see it), and its solution (as problem solvers believe they can deliver it). The newsletter/seminar launch is used when the solution has not been developed and when the people with the problem are not ready to pay for its solution. They need more information about the problem.

Sheldon Adelson founded *The Interface Group* in the mid-1970s to sponsor COMDEX (Computer and Data Processing Expos), the largest seminar in the computer industry. Adelson entered into strategic alliances with hotels in Las Vegas, where the first expos were held, and with airlines.

When I first learned that I could solve problems for entrepreneurs, only one aspect of the problem appeared to me: raising venture capital for them. I subsequently learned that the universe of entrepreneurs was broad, and some segments of it needed entirely different kinds of solutions than other segments. For example, I estimated that approximately one million people in the United States annually consider the possibility of becoming entrepreneurs. I based this on the readership of entrepreneur-oriented magazines and the attendance figures for franchise, small business, and new technology conferences. These people were probably at the dissatisfaction and dance figures for franchise, small business, and new technology conferences. These people were probably at the dissatisfaction and energy peaks of their personal development curves, but lacked insight as to what to do about it. A possible solution was to steal a page from Gloria Steinem: Index the problems of becoming an entrepreneur and the many resources available to entrepreneurs, how to access them, and when. The perfect product was a book, which I called *Upfront Financing*.*

A smaller group of would-be entrepreneurs, perhaps one hundred thousand per annum, has a different set of problems. They want to share their problem with others, discuss specific areas such as attracting a manager, packaging a product, and dealing with suppliers. This group of entrepreneurs would prefer to come together in a conference room environment. The multiple solutions for this group are Venture Capital Clubs, conferences, and discussion groups. I started the Venture Capital Club of New Mexico at about the same time.

A yet smaller group of entrepreneurs has completed its journey through the tunnel, put it all together, and is ready to write a business plan and to raise venture capital. I estimated approximately 10,000 entrepreneurs go through this rite of passage each year.

And, finally, approximately 1000 entrepreneurs will seek the assistance of an investment banker each year to help them find a merger partner or raise venture capital or other forms of cash.

Thus, when I problem-formulated the market for my services, I saw four tiers, each interested in a separate and distinct product having its own price, payment terms, and means of conveyance. Table 3.2 tells the story better.

By addressing only one segment of the market, such as investment banking, I would have been ignoring much larger aspects of the market which not only feed into one another but also can easily be serviced profitably by the overall entity. The multiple niche method of problem-formulating seems to be applicable in a number of service industries.

Service companies are unique in two respects: (1) Many entrepreneurs are attracted to the idea of starting service companies, and (2) it is very difficult to raise serious amounts of capital for them. Venture capitalists have protested that the problem with service

---

*A. David Silver, *Upfront Financing* (New York: John Wiley & Sons, Inc., 1982).

Table 3.2. The Market of New Entrepreneurs

Market	Service
1000 need venture capital.	Investment banking services
10,000 are ready to write a business plan.	Business plan preparation
100,000 are actively considering launching a new business.	Seminars, conferences, tapes, study materia
1,000,000 are dissatisfied and energetic, but have no insight.	Books, magazines, indexes

sums of start-up capital lavished on their fellow entrepreneurs who have tires to kick, have in desperation come up with unique financing methods. Coincidentally, the sources of capital come from the people with the problem, that is, customer financing. Approximately 20 percent of the greatest entrepreneurs of the last 25 years relied on customer financing for their venture capital. A substantial number of successful service companies have been customer-financed because it occurred to the entrepreneurs that their customers could be persuaded to risk capital up front. The insurance industry was launched with customer financing. Many customer-financed companies are well-known, including Arthur Murray Dance Studios, Weight Watchers International, Century 21 Real Estate, EST, Esprit, Evelyn Wood Reading Dynamics, ComputerLand Corporation, CMP Communications, Renovators Supply, Mary Kay Cosmetics, Avon Products, Shaklee, Time, Maxicare, and others.

12. Franchise on OPA

Why invest in capital equipment or bricks and mortar to start a new business when you can obtain a franchise on OPA—other people's assets?

ActMedia was started in 1979 by the Bruce Failing family as an in-store media company. The Failings convinced large consumer products companies of the potency of placing their ads at the point of purchase. The entrepreneurs beta-tested the idea in several large supermarkets and calculated the results. Product sales increased dramatically in stores where shopping carts had advertisements. The

Failings entered into strategic alliances with all of the major supermarket chains, which benefited by earning fees on their shopping carts. With very little investment at the front end, most of which I raised from Allstate Insurance Corporation's venture capital division, ActMedia's market value exceeded $250 million in 1986 when it was acquired by a cable television company.

The essence of ActMedia's success was in the strategic alliances it forged with major supermarket chains such as Dominicks and Jewell in Chicago, Ralph's and Von's in Los Angeles, and Winn-Dixie in Atlanta.

4

Writing a Business Plan for the Strategic Investor

The Five Questions of Financial Investors

When an entrepreneur approaches them for an investment, all *financial investors* ask at least these five questions:

1. How much can I make?
2. How much can I lose?
3. How do I get my money back?
4. Who says you're good, honest, hardworking?
5. Who else is in the deal?

In asking these questions, financial investors are attempting to accept or turn down the investment opportunities quickly to maximize their time. It is in their interest, as much as that of the entrepreneur's, to avoid 30 days of investigation that result in a turndown. Thus, their mindset is to turn down a deal quickly if at least one of the answers to these five questions is not on point.

How Much Can I Make? The first question could result in a turndown if the operating statement projections are too flat, making the rate of return inadequate. Or, if the projection ramp is too steep, the turndown may be the result of unrealistic projections.

How Much Can I Lose? The answer to this question has to do with the use of proceeds of the financing. The entrepreneur may need product development money at a time when the portfolio of the investor has too many companies at the earliest stage of risk.

How Do I Get My Money Out? The investor is wondering if this company can be taken public or sold to a larger company—the conventional means of capitalizing on an investment—or if it will be a cash cow.

Who Says You're Good, Honest, Hardworking? By asking about management track record, the investor would like the answer to be that the entrepreneurs were involved in the founding of Hewlett-Packard or Federal Express and that they have blessed the investor with the opportunity to finance their second company. This does not happen on a daily basis. In fact, investors are faced with lesser of evil choices most of the time because most entrepreneurs have track records ranging from none to poor. What the investor likes to see, however, is that the entrepreneur exhibits good enough judgment to hire skilled managers, primarily in the areas of marketing, manufacturing, finance, and engineering.

Who Else Is in the Deal? The purpose of the fifth question is for the investor to find others who have endorsed the company by agreeing to provide products, credit, contracts, purchases, or time on the board of directors.

If all of this sounds wooden and mechanical, then how did one Fred Smith, age 29, raise $96 million from Prudential Insurance, General Dynamics, and 26 venture capital funds to launch Federal Express Corporation in the pit of the 1973 recession on the basis of a term paper he had written in college and without any substantive previous business experience? The relationship that Smith forged with General Dynamics was the key to further capital raising. Smith correctly perceived that General Dynamics would make a ton of money selling Falcon jets to Federal Express, and he approached them for a strategic alliance before lining up his venture capital investors. His plan worked.

Or why did it take Chester Carlson, the patent lawyer, 12 years to raise capital to finance the development of the first Xerox machine? Perhaps it had something to do with the fact that there was no business plan, merely a demonstration by a tall, cragged man in a wrinkled raincoat, involving a small piece of stainless steel, a rabbit's foot, some dark powder, and a piece of paper.

Some small companies have trouble paying for postage, while others have to send back offers to invest because they are oversubscribed. Apple Computer, Inc. raised more venture capital between 1978 and 1980 than the rest of the personal computer industry in total. Its founders were two unseasoned engineers under age 26, but the manager they hired to run Apple, Mike Markulla, was considered one of the marketing stars at Intel Corporation and he attracted venture capital from Arthur Rock, Tommy, Davis, and Don Valentine.

Peter Farley, the molecular biologist who founded Cetus Corporation, raised over $36 million from strategic investors and venture capitalists in the mid-1970s. He then went on to secure $125 million from the public in early 1981—without a product or more than a few million dollars in contracts. Dr. Leonard Schoen, founder of the U-Haul System, raised all of U-Haul's capital privately through tax-shelter-oriented limited partnerships that own the trucks and trailers and lease them to the company. The seed capital for *Psychology Today* came very rapidly from recipients of a direct mail test who subscribed to the magazine at an overwhelming rate, thus providing the cheapest of all forms of capital: customers' money.

Yet in the shadow of these success stories lies the wreckage of thousands of economically viable, socially useful businesses that have been unable to attract financing. Their entrepreneurs did not have correct answers to the five questions.

The basis for these five questions is that financial investors by necessity are *risk averse*. That is, although it is their business to "rent out" their fund's money (their "inventory"), an investor's *raison d'etre* (or "reason for existence") is to make absolutely certain the money brings back a profit. The greater the risk, the greater the projected return.

Strategic investors require answers to these five questions, as do financial investors. In addition, they need to know how it will benefit their companies. This requires adding a strategic partnering section to the business plan.

The Launch Plan

Many ventures fail because entrepreneurs leap from designing the solution to a large problem right to raising capital. This wastes capital and time, and raises tempers. It is the equivalent in baseball of putting seven fielders on first base, batting the pitcher in the cleanup spot, having the catcher use the third baseman's glove, and so on. It won't work.

To launch your entrepreneurial company in the most effective way, you should follow an orderly progression of events, which we will call the *launch plan*. Here are the twelve steps in a launch plan:

1. Formulate the problem.
2. Develop the solution to the problem.
3. Select the solution delivery method.
4. Create a PERT chart.
5. Write a business plan.
6. Create a prototype of your solution and protect it with a patent or copyright, if necessary.
7. Beta-test your solution.
8. Debug the solution and modify your business plan.
9. Begin production in small volumes.
10. Hire a corporate achiever.
11. Raise the necessary capital; consider strategic partnering.
12. Begin full production and marketing.

To avoid losing time, wasting capital, and compromising your credibility, you should follow these twelve steps in order. If you scramble them, you are likely to end up with an unsuccessful launch.

1. Formulate the Plan

This is the most creative aspect of the entrepreneurial launch. It requires your analyzing the problem that you have chosen to solve and studying it from various angles. You can accomplish this most effectively by asking yourself a number of questions:

- Are people aware of the problem?
- Do they know what the problem costs them?
- Is the problem equally severe and costly to all of them? Most of them? None of them?
- Is the problem discussed in a newsletter, a trade journal, newspapers, or television?
- Is the problem common to a widespread geographic area?
- Do people who have the problem customarily buy solutions from entrepreneurs? From consultants? From large companies?
- Do people who have the problem attend seminars or industry-wide conferences where solutions and new ideas are discussed, or do they wait for solutions to come to them?
- Is there a trade association or any other institutional barrier that mitigates the flow of new ideas into this marketplace?
- Will this product need to be accompanied by a service or instruction manual?

2. Develop the Solution to the Problem

What you do at this stage of the launch will depend in part on the sort of problem and solution you have chosen. If you are working on a high-tech startup, for example, you will now seek and hire a scientific team to help you develop your product. If you have chosen a consumer product or capital equipment solution, now is the time either to assemble a product development group or to license the right to produce and market a product that someone else has developed.

Whatever solution you have chosen, you should at this point standardize your solution so as to make it useful to the largest possible number of people. Also, if your product is to contain a component that must occasionally be replaced—like the blade in a razor or the ribbon in an office machine—spend some time right now developing replacement parts that are efficient, reasonably priced, and easy to install.

Keep going over the DEJ Factors. Analyze your solution from every possible angle, always remembering that it will be successful only if it has as many DEJ Factors as possible—preferably all eight of them.

3. Select the Solution Delivery Method

Now ask yourself exactly what kind of business this should be. In other words, choose your Solution Delivery Method. Study the SDMs until you are certain of the one that will be right for your solution. Use the following list for quick reference:

1. Facilities management
2. Prepaid subscription
3. Franchising
4. Party plan
5. Celebrity-endorsed consumer product
6. Consumer product start-up
7. High-technology start-up
8. Cookie cutter
9. Capital equipment
10. Tollgate
11. Newsletter/seminar
12. Franchise on OPA

You may decide to combine several SDMs into one business plan, especially if you are an information or franchise entrepreneur. For example, newsletters are usually marketed on a prepaid subscription basis, and franchising chains occasionally rely on celebrity endorsement.

4. Create a PERT Chart

The word *PERT* is an acronym for *program evaluation and research tool*. Diagram all the steps in your business launch, plotting each move against a time frame and keeping the tasks organized into categories such as finances, facilities and equipment, and product. Assign a cost to each activity, and include all 12 launch steps in your PERT.

Schedule each move carefully, taking time to consider the worst-case scenario for each step. Remember that if one event, such as developing the prototype, takes two months longer than you planned, your company will need additional capital to cover rent, salaries, and other expenses for those extra eight weeks.

PERT charting will encourage you to temper your optimism with "downside planning." This healthful exercise consists of continually asking yourself a question: If this move backfires, what can I do to repair the damage or cover the shortfall?

5. Write a Business Plan

In writing a business plan, your objective is to take the skeleton of a PERT and put flesh on it by adding descriptive material, which will include detailed financial information. Your PERT plots events against time, and each of those events will cost a certain amount of money. Revenues and cost of goods sold will at some point begin to appear. The result will be a cash flow projection of 36 to 60 months. Figure 4.1 shows you how to diagram this flow numerically and graphically.

The key considerations in preparing a business plan are the components of:

- Revenue.
- Variable costs.
- Fixed costs.

These components are a function of the events of the launch process that you have developed up to this point.

Revenue. The components of revenue include:

- *Sales*: Cash, installment, or terms.
- *Rental*: Down payment, terms, bankability of future rentals.

Table 4.1. Sales and merchandising plan

Sales and merchandising plan	Sales plan	Channels selected	Salesmen
			Representatives
			Distributors
			Dealers
			Direct mail
		Location of sales	Trained salesmen vs. untrained salesmen
			Training program
		Accounts and territories by sales forces	
		Incentive plans	Quotes
			Commissions
			Incentives
		Major customer selection	Rationale
			Strategy
		Sales forecast	In dollars and unit total (include assumptions)
			By major customer in dollars and units
			Major customer action plans
			Document unit and dollar histories of similar companies to support
	Merchandising plan	Sales contracts	
		Benefits to customer	
		Sales aids (written)	For salesmen
			Distributable
		Sales aids (other)	
		Other support for sales forces	From technical
			From manufacturing
			Other

Table 4.1. Sales and merchandising plan *(Continued)*

			Quantified by impact on P&L	
			Ranked by impact on P&L	Action to be taken to minimize uncertainty
Management information and control systems	Description of accounting and control practices			
	Critical measures of performance			Organization plan
			Product plan	
			Technology plan	
			Manufacturing plan	
			Sales and merchandising plan	
			Financial plan	
	Management reports	Operating reports		Contents
				Distribution
				Frequency
				Purpose
				Effectiveness
		Financial reports		Contents
				Distribution
				Frequency
				Purpose
				Effectiveness
	Meetings	By functional area		Contents
				Attendance
				Frequency
				Purpose
				Effectiveness
P&L	Historical	1st year by month		Assumptions
	Forecast	2nd year by quarter		
		3rd, 4th and 5th years annually		
		Inventories		Materials
				Work in process
				Finished goods

Table 4.1. Sales and merchandising plan *(Continued)*

		Fixed assets schedule	Cost
			Improvements
			Additions
			Write-offs
			Depreciation
		Payables aged	
		Schedule of all loans and debts	Bank line
			Bank officer
			Notes payable
			Interest rates
		Lease commitments	Obligations terms
			Obligations amount
			Payment terms
			Interest rate
		Good will	
Cash flow	Receipts		
	Disbursements		
Break-even analysis			
Accounting system	Accounting		
	Cost accounting		
	Cash management		
	Budgeting		
	Auditing		
	Inventory methods		
	Depreciation		
	Valuation of tangible assets		

- *Fees collected*: Set annual minimums.
- *Service income*: Collected or contractual.
- *Peripheral sales*: Ratio to primary sale.
- *Meter income*: Can you make, install, and service the meter?
- *Royalties collected*: Set annual minimums; renewal conditions.

You can make a revenue projection by asking yourself the following questions:

1. How many units can I expect each representative, tele-marketer, or mailing piece to sell each month?
2. Can my company gradually build up its sales to 5 percent of the total market?
3. What is the experience curve of other companies that are similar to mine?
4. How much should my company spend on marketing?
5. How large a test mailing will I need?

Keep in mind, however, that your revenue projections must be based on valid, meaningful assumptions; otherwise your cash flow projections will lack credibility. If that happens, sophisticated investors will not back your business, and good managers will not join your company.

Variable Cost. The costs of production alone will include:

- Cost of materials: Try to have vendors ship just-in-time.
- Cost of labor: Maybe your state will foot the bill for training.
- Cost of shipping and handling: Pass these costs along to the customer, but stick a newsletter and subscription form in the box, a la Pinnacle, to achieve ongoing revenues.

It is helpful to have cost estimates prepared or reviewed by the person who will be responsible for manufacturing. Also, be sure to locate alternative sources of key components, and make certain that their prices will fit into your business plan.

In addition to your production costs, you will have to bear the variable cost components of selling and marketing. The costs of selling will include support and commission for all or some of the following employees:

- Direct sales representatives
- Marketing representatives
- Dealers
- Franchisees
- Party plan representatives

Your variable marketing costs will be spread among these functions:

- Advertising
- Direct mail
- Public relations
- Consultants

Depending on the nature of your entrepreneurial company, you may have additional variable cost components.

Fixed Costs. Your business will most likely incur the following fixed costs:

- Management salaries, FICA, and benefits
- Administrators' salaries, FICA, and benefits
- Insurance
- Legal fees
- Accounting
- Rent
- Office equipment, furnishings
- Utilities
- Telephone
- Sanitation
- Factory overhead
- Shrinkage
- Postage
- Stationery and consumables

A credible basis for these costs is as important as for any other. Attention to detail is one of the most prized skills of successful entrepreneurs.

Do your business plan projections by hand. Do not use a software package. The old-fashioned method will result in a more thorough understanding of the business plan. When it is finished, ask your board of advisors or directors to evaluate it.

6. Create and Protect Your Prototype

The Product Prototype. If your solution is a product, you must at this point design, build, and assemble a *prototype*—an original model on which all others will be fashioned. As soon as you have accomplished this, you should patent your device. A patent attorney can help you file the necessary materials with the U.S. Patent Office. The patent is absolutely vital if you wish to prevent others from infringing on your right to the exclusive use of your idea. You may wish to introduce complications into your patent application in order to make your device difficult for others to copy. *Do not go public with your product until you have filed with the Patent Office.*

Service and Information Prototypes. If your solution is a service, you will have to describe it in complete detail in a manual. You may wish to obfuscate it a bit so as to make it difficult for imitators to copy. When you are satisfied with your description, get it into copyright by filing it with the U.S. Copyright Office. Again, the services of an attorney or a how-to book will be useful here.

If your solution is information, it should be described in elaborate detail in a manual and then copyrighted like the service solution.

7. Beta-Test Your Solution

When you have created your product or service, you should test it thoroughly in your plant or office to see (1) if it works, and (2) if it is innovative. These are known as *alpha tests*.

The *beta tests* are conducted outside your plant or office. A beta test involves putting your solution into the hands of potential consumers and letting them use it. Probably the most common type of beta test is the focus group. For this test, you simply assemble a group of potential customers in a conference room or in someone's house. Put the product into their hands, show them how to use it, and then watch them and listen to what they say about your solution. This way you can find out what they think of these aspects of your product:

- The name of your product or service.
- The packaging and general appearance.
- Its price.
- The directions that come with the product.
- Its usefulness.
- The way it feels in their hands.
- The degree of ease with which it can be operated.
- How well it does what it is supposed to do.

Decide ahead of time what you want to learn through your beta tests. Choose your focus groups and your meeting places so as to be sure of getting the information you need. You may want to offer your beta testers a discount on future purchases in return for testing your product.

If your solution is a magazine or newsletter, you can beta-test it by preparing a dummy issue that includes a questionnaire. Mail copies to a small target audience, and ask people to fill in the questionnaires and return them to you. Spend a good deal of time formulating the questionnaire so that the respondents' answers will tell you what you need to know about their opinion of the issue.

8. Debug the Solution and Modify Your Business Plan

The chances are good that the beta tests will turn up one or more weaknesses in your solution. If so, your next step is to debug your product or service; in other words, correct any weaknesses, and rebuild or rewrite the solution so as to incorporate any necessary changes. Once you have done that, you will need to run a second wave of beta tests on your debugged product.

When you finally get your solution into working condition, you will need to modify your business plan to reflect all changes, cost differences, and delays. The modified business plan—which, by the way, might have to be revised many times—will become your company's strategy. You will use it to hire key managers, and you will show it to banks and other sources of capital.

9. Begin Production in Small Volumes

At this stage you need to put your production system into operation, not so much to turn out goods as to gain information about the production process. Here are just a few things you will be looking for at this stage:

- How good is the production team? Are they adequately trained? Do they work well together?
- What problems, if any, are likely to crop up in the mass production process?
- How good are the suppliers? Will the production process be slowed down because of delayed delivery of supplies? How many alternative suppliers are available?
- Are raw materials in abundant supply? How many alternative sources are available?
- What kind of quality control mechanism works best for this particular team?

Depending on the nature of your solution, you may have to add to or subtract from the list. Compile a detailed list of things you want to learn from this small-volume production process. During this stage, make whatever adjustments seem necessary to achieve the most efficient and satisfactory production operation.

10. Hire a Corporate Achiever

Now you are ready to choose a corporate achiever or a business partner to manage your company. This person must already have demonstrated a high level of ability in the corporate world, preferably in a field related to the one your new company is about to enter. He or she should possess skills that complement your own. For example, if you are a very creative, high-energy person, the corporate achiever should be thorough and meticulous.

Don't make the mistake of hiring someone who is less capable than you are or who lacks the strength of character to stand up to you when he or she believes you are wrong. Try to find someone who is as courageous, intelligent, and capable as you are. Your business partner should review the business plan and modify it as necessary, with your guidance. You may call on the corporate achiever to support the plan before commercial banks and venture capitalists.

In most instances, corporate achievers are older than entrepreneurs and more conservative. They usually have greater personal assets to protect, and they may be more meticulous in dress, speech, and demeanor. Their reasons for joining an entrepreneurial company should include a desire to build something, to become a member of a problem-solving organization, and to regain their sense of purpose. The glue that binds them to the entrepreneur is equity—a piece of the action.

11. Raise the Necessary Capital from a Strategic Partner

At this stage of your company's development it is important to turn to the Directory of Strategic Partners in the back of the book, and on a separate pad of paper write down the names of the corporations that have a need for your product, those whose customers you would like to sell to and service. Then order the annual reports, 10-K and 10-Q reports, and securities analysts' research reports on these companies *and* their competitors. Study them analytically. Look for changes in their gross profit margins. If you see declines over the last few years, then you have spotted a serious need for new product innovation. Carefully document this. Analyze the corporations' sales per employee and profit per employee ratios. If you notice declines in these ratios, then you have once again spotted a weakness that you may be able to sell your way into. You are now ready to contact them with your business plan.

12. Begin Full Production and Marketing

You are ready to roll out your product or service, giving your entrepreneurial gift to the audience whose problem you have set out to solve. If you have taken care to complete every step in the entrepreneurial process to the best of your considerable ability, your launch will be a success.

During the roll-out, you will want to keep in mind the following tips from successful entrepreneurs who I have worked with over the years:

1. Tell your spouse and family to bear with you for 12 to 18 months while you live fanatically and cut-off from the world.
2. Seek helpers, cooperators, networkers, alliances, boosters, cheerleaders, and door-openers from people who will benefit if your new company succeeds.
3. Turn-around the turn-downs. If you receive a "no," it is because you did not convince the buyers. Try again. The sale begins with the "no."
4. Keep moving forward. Keep the ball in play. Climb some walls, go around others, and tunnel under still others.

5
Closing the Strategic Partner

Once you have clearly identified your company's SDMs and matched your company's elegant solution to the needs of the most likely strategic partners, send them your strategic plan and call for a meeting.

Six Steps to a Successful Closing

When Eli Lilly & Co. paid 15 times revenues for Hybritech in 1987, it did so to obtain a presence in genetic engineering. When Pillsbury paid 26 times earnings for Steak 'n Ale in 1980, it did so to add a dinner house chain to its restaurant division. When Medtronics paid eight times revenues for Versaflex in 1990, it did so to broaden its product line and reduce its concentration on pacemakers. Something takes possession of the minds of large corporations when they are on the prowl. Rather than call an exorcist to remove the passion to overpay for a niche business, they pay the price because the egos of the managers drive them to it. Their egos compel them to take over small, interesting niches and regional business with their capital.

In every situation in which two people communicate, one is always "selling" and the other is potentially "buying." *Selling* includes persuading, teaching, motivating, urging, or convincing the other person to trust, accept, believe in, loan or invest money in, approve or recognize the idea, concept, outline, or description of some event that may occur in the future.

There are six critical steps necessary to closing a deal. The following steps describe the tools used in deal making and explain how the winner can be selected:

1. Determine your product's *Demonstrable Economic Proposition* (the DEP Factor).
2. Gather data about your potential strategic partner—the target of your sale.
3. Find the gatekeepers who can block your deal, and develop a strategy for "shunning their pikes."
4. Leverage others who can lose if your deal doesn't close.
5. Control the closing meeting with questions.
6. Add a dose of third-party endorsement to your deal.

Let's look at each of these steps more closely.

Step 1: Find the DEP Factor

If you were to write a headline about your product or service, what would it say? What single statement would compel people to buy what you are selling? The headline must be the precise solution to the problem shared by your intended buyers. The Demonstrable Economic Proposition (the DEP Factor) is a *succinctly stated solution or need that the strategic partner is looking for, but that may be, and probably is, unstated.*

Many sellers ignore the issue of finding their unique selling proposition, and attempt to close the buyer with other premises such as lower price, more features, after-sale support, more locations, or 24-hour service. But these side issues take profit out of a deal. A brilliantly conceived DEP Factor enables the seller to maintain a high profit margin.

Still other sellers, particularly those with industrial or technology-based solutions, obfuscate their headlines with a lengthy explanation of a complex factory bottleneck, such as: "If you're using six throws on your 4(XX) hp reciprocal compressor but only pulling 400 bps, then you need a Ramaframas Compressor with more pull for less hp." Apparently, the unique feature of the Ramaframas Compressor is more power for less cost, but the prospective buyer usually cannot make the mental conversion because the features are hidden in an overly detailed description of the problem. Buyers want the message conveyed in easily recognizable patterns.

Federal Express was burning advertising money between 1972 and 1974 with headlines that touted, "We Own Our Own Planes." The target customer did not give a hoot for such a grand and egocentric statement, and Federal Express was bleeding red ink while searching desperately for its DEP Factor: the headline that would set it apart from freight forwarders. Finally, it discovered that what it was selling was a solution to the anxiety of the shipping clerk, whose job rested precariously on the prompt and certain arrival of the company's package at its destination the following day. Federal Express discovered its headline on the verge of filing for bankruptcy protection: "Absolutely, Positively, Overnight"—a money-back guarantee of next day delivery by 10:30 A.M. The rest, as they say, is history.

Every deal must have a headline. Every deal must state a demonstrable economic proposition and answer the question: What opportunity or need does your deal address? The DEP factor should compel the strategic partner to close from the moment she sees or hears the headline. However, 90 percent of all sellers either overstate or complicate the problem. Many of us know the headline "The Heartbreak of Psoriasis," but few of us know the product that is used to solve it. Looking inward at the mechanics of the concept is *centripetal* projecting, as opposed to *centrifugal* projecting, looking at a description of the solution from the strategic partner's point of view.

Chester Carlson, the founder of xerography, found his strategic partner in Haloid Corp., a Rochester, New York photographic equipment manufacturer whose prospects lay in an inconclusive fog. The more likely candidates, Bell & Howell, IBM, and RCA, were doing too well in their basic businesses to be scouting for new innovations.

Craig McCaw, the founding CEO of McCaw Cellular Communications, Inc., the nation's leading cellular telephone company, did not invent wireless communications; AT&T did. But McCaw has transformed how we think about telecommunications by putting portable telephones in our hands, so that we can make or receive telephone calls (or send/receive data or documents) wherever we may be. AT&T watched McCaw control AT&T's future. What a perfect strategic alliance when AT&T bought a little more than one-third of McCaw's common stock in late 1992.

Carlson and McCaw found strategic partners because they found the key DEP Factor. If you want to close a deal with a strategic partner, call on a company to whom you can give a *future*.

Step 2: Collect Data on Your Potential Strategic Partner

Who are your prospective strategic partners? Are they "open to buys" to what you are selling? Can they pay for it? Once you have found them, how do you qualify them inexpensively? There are horror stories of entrepreneurs who spent months and months trying to sell a strategic buyer, only to learn at the closing that there was yet another hurdle to jump.

A fast "no" is as good as a prolonged "yes." If you know all the strategic partner's objections up front, then you have qualified him or her in full. You know exactly what aspects of your deal are going to present the most difficulty: price, terms, delivery schedule, involvement of the buyer, labor intensivity of the buyer, timing, or other drawbacks. Clarity is critical to closings. Demand it.

The needs of prospective strategic partners may change suddenly due to external events. They may have been open to buys yesterday, and you are too late. In a great number of situations, an entrepreneur arrives at the prospect's door too early, and will have to help the proposed partner see the need for the deal. That costs money.

If your deal is too ahead of its time or too out front of the strategic partner's perception of the problem, you will waste a lot of time and money in qualifying. Pioneers get arrows in their backs. The second guy who enters a market frequently does better than the first because the buyers have been prequalified.

A good example of this is the Honda Motor Company's introduction of the Cub Cadet into the United States in the early 1960s, a few years after the introduction of the Italian Vespa. The postwar baby boom had created a population of millions of young adults who could not afford cars, yet whose lifestyles beckoned excitement and freedom. They could afford motorbikes or mopeds, but people had a negative image about motorbike owners, associating them with the Hells' Angels and social ostracism. All of this negatively impacted moped sales in the United States. Honda countered the negative myth with a positive one of its own—"You meet the nicest people on a Honda"—which blazed the way for Honda to close deals with thousands of bicycle dealers, who subsequently closed their deals with millions of Cub Cadet owners.

To collect data on your prospective strategic partner requires one or more forms of market research. Order their annual reports, 10-K and 10-Q reports, and securities analysts' research reports. Study trade journals. Review the names on the boards of directors to see if you or one of your board members has a contact.

What does it actually mean to "qualify prospective strategic partners"? It means asking enough questions up front to find out what they like and do not like about your deal, without turning them off by appearing ill informed or naive. This is frequently done with *either/or* questions.

For example, if I ask you, "What is your favorite food?" you may have difficulty being specific. But suppose I ask you, "Do you like meat better than fish?" and you say, "Yes." Then I follow with, "Do you like steak better than hamburgers?" Given the answer, I have qualified you for steak sauces, barbecue grills, and a whole host of related products.

Clarity up front, even if it is a quick "no," is critical to getting a "yes" out of the strategic partner. If you substitute assumptions for clarity, you could be going down a blind alley, burning up money and time.

The Directory of Strategic Partners lists the names and telephone numbers of the chief executive officers of entrepreneurial companies that have raised strategic partner capital. One of the reasons for this is so that you will pick up the telephone and call them. When you do, ask them how they made contact with their partner. How long did it take? What stage of development was their company in when it raised capital from them? Did they have a working prototype? Did they have any sales? Did they have other outside capital? Do they recommend that you make a frontal assault, call an investment banker, or use our accounting firm to introduce us?

Of course, you may have identified several strategic partners whose names do not appear in the Directory. This is a tougher assignment because you will face the *gatekeeper problem*.

Step 3: Find the Gatekeepers and Go Around Them

There are tollgates in front of every deal. These are erected by either commercial or government opportunists who have seized an opportunity to block deals—that is, charge a toll for access to the buyers—unless the gatekeeper can be persuaded to turn the pike and let the entrepreneur pass. The "tollgate" is the gatekeeper's *gut values*. These values can block an innovative plan as thoroughly and completely as can the FDA, one of the most powerful gatekeepers in the country, from stopping an innovative drug from getting to the market. But the entrepreneur can gain the *cooperation* of the corporate gatekeeper by using a combination of strategies including endorsement, sponsorship, and leverage.

When Frederick W. Smith was hammering together the initial $96 million necessary to launch Federal Express Corp., his cooperative strategy involved the following collaboration:

1. *Endorsement*: A report was prepared by a well-known consulting firm with freight forwarding experience that blessed Smith's business plan.
2. *Overcome the "inexperience" turndown*: Industry-experienced managers joined forces with the 29-year-old Smith and began lining up early customers. (The name "Federal Express" was selected because Smith and his team were convinced that the Federal Reserve would be the company's most important customer; but it never did play an important role, except as an interested, potential customer that other players could look to as a source of endorsement.)
3. *Second-level endorsement*: The company's investment banker, Rothschild, Inc., tested the money-raising waters for Federal Express and determined that potential investors were uncomfortable with the concept of flying all packages into a single hub in the middle of the night, sorting them, and flying them out to their

destinations in the early hours of the morning. Thus, a nationally known management consulting firm was hired to study the concept. It did and it blessed it.

4. *The targeted strategic partner*: A strategic alliance with General Dynamics Corp. was sought to provide a fleet of airplanes, a portion of the capital to buy them, and long-term financing for the balance. But General Dynamics wanted some company in the deal. It didn't want to be alone.

5. *Leverage*: General Dynamics' "Maybe I'm in" was communicated to Prudential Insurance Co., which agreed to provide a layer of long-term debt subject to the rest of the financing, which was mostly venture capital, coming together. Smith took the "subject-to-commitment" from Prudential back to General Dynamics. The financing arrangements with General Dynamics were improved to the company's advantage.

6. *Raising the tollgate*: Given strong managers to supplement Smith's inexperience, two management consultant studies that said the concept would fly, a highly regarded investment banker shaking the trees for start-up equity capital, and an insurance company willing to provide a layer of long-term debt between the equipment financing and the equity, the supplier of airplanes put up some launch capital to make sure that Federal Express lifted off the ground with its airplanes. The $96 million deal that launched Federal Express closed in 1972.

The date of the Federal Express deal is significant because when the price of oil quadrupled two years later, the company almost went bankrupt. However, it had such a broad range of deep pocket investors that a handful of them was all that was necessary to keep the company afloat.

Gatekeepers exist in every market, and *every deal that is turned down is done so by a gatekeeper*.

I will show you how to get around them. The most rigid gatekeepers are people who sit on decision-making committees and who find it *safer* for their careers to say "no" and to block deals. If your idea has career advancement opportunities for them, they will approve it. But if you can't present your deal to them directly to show them its sound personal benefits, the risk of a turndown is heightened.

You may think you have corporate venture capital officers sold when they hear your deal and say, "I like it." But if you let the matter drop there, you will probably not close your deal because you haven't learned anything about what the gatekeepers are thinking. You should ask the following questions of the "deal messenger":

- Do you have to present this deal to committee?
- Who is on the committee?
- When does it meet?
- Does a deal require 100-percent approval to close?
- Who is most likely to block it?
- What can we do to get his or her approval?

You can pose a great number of questions, including how to gain permission to present your deal to the entire committee rather than have the "deal messenger" handle it alone.

To assist you in creating a flying wedge to carry your deal to the decision makers, the Directory of Strategic Partners provides you with names of outside directors and the company's accounting firm. You may know one of the outside directors or someone who does. The same applies to the company's accountants. Perhaps you went to the same school or grew up in the same town as one of them.

In the Spring of 1992 as a Lamar start-up biopharmaceutical company, decided to develop hyperimmune intravenous immunoglobulins (IVIGs) by breeding tens of thousands of swine and injecting them with the company's proprietary vaccines. The IVIGs are intended to provide an immune system for HIV-positive people. To raise venture capital, the Company's senior management asked me for my thoughts. I suggested a mix of debt financing to build and equip the swine breeding and processing facilities, venture capital from knowledgeable, start-up health care investors, and at least two strategic partners. As to the latter, I contacted several catheter manufacturers because each swine needed a subcutaneous implantable catheter; and I contacted every pharmaceutical company that did not appear to be searching for an AIDS vaccine or remission product, yet had a history of doing strategic alliances. The IVIG deal suggested itself for two kinds of strategic partners: a production stage partner and an R&D stage partner.

Step 4: Leverage Others to Help Close

You can increase your closing ratio if you are willing to give up some of the credit. More to the point, most deals crater when the seller seeks to retain all the credit.

In the halls of Congress, where there are 100 senatorial and 521 congressional gatekeepers, the President's acolytes know that, to get the President's ideas sponsored as bills, they have to give up the credit to certain senators or representatives. The trade-off is not credit for cash flow; it is an IOU for Presidential endorsement at election time.

The same technique applies in business. Involve investment bankers. Ask your accounting firm to prepare projections to describe to the strategic partner what future royalty payments it might receive. Have your attorney prepare a license agreement, or use the one provided in Appendix B. Your insurance agent may be helpful in making a contact if his or her firm also insures the strategic partner.

Consider forming a board of directors and board of scientific advisors, bringing a handful of consultants together, and issuing them stock but paying them very little for their time. Then your network of advisors has lots to gain and the value of their time to lose if they don't make things happen for you. If the directors, advisors, and consultants lend their names, their skills, their contacts, and their networking abilities, they will open doors that you, acting separately, may not have known existed. Nowhere is this more prophetic than when your company operates in a small town, where its success could make the entire region blossom with employment, productivity, and purchases of local goods and services.

In this environment some of the more exceptional networkers to put onto your boards are the president of the local community college or vocational schools, the top real estate broker, and the leading insurance agent. The educator knows the nuances of government-guaranteed loan and grant programs, and he or she can place the college's graduates in your company for years to come. The real estate broker wants to sell you land for your buildings over the next 10 years. To make her goal come true, she will introduce you to deep-pocketed real estate investors who she thinks may want to diversify into commercial businesses with big upsides. And the insurance agents want to write your property and casualty and key person life insurance policies. To win that prize, he will introduce you to the investment officer of his firm who will reintroduce you to venture capital firms it has invested in. Your network of advisors, consultants, and directors will be rewarded in two ways for manning the laboring oars for you: to provide services to your company and, in so doing, win with your common stock.

Be certain to point out these possible conflicts of interest. You do not want anything hidden from any investor that could embarrass you later.

Step 5: Just Ask

Closing can be equated with negotiating. And the key to successful negotiating is to control conversations by asking the following questions:

- Are you looking for this kind of technology at this time?
- What is your overall budget for this kind of deal?
- Have you ever done this kind of deal before?
- What are your constraints in qualifying this technology for your R&D department to work on?
- Do you have decision-making responsibility in this area?
- What kind of information do you need to take this deal to committee?
- When does the committee next meet?
- Will this deal be presented at that committee meeting?
- Would it be appropriate for me to attend? Do you need to meet some of the other players, see the site, or do you need other back-up data?

Someone (who stands to benefit if there is a closing) should attend the deal meeting with you and take thorough notes on the buyer's responses. The notes can be reviewed later to see whether you failed to follow up on one or more of the buyer's answers or statements. You can then ask for another meeting or make a telephone call to clarify a point.

When you take colleagues to a deal meeting, do not let them sit idly by twirling their thumbs. They should pull out a legal pad and take notes. Should you miss a point, they should politely interject. When the meeting is over, they can critique your performance. If they are actively writing, it encourages the "buyer" to write as well.

Another axiom in successful negotiating is that the party with the most time to spend wins. You should stay at the deal meeting until the other side has to leave. An early departure by you will not sit well with the buyer.

Bring one or more of your sponsors to the meeting. If you are trying to close a technology license, bring evidences of customer satisfaction with you. Better yet, bring a customer. Discuss with the customer in advance what you are expecting him or her to say.

The type of conference that you want to achieve at the deal meeting is one that is highly orchestrated, yet animated, with lots of questions and give and take. This is the time to demonstrate your competence as orchestra leader.

The buyer is likely going to hand you a Confidential Disclosure Agreement to sign before you begin making your presentation. It will probably say that, no matter what secrets you impart to the buyer, he probably knew them any way, and no matter what the buyer tells you in confidence, you are liable if they leak out. The Confidential Disclosure Agreement will be very one-sided. Big companies do things that way because they have a fortress mentality. As long as the agreement does not absolutely strip you of your company's rights without consideration, then go ahead and sign it. The deal meeting will not move forward unless you do.

A sample Confidential Disclosure Agreement used by a large tehnology-based firm appears in Appendix A.

Step 6: Use a Third-Party Endorsement

In many instances, the deal meeting will not be decisive. A decision will come later when the buyer has a committee meeting to decide whether to accept or kill the deal. In the interim period, it is essential that you provide the deal with the *myth of authority*. If you're not selling Sears' paints, then you cannot endow your deal with the same 100 years or so of trustworthy service. But you can get the local media—the newspapers that are read and the television shows that are watched by the people on the committee—to give you a mention, at the very least.

When I fly into Columbus or Dubuque for a deal meeting, I sometimes have my secretary call one or two writers and TV journalists in these cities to schedule an interview. The subject of the interview is the benefit to the community if my deal closes. In most instances, the story will run prior to the committee meeting and my deal will have the third-party endorsement of the press and thus the ring of authority. This is critical to providing information to the gatekeepers on the decision-making committee whom you may not be permitted to sell to in person.

For technology deals, you will want the endorsement of a reviewed or scholarly scientific journal to bless your field of investigation and your discoveries, up to the point of negatively impacting your patent applications and trade secrets. The whiff of gunpowder from the bullets you fire at the deal meeting may have drifted away in a week's time, and you will want to turn the committee's heads with a positive article about your new product or company in a respected publication. In the hermetically sealed board rooms of many large corporations, where innovative deals are few and far between, a positive story in the newspaper or trade journal will appear coincidental but spark a positive recall of your presentation. Public relations reinforcement after the deal meeting will push your deal to the very vanguard of ideas that the board next decides to invest in.

APPENDIX A
Sample of Confidential Disclosure Agreement

This Agreement ("Agreement"), is made this ____ day of _____, 1993, by and between Entrepreneurial Ideas, Inc. ("EII"), a Delaware corporation, with its principal place of business at _____ and ADS Financial Services, Inc. ("ADSFIN"), with a principal place of business at 524 Camino del Monte Sol, Santa Fe, NM 87501. Hereinafter, EII and ADSFIN are jointly referred to as "The Parties."

The Parties to this Agreement hereby agree as follows:

The Parties have developed or otherwise obtained certain confidential information including but not limited to business plans, strategies, contracts, and financial information. The Parties wish to discuss, and possibly enter into certain business agreements. In order to do so, it is necessary that The Parties disclose some or all of this confidential information. The Parties do not wish to lose the confidentiality or diminish their rights in the confidential information, and require assurances that their rights in this information will not be diminished or impaired.

Therefore, in return for fair and adequate consideration, The Parties agree as follows:

1. "Confidential Information" means any and all information The Parties provide to each other which The Parties identify as confidential. However, a Party will be under no obligation to maintain the confidentiality of such information which it can prove, by clear and convincing evidence
   a. was previously known to The Party free of any obligation to keep it confidential; or
   b. is or becomes available by any means other than unauthorized disclosure; or
   c. is developed by or on behalf of The Party independent of any information furnished under this Agreement; or
   d. is received from a third party whose disclosure does not violate any confidentiality agreement or obligation.
2. All Confidential Information is and shall be the sole and exclusive property of the disclosing Party. The Parties shall not take or cause any action which would be inconsistent with or tend to diminish or impair the disclosing Party's rights in the Confidential Information.
3. Confidential Information is provided solely for the purpose of the discussions, negotiations, and possible business agreements. The Parties shall not use, or induce others to use, any Confidential Information for any other purpose whatsoever.
4. The Parties shall not, directly or indirectly, print, copy or otherwise reproduce, or commit to hard copy in whole or in part, or embody in any product any Confidential Information, without The disclosing Party's prior written consent.
5. The parties shall not disclose or reveal any Confidential Information to anyone except those of their employees or agents with a need to know in order to effectuate the business purposes contemplated by The Parties. Further, prior to revealing or disclosing Confidential Information to such persons, The Parties will require them to agree to and be bound by the terms of this Agreement.
6. Upon a Party's request, the other Party will deliver to the requesting Party all Confidential Information, as well as all documents, items, of whatever media comprising, or relating to the Confidential Information as well as any other documents or materials belonging to the requesting Party that may be in the other Party's possession. The other Party shall not retain any copies.

7. The Parties acknowledge that any unauthorized disclosure or use of Confidential Information would cause The Parties immediate and irreparable injury or loss.
8. This Agreement may be amended only in writing signed by The Parties, and there are no other understandings, agreements, or representations, expressed or implied.
9. If any clause or provision of this Agreement is or becomes illegal, invalid, or unenforceable, such clause or provisions shall be severed and the remaining provisions of this Agreement shall continue in full force and effect.
10. This Agreement shall be governed by and construed in accordance with the laws of the State of _____.

IN WITNESS WHEREOF, The Parties hereto have caused this Agreement to be executed as of the day and year first above written.

By: _____
Title: _____
President
ADS FINANCIAL SERVICES, INC.

ENTREPRENEURIAL IDEAS, INC.
By: _____
Title: _____

APPENDIX B
Sample Licensing Agreement

THIS AGREEMENT is made between ENTREPRENEURIAL IDEAS, INC. (the "Company"), a Delaware corporation, whose business address is _____, and GIANT MARKETING CORP. (the "Sponsor"), a corporation, whose address is _____.

WITNESSETH:

WHEREAS: The Company has pioneered the development of an alcohol-on-the-breath analyzer for automobile dashboards, as well as related technologies to mitigate DWI-related deaths and accidents; and

WHEREAS: The Company owns the exclusive rights to the product named the DWI-MITIGATOR, and

WHEREAS: The Sponsor is the largest producer of automobiles in the world; and

WHEREAS: Sponsor has examined the DWI-MITIGATOR device and is agreeable to implant it on a test basis in 100,000 of its 1994 model St. Tropez sports cars.

NOW THEREFORE:

1. Sponsor shall make itself available for up to 80 hours per month in the twelve-month period commencing with the signing of this Agreement, and for each of the following years of this Agreement so long as the minimum royalties are paid by Company to Sponsor, for the purpose of preparing advertisements, endorsements, testimoni-

als, public relations and commercials on behalf of the Company and its DWI-MITIGATOR (the "Product").

2. Sponsor's image and name may be used on the packaging of the Product and on the printed matter that accompanies the Product, but Sponsor shall have the right to edit such packaging and printed matter. Sponsor shall return all edited materials to the Company within 15 days, or failing to do so, the Company will assume that Sponsor has approved it.

3. Sponsor shall have the right to approve any and all advertisements, endorsements, testimonials and commercials for the Product.

4. Sponsor shall not unreasonably delay its review of editorial material sent to Sponsor by the Company and shall cooperate to the best of its ability toward the mutual objective of generating sales for the Product.

5. In consideration therefore, the Sponsor agrees to purchase DWI MITIGATORS from the Company for twenty dollars ($20.00) per unit up to 100,000 units per annum, thereafter the price drops to sevendeen dollars and fifty cents ($17.50) per unit; and Sponsor agrees to advance the Company the sum of $1 million to be applied to the first 50,000 units.

6. Sponsor agrees to make the DWI MITIGATOR available through its North American dealers as a retrofit product and any sales that Sponsor makes to its dealers shall entitle the Company to receive a royalty from Sponsor of two and one-half percent (2.5%) per annum.

7. Sponsor shall pay to Company a royalty advance of one hundred thousand dollars ($100,000) and a minimum royalty of $450,000 per annum for three years to secure exclusive rights to make, use, and sell the DWI MITIGATOR to the North American aftermarket.

8. In calculating the royalty, the gross selling price shall be defined as the gross sales receipts paid to the Company by dealers, less returns, unpaid taxes, shipping and handling charges, and dealer's duties, if any.

9. The Sponsor shall summarize all sales data in dollars and units on a monthly basis and deliver it to Company within 20 days after the last day of each month at the above address.

10. Sponsor shall be given fifty (50) models of the Product, without charge, for its professional use.

11. Sponsor may not endorse a competitive product unless the Company ceases operations. Company may request an examination

of the Sponsor's books and records having to do with the Product, to be conducted by qualified representatives skilled in accounting. The examination shall take place following two weeks' written notice at the Sponsor's principal place of business, during usual business hours, at Company's expense.

12. The Company agrees that it will not sell the DWI MITIGATOR to any other automobile manufacturer other than Sponsor for one full year and that it will not sell the DWI MITIGATOR through any other channel to the automobile aftermarket than through the Sponsor's dealer network for three full years from the date below; however, the Company may sell the DWI MITIGATOR under another name via direct mail to the do-it-yourself market, but not to other automobile dealership networks for three full years.

13. This Agreement shall constitute the entire agreement between the Parties and shall be construed under the laws of the State of _____.

ENTREPRENEURIAL IDEAS, INC.   _____
                                                     Date

by:_____

GIANT MARKETING CORP.   _____
                                       Date

by:_____

Appendix C
Directory of Strategic Partners

Abbott Labs

One Abbott Park Rd.
Abbott Park, IL 60064-3500
Phone: (708) 937-6100
Fax: (708) 937-1511

Contact: Richard H. Morehead, Vice President Corporate Development and Planning

Annual Revenues (mill $): $6876.6

Annual Net Income (mill $): $1544.2

Description of Business: Abbott Labs is a leader in the Healthcare industry developing and manufacturing pharmaceuticals, nutritional products, as well as hospital and laboratory products.

CPAs: Arthur Andersen & Co.

Advisors and Gatekeepers:
- Laurance Fuller, CEO Amoco Corporation, Chicago
- Bernard J. Hayhoe, British Member of Parliament
- David A. Jones, CEO Humana, Inc., Louisville
- Arthur E. Rasmussen, Director Executive Committee, Household International, Inc., Chicago

- W. Ann Reynolds, PhD, Chancellor, The City University of New York
- William L. Weiss, CEO Ameritech Corp., Chicago

Strategic Alliance: **North American Biologicals** is a plasma provider based in Miami. North American, in exchange for $2 million worth of the company's stock (a 16-percent stake), will receive rights to a proprietary Abbott product known as hepatitis B globulin or H-BIG, which is used to prevent people exposed to hepatitis B from coming down with the disease. The Miami concern also gets the exclusive right to acquire Abbott's experimental HIV immune globulin, or HIVIG, once certain liability matters are cleared up.
North American CEO: Mr. David Gury
Phone: (305) 625-5303

Adobe Systems, Inc.
1585 Charleston Rd.
PO Box 7900
Mountain View, CA 94039-7900
Phone: (415) 961-4400
Fax: (415) 961-3769

Contact: Daniel Putman, Senior Vice President New Product Development

Annual Revenues (mill $): $229.0

Annual Net Income (mill $): $51.6

Description of Business: Adobe Systems develops, markets, and supports computer software products and technologies that enable users to create, display, print, and communicate all forms of electronic documents.

CPAs: KPMG Peat Marwick

Advisors and Gatekeepers:

- William Hambrecht, Director
- William Krause, Director
- Robert Sedgewick, Director
- Delbert Yocam, Director

Strategic Alliance: **Electronics for Imaging, Inc. (EFI)** was founded to develop innovative solutions to enable color desktop publishing analogous to the way that page layout software, PostScript software, and laser printers enabled black-and-white desktop publishing in the mid-1980s. Adobe and EFI entered into an agreement pursuant to which each granted the other a nonexclusive, royalty-free cross license expiring in January 1996 with respect to any patents owned by either of the companies. In conjunction with this agreement Adobe purchased series A preferred stock convertible into 285,720 shares of common stock in EFI.

EFI CEO: Efraim Arazi

Phone: (415) 742-3400

Alpha Therapeutic Corp.
5555 Valley Blvd.
Los Angeles, CA 90032
Phone: (213) 225-2221
Fax: (213) 223-9228

Contact: Ed Matveld

Annual Revenues (mill $): $172

Annual Net Income (mill $): N/A

Description of Business: Alpha Therapeutic is one of the world's largest plasma fractionators.

CPAs: Deloitte & Touche

Advisors and Gatekeepers:

- Hachiro Ishigaki, Chairman
- Sam Anderson, President
- Hikosuka Yorihiro, Executive Vice President
- Marietta Carr
- William Hartin

Strategic Alliances: **Univax Biologics, Inc.** is focused on the development of proprietary vaccines and immunotherapeutic products for the prevention and treatment of serious infectious diseases and conditions. Alpha Therapeutic Corp. (ATC) is a wholly owned subsidiary of Green Cross Company of Japan, and is one of the world's largest plasma fractionators. Univax and ATC are cooperating in the development of a hyperimmune IGIV for use in the prevention and treatment of adult sepsis. ATC has agreed to help fund Univax's research and clinical testing of the vaccines by making quarterly advances to Univax through 1992 up to a total of $2.747 million. As of December 1991, Univax had received $1.692 million in such funding. Milestone and royalty payments are also involved.
Univax CEO: Thomas Stagnaro
Phone: (301) 770-3099

American Cyanamid Company

One Cyanamid Plaza
Wayne, New Jersey 07470
Phone: (201) 831-2000
Fax: (201) 831-2210

Contact: Terence D. Martin, CFO

Annual Revenues (mill $): $4986

Annual Net Income (mill $): $358

Description of Business: American Cyanamid is a research-based biotechnology and chemical company which develops and markets medical, agricultural and chemical products.

CPAs: KPMG Peat Marwick

Advisors and Gatekeepers:

- David M. Culver, Chairman CAI Capital Corp.
- Allan R. Dragone, former Chairman Arcadian Corp.
- Ronald Halstead, former Chairman Beecham Group
- Arnold J. Levine, Chairman Department of Molecular Biology, Princeton University
- Paul W. MacAvoy, Professor of Management Studies, Yale University
- Morris Tanenbaum, retired Vice Chairman AT&T
- Anne Wexler, Chairman The Wexler Group

Strategic Alliances: **ImClone Systems Inc.** is a biopharmaceutical company engaged primarily in the research and development of therapeutic products for the treatment of selected cancers, disorders of the hematopoietic system, and inflammatory diseases. In December 1987, ImClone entered into a vaccine development and licensing agreement with American Cyanamid Company, which provides American Cyanamid an exclusive worldwide license to manufacture and sell vaccines developed during the research period of the agreement. ImClone is entitled to royalties from the sale of these vaccines and has received $900,000 to date under this agreement from American Cyanamid.
ImClone CEO: Samuel Waksal
Phone: (212) 645-1405

American Telephone & Telegraph
32 Avenue of the Americas
New York, NY 10013-2412
Phone: (908) 221-6203
Fax: (908) 221-5217

Contact: Richard Bodman

Annual Revenues (mill $): $63,089

Annual Net Income (mill $): $522

Description of Business: AT&T is a global company that provides communications services and products, as well as network equipment and computer systems.

CPAs: Coopers & Lybrand

Advisors and Gatekeepers:

- Kathryn Eickhoff, President Eickhoff Economics, Inc.
- Walter Elisha, CEO Springs Industries, Inc.
- Louis Gerstner, Jr., CEO RJR Nabisco Holdings
- Philip Hawley, CEO Carter-Hawley Hale Stores
- Edward Jefferson, retired CEO E.I. du Pont de Nemours and Co.
- Belton K. Johnson, Owner Chaparossa Ranch
- Drew Lewis, CEO Union Pacific Corp.
- Henry B. Schacht, CEO Cummins Engine Co., Inc.
- Michael Sovern, President Columbia University
- Franklin Thomas, President The Ford Foundation
- Joseph Williams, Chairman Warner-Lambert Co.
- Gilbert Williamson, CEO NCR Corp.

Strategic Alliance: **McCaw Cellular Communications, Inc.** is the largest cellular phone service provider in the United States. AT&T has announced plans to purchase a $3.73 billion equity stake in the cellular company enabling McCaw Cellular to continue to expand and update its equipment in an industry of rapidly changing technology. The move by AT&T will allow it entry into the rapidly growing cellular market with the potential for AT&T to bypass local telephone companies for regional business. "We invented cellular,"

said Lewis M. Chakrin, AT&T's vice president for personal communications services. "McCaw capitalized on it and understands it. This is a very natural alliance." (*The New York Times*, November 15, 1992, p. F-5)
McCaw CEO: Craig McCaw
Phone: (206) 827-4500

A. Menarini SRL
Via Sette Santi 3
50131 Florence, Italy
Phone: 011-3955-56801
Fax: 011-3955-5680385

Contact: Raul Alvarez, Managing Director

Annual Revenues (mill $): $1000

Annual Net Income (mill $): N/A

Description of Business: International health care company based in Italy.

CPAs: N/A

Advisors and Gatekeepers: N/A

Strategic Alliances: **Chemtrak Incorporated** manufactures and markets quantitative, easy-to-use, disposable diagnostic tests for the worldwide point of care markets, including the consumer retail and physician office markets. ChemTrak is launching its first product, the AccuMeter Total Cholesterol Test. A. Menarini SRL and ChemTrak have entered into a corporate alliance in which A. Menarini SRL will market and sell Chemtrak's AccuMeter Total Cholesterol Test.
ChemTrak CEO: Prithipal Singh, PhD
Phone: (408) 773-8156

American Home Products Corp. (AHP)
685 Third Avenue
New York, NY 10017
Phone: (212) 878-5000
Fax: (212) 878-6642
Contact: John Adams
Annual Revenues (mill $): $7079
Annual Net Income (mill $): $1375
Description of Business: American Home Products Corp. is a leading researcher, manufacturer and marketer of products that meet important health needs.
CPAs: Arthur Andersen & Co.
Advisors and Gatekeepers:
- Frank A. Bennack, Jr. CEO The Hearst Corporation
- John W. Culligan, retired former Chairman of the Board
- John D. Feerick, Dean, Fordham University School of Law
- Edwin A. Gee, retired former Chairman International Paper Company
- John R. Torell III, Chairman Torell Management, Inc.
- William Wrigley, CEO William Wrigley J. Company

Strategic Alliances: **Athena Neurosciences, Inc.** is an early-stage pharmaceutical company committed to the field of neurology. American Home Products Corp. (AHP) entered into a collaborative research agreement with Athena to develop diagnostic and therapeutic products for stroke, migraine, and spinal cord trauma. AHP has committed to provide $6.4 million to Athena.
Athena CEO: John Groom
Phone: (415) 877-0900

Ameritech Development Corp.
10 S. Wacker Drive
Chicago, IL 60606
Phone: (312) 609-6000
Fax: (312) 207-0615

Contact: Thomas Touton

Annual Revenues (mill $): $4886

Annual Net Income (mill $): $1165

Description of Business: Ameritech, one of the world's leading information companies, is the parent of five Bell companies serving the Great Lakes region, and other information businesses. Ameritech also is a principal in several international businesses, including Telecom Corporation of New Zealand.

CPAs: Arthur Andersen & Co.

Advisors and Gatekeepers:

- Weston R. Christopherson, retired Chairman Northern Trust Corporation
- Donald C. Clark, CEO Household International, Inc.
- Robert C. Ernest, retired President Kimberly-Clark Corporation
- Richard M. Gillett, retired Chairman Old Kent Financial Corp.
- Hanna Holborn Gray, PhD, President University of Chicago
- James A. Henderson, CEO Cummins Engine Company, Inc.
- Hal C. Kuehl, retired Chairman Firstar Corp.
- John B. McCoy, CEO Banc One Corporation.

Strategic Alliances: **Triconex** develops, manufactures, and markets fault-tolerant safety and control systems used in critical industrial process applications such as the chemical, fuel, and electric utility industries. Ameritech invested approximately $750,000 to purchase 130,849 or 4.2 percent of the shares of common stock of Triconex Corp.
Triconex CEO: William K. Barkovitz
Phone: (714) 768-3709

Amgen, Inc.
1840 Dehavilland Drive
Thousand Oaks, CA 91320-1789
Phone: (805) 499-5725
Fax: (805) 499-9315
Contact: Lowell Sears, Vice President, CFO
Annual Revenues (mill $): $682
Annual Net Income (mill $): $97.9
Description of Business: Amgen is a global pharmaceutical company that develops, manufactures, and markets human pharmaceuticals based on advanced cellular and molecular biology.
CPAs: Ernst & Young
Advisors and Gatekeepers:
- Raymond F. Baddour, Lammot du Pont Professor Emeritus, MIT
- William K. Bowes, Jr., General Partner, U.S. Venture Partners
- Franklin P. Johnson, Jr., General Partner, Asset Management Partners
- Steven Lazarus, CEO Argonne National Laboratory/University of Chicago Development Corp.
- Edward J. Ledder, retired CEO Abbott Labs.
- Gilbert S. Omenn, Dean, School of Public Health and Community Medicine, University of Washington
- George B. Rathmann, CEO ICOS Corp.
- Bernard H. Semler, Independent Management Consultant

Strategic Alliances: **Regeneron Pharmaceuticals, Inc.** is a company formed to develop and commercialize products for the treatment of neurological diseases. Amgen made a $15-million equity investment in Regeneron translating to a 7-percent equity interest. Amgen will receive a certain percentage of revenues for Regeneron products that it distributes.

Apple Computer, Inc.
20525 Mariani Avenue
Cupertino, CA 95014
Phone: (408) 996-1010
Fax: (408) 974-2483

Contact: Michael Spindler

Annual Revenues (mill $): $6308

Annual Net Income (mill $): $309.8

Description of Business: Apple is one of the largest manufacturers of personal computers.

CPAs: Ernst & Young

Advisors and Gatekeepers:

- Peter Crisp, General Partner Venrock Associates
- Bernard Goldstein, Partner Broadview Associates
- A.C. Markkula, Chairman ACM Aviation, Inc.
- Arthur Rock, Principal Arthur Rock & Co.
- John Rollwagen, CEO Cray Research, Inc.

Strategic Alliance: **Adobe Systems Inc.** is a producer of font and printer software. In 1984 Apple Computers bought a 15-percent equity interest in Adobe for a total of $2.5 million. As part of the agreement, Apple Macintosh Computers all used Adobe Systems, Inc. font and printer software. After extraordinary growth in both companies, Apple sold its stake in Adobe for $89 million.
Adobe CEO: John Warnock
Phone: (415) 961-4400

Baxter International, Inc.
One Baxter Parkway
Deerfield, IL 60015
Phone: (708) 948-2000
Fax: (708) 948-2005
Contact: Robert J. Lambrix, CFO
Annual Revenues (mill $): $8921
Annual Net Income (mill $): $591
Description of Business: Baxter International is the world's leading manufacturer and marketer of health care products and services for use in hospitals and other health care settings.
CPA: Price Waterhouse
Advisors and Gatekeepers:

- Silas S. Cathcart, retired CEO Kidder, Peabody Group, Inc.
- John W. Colloton, Director, University of Iowa Hospitals and Clinics
- Harrington Drake, retired CEO Dun & Bradstreet Corp.
- James D. Ebert, Director Chesapeake Bay Institute of Johns Hopkins University
- Mary Johnston Evans, former Director and Vice Chairman Amtrak
- David W. Grainger, CEO W.W. Grainger, Inc.
- Charles F. Knight, CEO Emerson Electric Company
- Blaine J. Yarrington, retired Executive Vice President, Amoco Corp.

Strategic Alliances: **Applied Immune Sciences, Inc. (AIS)** is engaged in the development of proprietary, single-use therapeutic devices and related cell therapy laboratory services for the treatment of diseases by manipulation cells and proteins of the immune system ex vivo (outside the body). In August 1987 Baxter and AIS entered into an agreement that granted Baxter exclusive rights to market the Icelerator-rPA worldwide, with the exception of Japan and Israel. In return AIS has received an undisclosed fee from Baxter.
AIS CEO: Thomas B. Okarma
Phone: (415) 326-7302

In 1991, Baxter entered into an unprecedented agreement with **Argonne National Laboratory**, a federal research center in Argonne, Illinois—the first time a national laboratory and a private firm have entered into a commercial agreement. Argonne and Baxter are undertaking a study of the use of light-sensitive chemicals to sterilize donated blood to protect recipients from AIDS, hepatitis, and other viral diseases. Baxter acquires the right to license any products derived from the project in exchange for monetary support.
Argonne Labs CEO: Dr. Schriescheim
Phone: (708) 252-2000

Applied Immune Sciences, Inc. (AIS) is engaged in the development of proprietary, single-use therapeutic devices and related cell therapy laboratory services for the treatment of diseases by manipulation cells and proteins of the immune system ex vivo (outside the body). Caremark, a subsidiary of Baxter, and AIS entered into a joint venture agreement to establish cell therapy laboratories in North America. Caremark will provide the funding for initial start-up costs and working capital and will operate the laboratories. AIS will have responsibility for quality control and will supply its AIS CELLEC- TOR- AIDS to the laboratories. Any profits will be divided equally.
AIS CEO: Thomas B. Okarma
Phone: (415) 326-7302

BCE

2000 McGill College Ave.
Ste. 2100
Montreal, Quebec H3A3H7
Phone: (514) 499-7000
Fax: (514) 499-7223

Contact: Bernard Gregoire

Annual Revenues (mill $): $19,884

Annual Net Income (mill $): $3282

Description of Business: BCE is a management holding corporation whose core businesses are telecommunications services and the manufacture of telecommunications equipment. BCE also has major interests in financial services and in a number of other businesses.

CPAs: Deloitte & Touche

Advisors and Gatekeepers:
- Peter A. Allen, CEO LAC Minerals Ltd.
- Ralph M. Barford, President Valleydene Corp.
- Laurent Beaudoin, CEO Bombardier Inc.
- Marcel Belanger, President Gagnon and Belanger, Inc.
- Jeannine Guillevin Wood CEO Guillevin International, Inc.
- Donald J. Johnston, Legal Counsel Heenan Blaikie.
- Gerald J. Maier, CEO TransCanada PipeLines Ltd.
- E. Neil McKelvey, Counsel Stewart McKelvey Stirling Scales
- J. Edward Newall, CEO NOVA Corporation of Alberta

Strategic Alliance: **CLEAR Communications Ltd.** is a provider of competitive national and international telecommunications services in New Zealand. BCE Telecom International, Inc., a wholly owned subsidiary of BCE, holds a 25-percent share in CLEAR Communications. CLEAR began offering private line services in January 1991, then in May launched national and international long distance services.

CLEAR CEO: G.H. Newton
Phone: 011-649-358-0189

Videotron Corporation is a British Company which has 12 cable television and telecommunications franchises, primarily in greater London as well as Southampton. BCE has purchased a 30-percent share in Videotron. In 1992, with BCE's help, a $128-million financing was announced that will permit expansion of the cable network.
Videotron CEO: Ross Jepson
Phone: 011-81-852-0123

Boehringer Ingelheim, Inc. (BII)

N/A
Phone: N/A
Fax: N/A

Contact: Dr. Claus Rohleder

Annual Revenues (mill $): $5225

Annual Net Income (mill $): $127

Description of Business: BII is an international producer and marketer of pharmaceuticals, chemicals, food, and other related products.

CPAs: H. Macke Wirtschaftsprufer

Advisors and Gatekeepers:
- Dr. Heribert Johann
- Dr. Rolf Krebs
- Dr. Claus Rohleder
- Dr. Eckart Schonduve
- Dr. Franz Waldeck

Strategic Alliances: **Alliance Pharmaceutical Corp. (Alliance)** is a leader in the development of proprietary pharmaceutical products based on (PFC) and emulsion perfleurocarbon technologies. In 1989 Alliance and BII entered into a series of agreements in which BII was granted the marketing rights to all the Imagent and Oxygent HT products in all countries outside North America. Alliance received $3 million upon entering the agreement and is entitled to an additional $12 million in four installments upon the achievement by Alliance or BII of certain regulatory and marketing objectives. In a related transaction BII purchased 700,000 restricted shares of Alliance common stock for $10 million.
Alliance Contact: Theodore Roth
Phone: (619) 558-4300

Boise Cascade Corp.
One Jefferson Square
Boise, ID 83728-0001
Phone: (208) 384-6161
Fax: (208) 384-4912

Contact: George Harad

Annual Revenues (mill $): $3950

Annual Net Income (mill $): ($79)

Description of Business: Boise Cascade Corporation is an integrated paper and forest products company headquartered in Boise, Idaho with operations located in the United States and Canada. The company manufactures and distributes paper and paper products, office products, and building products. It owns and manages timberland to support these operation.

CPAs: Arthur Andersen & Co.

Advisors and Gatekeepers:

- Anne Armstrong, former U.S. Ambassador to Great Britain
- William S. Cook, former Chairman of the Board Union Pacific Corporation
- Robert Jaedicke, former Dean Stanford Business School
- Paul Phoenix, CEO Dofasco, Inc.
- William Reynolds, CEO GenCorp, Inc.
- Frank Shrontz, CEO The Boeing Company
- Edson Spencer, former CEO Honeywell, Inc.

Strategic Alliances: **BMC West Corporation** was founded in 1987 to acquire 20 building materials centers owned and operated by Boise Cascade. In addition to distributing building materials made by others, BMC performs value added services such as fabrication of roof trusses and preassembling windows. As part of the purchase price, Boise Cascade was issued 650,000 shares, or approximately one-third of the common stock of BMC. BMC purchased $22.2 million with 16.7 percent of its cost of goods sold in the first year following the buyout. Boise Cascade gives the Company discounts

based on reaching milestones and rebates based on achieving sales goals.
President: Donald S. Hendrickson
Phone: (208) 338-1750

Bristol Meyers Squibb
345 Park Avenue
New York, NY 10154-0037
Phone: (212) 546-4000
Fax: (212) 546-4020

Contact: Richard L. Gelb

Annual Revenues (mill $): $11,159

Annual Net Income (mill $): $2056

Description of Business: Bristol Myers Squibb is a world leader in the development, manufacture, and marketing of pharmaceuticals.

CPAs: Price Waterhouse

Advisors and Gatekeepers:

- Robert E. Allen, CEO AT&T
- Ellen V. Futter, President Barnard College
- Louis V. Gerstner, Jr., CEO RJR Nabisco Holdings Corp.
- Alexander Rich, MD, Professor Biophysics, MIT
- James D. Robinson III, formerly CEO American Express
- Andrew C. Sigler, CEO Champion International Corp.

Strategic Alliances: **Advanced Magnetics, Inc.** is an early-stage company that develops, manufactures, and markets innovative biopharmaceutical products based on its proprietary colloidal superparamagnetic particle technology. Squibb Diagnostics, Inc., a wholly owned subsidiary of Bristol Meyers Squibb (Squibb), purchased exclusive worldwide rights from Advanced Magnetics, Inc. (except for Japan, Western Europe, and Brazil) to manufacture and sell two magnetic resonance imaging (MRI) products. Squibb has agreed to pay Advanced Magnetics up to $10 million in license fees, plus royalties based on Squibb's sales. In addition, Squibb paid $950,000 to buy 600,000 shares (roughly 9 percent) of the company's common stock. Advanced Magnetics CEO: Jerome Goldstein
Phone: (617) 499-1433

Chemtrak Incorporated manufactures and markets quantitative, easy-to-use, disposable diagnostic tests for the worldwide point of care markets, including the consumer retail and physician office

markets. ChemTrak is launching its first product, the AccuMeter Total Cholesterol Test. Bristol Myers Squibb and ChemTrak have entered into a corporate alliance in which BMS will market and sell ChemTrak's AccuMeter Total Cholesterol Test.
ChemTrak CEO: Prithipal Singh, PhD
Phone: (408) 773-8156

Burlington Industries, Inc.
PO Box 21207
Greensboro, NC 27420
Phone: (919) 379-2000
Fax: (919) 379-2245

Contact: Park Davidson, Treasurer

Annual Revenues (mill $): $535

Annual Net Income (mill $): $39.5

Description of Business: Burlington Industries is one of the largest and most diversified manufacturers of textile products in the world.

CPAs: Ernst & Young

Advisors and Gatekeepers:

- Joseph F. Abely, Jr., CEO of Sea-Land Corporation
- David Margolis, Chairman and CEO Coltec Industries, Inc.

Strategic Alliances: **Galey & Lord, Inc.** is a leading developer, manufacturer, and marketer of high-quality woven cotton and cotton-blended apparel fabrics. Burlington Industries owns a 5-percent interest in Galey & Lord after selling certain divisions of its own that now comprise Galey & Lord. Burlington now provides warehousing, distribution, data processing, communications, and computer services to the company for a fee.
Galey & Lord CEO: Arthur Wiener
Phone: (212) 465-3000

Centocor, Inc.
200 Great Valley Parkway
Malvern, PA 19355
Phone: (215) 651-6000
Fax: (215) 889-0895

Contact: James Woody

Annual Revenues (mill $): $53

Annual Net Income (mill $): ($195)

Description of Business: Centocor is a leading biopharmaceutical company that specializes in monoclonal antibody products to meet critical needs in human health care.

CPAs: KPMG Peat Marwick

Advisors and Gatekeepers:
- Anthony Evnin, General Partner Venrock Associates
- William Hamilton, Professor of Management and Technology at the Wharton School of Business
- Antonie Knoppers, former CEO Merck & Co.
- Lawrence Steinman, Professor of Neurology, Stanford

Strategic Alliances: **Corvas International, Inc.** is a biopharmaceutical company engaged in the design and development of a new generation of therapeutic agents in the field of thrombosis and associated vascular diseases. In November 1991, Corvas entered into an agreement with Centocor, a leader in the field of monoclonal antibody based products. Under the terms of the alliance, Centocor purchased what amounts to a 20-percent share of Corvas equity for $9.25 million, plus $750,000 for the licensing rights to Corsevin M. Centocor is also required to pay royalties on sales of such licensed products to Corvas.

Corvas CEO: David Kabakoff
Phone: (619) 455-9800

Chemlawn Corporation
855 Ridge Lake Blvd.
Memphis, TN 38120
Phone: (901) 681-1800
Fax: N/A

Contact: Chemlawn was acquired by ServiceMaster on May 23, 1992 and subsequently restructured.

Annual Revenues (mill $): N/A

Annual Net Income (mill $): N/A

Description of Business: Manufacturer and distributor of lawn products and services.

CPAs: N/A

Advisors and Gatekeepers: N/A

Strategic Alliances: **Ecogen** develops and markets biological pesticides derived from naturally occurring or genetically modified microorganisms for use in controlling insects, diseases, and weeds that affect agricultural crop production, and forestry. Ecogen has entered into an agreement with Chemlawn for the development of Bt-based insecticides for several turf pests. Any such products that may be developed under the agreement will be manufactured by Ecogen and supplied exclusively to ChemLawn over a 15-year period. Funding by Chemlawn ended in March 1990; however development work is ongoing, including field trials.
Ecogen CEO: John Davies
Phone: (215) 757-1590

Ciba-Geigy
444 Saw Mill River Road
Ardsley, NY 10502-2699
Phone: (914) 479-2113
Fax: (914) 479-4218
Contact: Charles Keene
Annual Revenues (mill F): F21,077 (Swiss francs)
Annual Net Income (mill F): F1280 (Swiss francs)
Description of Business: Ciba-Geigy operates worldwide in the areas of pharmaceutical, biological, and chemical specialties.
CPAs: Swiss Auditing and Fiduciary Company
Advisors and Gatekeepers:
- Alex Krauer, Riehen, Chairman and Managing Director
- Albert Bodmer, Binningen, Deputy Chairman
- Professor Max M. Burger, Bottmingen
- Kaspar V. Cassani, Uitikon, ZH
- Franz Galliker, Oberwil BL

Strategic Alliances: **ISIS** is a leader in the discovery and development of a new class of drugs, antisense oligonucleotides, which may form the basis for therapeutic drugs with greatly increased selectivity and additional advantages over existing drugs. Ciba-Geigy and ISIS entered into a collaborative research agreement in which Ciba-Geigy has agreed to provide financial support for the research relating to the CG Compounds at ISIS and to commit substantial resources of its own to the application of medicinal chemistry to antisense drugs. ISIS has granted Ciba-Geigy the option, exercisable prior to clinical development, to obtain an exclusive license in all countries except the United States.
ISIS CEO: Stanley Crooke, MD
Phone: (619) 931-9200

Marsam Pharmaceuticals, Inc., founded in 1985, develops and manufactures generic injectable prescription drugs. Generic drugs, the chemical and therapeutic equivalents of brand name drugs, are sold after the patents on the related brand name drugs have expired. The company currently manufactures or markets 22 generic injectable drug products. The products are distributed by Geneva Pharmaceuticals, Inc., a wholly owned subsidiary of CIBA-Geigy, to hospitals and other health care institutions in the United States. CIBA-Geigy purchased 794,116 shares or 10.6 percent of the Company's common stock in June 1990 for approximately $9 million, and Geneva dedicated 18 of its sales personnel to sell the company's products. Geneva pays the company's cost plus 10 percent, with some variances. The agreement runs through July 2000, but may be extended for an additional five years.

Marsam CEO: Marvin Samson
Phone: (609) 424-5600

Com Net S.p.A.
Viale Erminio Spalla, 4100142
Rome, Italy
Phone: 011-39-6-503-6192
Fax: 011-39-6-503-7184
Contact: Andre Scheevo
Annual Revenues (mill $): N/A
Annual Net Income (mill $): N/A
Description of Business: Com Net manufactures and markets applications software products.
CPAs: Coopers & Lybrand
Advisors and Gatekeepers: N/A
Strategic Alliances: **Satellite Technology**, founded in 1982, designs, manufactures, and markets satellite communications networks composed of two-way small earth stations, referred to as "VSSATs" and marketed throughout the world. COM NET entered into a representation agreement with Satellite Technology Management, Inc. in 1988, which provided for the exclusive distribution of the company's products in Italy. COM NET purchased $4.5 million of products from Satellite Technology and purchased 817,723 or 7.2 percent of the company's common stock for approximately $1 million.
Satellite Technology CEO: Emil Youssefzadeh
Phone: (714) 557-2400

Corning, Inc.
Houghton Park
Corning, NY 14831
Phone: (607) 974-9000
Fax: (607) 974-8830

Contact: Roger Ackerman, COO

Annual Revenues (mill $): $3294.9

Annual Net Income (mill $): $316.8

Description of Business: Corning, Inc. is an international corporation focused in four business segments: specialty materials, communications, lab services, and consumer products.

CPAs: Price Waterhouse

Advisors and Gatekeepers:

- Robert Barker, Director Center for the Environment, Cornell University
- Mary L. Bundy, Clinical Social Worker
- Barber B. Conable Jr., retired President World Bank
- Gordon Gund, CEO Gund Investment Corp.
- John M. Hennessy, CEO CS First Boston, Inc.
- James W. Kinnear, CEO Texaco, Inc.

Strategic Alliance: **Unilab Corporation** is a leading clinical laboratory testing company serving the western region of the United States. During the past year (1992) Metpath, through its parent company Corning, Inc., increased its ownership in Unilab. The latest purchase increased Corning's ownership of Unilab to just about 50 percent, representing Corning's continued commitment and support to Unilab. Unilab also benefits from the sharing of many of Corning's corporate resources, including the technical and scientific resources from MetPath's national reference testing center in New Jersey.
Unilab CEO: Andrew Baker
Phone: (212) 832-3130

C.R. Bard, Inc.
730 Central Ave.
Murray Hill, NJ 07974
Phone: (908) 277-8000
Fax: (908) 277-8363

Contact: Robert Ernest, Vice President Business Development

Annual Revenues (mill $): $876

Annual Net Income (mill $): $57

Description of Business: C.R. Bard, Inc. is a leading multinational developer, manufacturer, and marketer of health care products. Bard holds strong positions in cardiovascular, urological, and surgical products.

CPAs: Arthur Andersen & Co.

Advisors and Gatekeepers:

- Joseph F. Abely, Jr., retired Chairman Sea Land Corp.
- William T. Butler, MD, CEO Baylor College of Medicine
- Raymond B. Carey, Jr., retired CEO ADT, Inc.
- Daniel A. Cronin, Jr., President Northbridge Management Company
- Regina E. Herzlinger, Professor Harvard Business School
- Robert P. Luciano, CEO Schering-Plough

Strategic Alliances: **Intromed**, founded in 1987, develops, manufactures, and markets single-use, miniature endoscopes for minimal invasive surgery, diagnosis and treatment monitoring. It markets its products to vascular and general surgeons. Its urology products are marketed through a corporate partnership agreement with C.R. Bard, Inc., which owns 8.8 percent of the Company's common stock plus additional warrants. Bard has loaned Intromed $835,000. Intromed CEO: Stuart L. Foster
Phone: (619) 455-5000

Defense Software & Systems
200 Route 17
Mahwah, NJ 07430
Phone: (201) 529-2026
Fax: (201) 529-3163

Contact: George Morgenstern, CEO

Annual Revenues (mill $): $11.1

Annual Net Income (mill $): $1.2

Description of Business: DSS provides sophisticated computer software services to customers by furnishing qualified software engineers.

CPAs: Price Waterhouse

Advisors and Gatekeepers:

- George Gertner, CEO Gertner Investments Ltd.
- Robert Kuhn, President Geneva Companies

Strategic Alliances: **Millimeter Wave Technology (MWT)**, based in Marietta, Georgia, is a manufacturer of radar-absorbent materials and coatings for the U.S. military and of portable units that measure the radar absorbability of materials. Defense Software & Systems, Inc. (DSS) and MWT have engaged in joint marketing of their products and system development services and resources, primarily to military customers in the United States and abroad. DSS owns approximately 14.3 percent of the outstanding Common Stock of MWT and holds a proxy to vote an additional 8.8 percent of such stock.

MWT CEO: Dennis Kozakoff
Phone: (404) 425-9382

Digital Equipment Corporation
146 Main St.
Maynard, MA 01754-2571
Phone: (508) 493-5111
Fax: (508) 493-8780
Contact: John Smith, Senior Vice President Operations
Annual Revenues (mill $): $13,931
Annual Net Income (mill $): ($2796)
Description of Business: Digital Equipment Corporation is the leading worldwide supplier of networked computer systems, software, and services.
CPAs: Coopers & Lybrand
Advisors and Gatekeepers:
- Vernon R. Alden, former Chairman The Boston Company, Inc.
- Colby Chandler, retired CEO Eastman Kodak
- Robert Everett, retired President Mitre Corporation
- Thomas P. Gerrity, Dean Wharton School of the University of Pennsylvania
- Thomas Phillips, retired CEO Raytheon Company

Strategic Alliances: **Ross Systems, Inc.** is a leading supplier of business application software and services to users of Digital Equipment Corporation. Ross Systems is currently negotiating a development agreement with Digital to convert certain of its applications to Digital's ULTRIX operating system. The terms of this proposed agreement call for Digital to pay to the company $600,000 in installments, provide equipment, software, and maintenance. In return the company will pay Digital a royalty on software licenses of such systems.
Ross Systems CEO: Dennis Vohs
Phone: (415) 593-2500

StrataCom, Inc. designs, manufactures, markets, and services IPX FastPacket cell switching systems for private wide area networks and public carrier high-speed data service offerings. In May 1990 Digital Equipment bought 625,000 shares of series F preferred stock for $8 per share. In connection with this investment DEC and Stratacom

entered into a series of agreements that provide both entities with various dependent options as well as restrictions when dealing with one another.
StrataCom CEO: Richard Moley
Phone: (408) 294-7600

Dow Chemical Company
2030 Dow Center
Midland, MI 48674
Phone: (517) 636-1000
Fax: Not Disclosed

Contact: Fred P. Corson, Vice President Research & Development

Annual Revenues (mill $): $18,807

Annual Net Income (mill $): $935

Description of Business: Dow manufactures and supplies more than 2000 products and services, including chemicals and performance products, plastics, hydrocarbons, and energy and consumer specialties. The company operates 181 manufacturing sites in 33 countries, and employs 62,000 people around the world.

CPAs: Deloitte & Touche

Advisors and Gatekeepers:

- Bernard B. Butcher, Senior Consultant
- Willie D. Davis, CEO All Pro Broadcasting, Inc.
- Michael L. Dow, Chairman General Aviation, Inc.
- Harold T. Shapiro, President, Princeton University

Strategic Alliances: **Ecogen** develops and markets biological pesticides derived from naturally occurring or genetically modified microorganisms for use in controlling insects, diseases, and weeds that affect agricultural crop production and forestry. In October 1986 Ecogen entered into an agreement with Dow Elanco, a joint venture of the Dow Chemical Company and Eli Lilly and Company, to study the feasibility of engineering Bt insecticidal genes into non-Bt microbes to yield a product useful in controlling certain crop pests. In exchange for Ecogen's work on the project, DowElanco is paying Ecogen's expenses over the 25-month project span. Both companies also retain a right of first refusal to establish a business relationship for commercialization of the covered technology.
Ecogen CEO: John Davies
Phone: (215) 757-1590

Polycon is working on the development of the new polymer cyclotene benzocyclobutene to be used as a dielectric in the emerging market

for high-density interconnects. The Dow Chemical Company and Polycon have entered into an agreement in which Polycon is provided with funding for research and development of Cyclotene while the two companies share all information regarding the application and development of this product.
Polycon CEO: William Snodgrass
Phone: (602) 731-9544

E.I. du Pont de Nemours and Company
1007 Market Street
Wilmington, DE 19898
Phone: (302) 774-1000
Fax: (302) 695-9840

Contact: Alexander MacLachlan

Annual Revenues (mill $): $38,695

Annual Net Income (mill $): $1403

Description of Business: Dupont is one of the largest global corporations in the world, operating in 40 countries and on six continents. Dupont manufactures and develops chemicals, fibers, and polymers, and takes part in various other diversified businesses.

CPAs: Price Waterhouse

Advisors and Gatekeepers:

- Andrew F. Brimmer, President Brimmer & Company, Inc.
- Charles R. Bronfman, Cochairman The Seagram Company, Ltd.
- Edgar M. Bronfman, CEO The Seagram Company, Ltd.
- Charles L. Brown, former CEO AT&T
- Margaret P. MacKimm, Senior Vice President Kraft General Foods, Inc.
- Dean R. McKay, Member Advisory Board of IBM

Strategic Alliances: **Crop Genetics International Corp. (CGI)** is involved with the discovery, development, and commercialization of crop protection systems that substitute biopesticides for synthetic chemicals. Dupont and CGI have entered into an alliance to develop and market insectical virus products worldwide. Under this agreement CGI will be the exclusive producer and Dupont the exclusive distributor and marketer of insectical virus products. Dupont is committed to pay $1.7 million to CGI in 1992 and $2.0 million in 1993 if the alliance continues.

CGI CEO: Joseph W. Kelly
Phone: (410) 712-7170

Eiken Chemical Company, Ltd.
26-20, Oji 5-Chome, Kita-ku
Tokyo, Japan
Phone: 011-813-3913-6491
Fax: 011-813-3914-7027

Contact: H. Kagawa

Annual Revenues (mill $): N/A

Annual Net Income (mill $): N/A

Description of Business: N/A

CPAs: N/A

Advisors and Gatekeepers: N/A

Strategic Alliances: **Advanced Magnetics** develops, manufactures, and markets innovative biopharmaceutical products based on its proprietary colloidal super paramagnetic particle technology. In 1988 Eiken purchased from Advanced Magnetics the exclusive right in Japan to manufacture and distribute the Feridex® liver contrast agent for $1.5 million plus royalties based on sales. In 1990, Eiken purchased the exclusive right to manufacture and distribute in Japan, Advanced Magnetics' GI contrast agent and any future MRI contrast agents, for which right Eiken paid a license fee of $1 million plus royalties on sales. In addition, Eiken invested $4 million in Advanced Magnetics common stock.
Advanced Magnetics CEO: Jerome Goldstein
Phone: (617) 499-1433

Eisai Company

Koishikawa 4, Bunkyo-ku
Tokyo, Japan
Phone: 011-813-3817-3700
Fax: 011-813-3811-7420

Contact: Haruo Naito

Annual Revenues (mill $): $1601

Annual Net Income (mill $): $113

Description of Business: Eisai is one of the largest pharmaceutical companies in Japan.

CPAs: Tomatsu & Co.

Advisors and Gatekeepers:

- Yuji Naito, Chairman Eisai
- Haruo Naito, CEO Eisai
- Akio Hiraku, Senior Managing Director
- Hitoshi Yamamoto, Managing Director
- Masaaki Tamura, Managing Director
- Akira Joumei, Managing Director

Strategic Alliances: **ISIS** is a leader in the discovery and development of a new class of drugs, antisense oligonucleotides, which may form the basis for therapeutic drugs with greatly increased selectivity and additional advantages over existing drugs. In December 1990, ISIS entered into a collaborative research agreement for a five-year research program with Eisai. Eisai has agreed to provide financial support for the necessary research at ISIS, plus one or two Eisai scientists to aid ISIS in its investigations. ISIS has granted Eisai the option to obtain an exclusive Japanese license and a coexclusive license in North America and Europe to manufacture, sell, and use any compounds discovered in this research collaboration. ISIS received an initial commitment fee in January 1991 and will receive milestone payments and royalties on sales of any products licensed to Eisai.
ISIS CEO: Stanley Crooke, MD
Phone: (619) 931-9200

Eli Lilly and Company
Lilly Corporate Center
Drop Code 2035
Indianapolis, IN 46285
Phone: (317) 276-9910
Fax: (317) 276-9317

Contact: Claire DeSelle

Annual Revenues (mill $): $5725.7

Annual Net Income (mill $): $1314.7

Description of Business: Eli Lilly manufactures pharmaceuticals such as insulin, medical devices, including pacemakers and prostate cancer monitors, plus veterinary vaccines. It invested $1.1 billion in R&D and new production facilities in the last 12 months.

CPAs: Ernst & Young

Advisors and Gatekeepers: Outside board members:
- Steven C. Beering, President, Purdue University
- George H. Conrades, Senior Vice President IBM Corp.
- James W. Cozad, CEO Whitman Corp.
- Karen N. Horn, CEO BancOne
- J. Clayburn LaForce, Jr., Dean UCLA-GBS
- Ben F. Love, retired CEO Texas Commerce Bank
- Randall L. Tobias, Vice Chairman AT&T
- Alva O. Way, Chairman IBJ Schorder Bank

Strategic Alliances: **Glycomed, Inc.** is a development-stage company that is attempting to develop a new class of pharmaceuticals based on complex carbohydrates. It is targeting clotting disorders, wound healing, and viral infections. Eli Lilly has agreed to fund Glycomed's research and development costs to discover novel oligosaccharide compounds in exchange for an exclusive worldwide license. Eli Lilly invested $4 million in Glycomed for 6 percent of its common stock. Glycomed CEO: Alan R. Timms
Phone: (510) 523-5555

Agouron Pharmaceuticals, Inc. is a development-stage company involved in protein structure-based drug design, which it intends to

apply to engineer drugs to treat cancer, AIDS, and other serious diseases. Eli Lilly has agreed to fund two of Agouron's research and development projects, which if commercialized will result in royalties to be paid to Agouron. Hybritech, a subsidiary of Eli Lilly, has a similar strategic alliance with Agouron. Eli Lilly purchased 5.2 percent of Agouron's common stock.
Agouron CEO: Peter Johnson
Phone: (619) 622-3000

COR Therapeutics, Inc. is focused on the discovery, development, and commercialization of novel biopharmaceutical products for the treatment and prevention of severe cardiovascular diseases. In May 1991, COR and Eli Lilly entered into research and development regarding a defined class of GPIIb-IIIa inhibitors. The agreement provides for Lilly to fund COR's research at annual levels that will be agreed upon jointly, but will not be less than $1.4 million per year. COR received an initial license fee of $1.25 million and is also entitled to receive development milestone payments and royalties on product sales. Lilly also purchased 400,000 shares of series D preferred stock of COR at $10 per share.
COR CEO: Vaughn Kailian
Phone: (415) 244-6800

Cytogen Corp. is a development-stage company engaged in the development of proprietary systems utilizing monoclonal antibodies of the targeted delivery of diagnostic and therapeutic substances in the treatment of cancer. Cytogen granted a limited field of use license to Eli Lilly to develop and market certain cancer therapy products using Cytogen's proprietary monoclonal antibody linker technology. Lilly agreed to make certain payments based on its achieving scientific milestones, and to pay royalties to Cytogen. Lilly also invested in Cytogen's common stock.
Cytogen CEO: George W. Ebright
Phone: (609) 987-8270

Ecogen develops and markets biological pesticides derived from naturally occurring or genetically modified micro-organisms for use in controlling insects, diseases, and weeds that affect agricultural crop production and forestry. In October 1986 Ecogen entered into an agreement with Dow Elanco, a joint venture of the Dow Chemical

Company and Eli Lilly and Company, to study the feasibility of engineering Bt insecticidal genes into non-Bt microbes to yield a product useful in controlling certain crop pests. In exchange for Ecogen's work on the project, Dow Elanco is paying Ecogen's expenses over the 25-month project span. Both companies also retain a right of first refusal to establish a business relationship for commercialization of the covered technology.
Ecogen CEO: John Davies
Phone: (215) 757-1590

Athena Neurosciences entered into a collaborative research agreement with Eli Lilly to discover compounds that may be useful in the prevention and treatment of certain neurological disorders, including Alzheimer's disease. Lilly is committed to provide Athena with approximately $19.3 million over the next five years for research, in addition to a $4-million equity investment in Athena.
CEO Athena: John Groom
Phone: (415) 877-0900

Organo-Genesis, Inc. is a pharmaceutical company developing an artery product called Graft Artery. Lilly agreed in 1987 to finance this human artery replacement in exchange for worldwide marketing rights. To date Lilly has provided $16.2 million and is obligated to provide $2.1 million more if certain tests of the arteries are successful. As of November 4, 1992, Lilly had suspended research payments to Organo-Genesis, but remains committed to the company's artery research. Upon reaching certain testing milestones and other conditions, Lilly will resume funding.
Organo-Genesis Inc.: Herbert Stein
Phone: (617) 575-0775

Shaman Pharmaceuticals, Inc. searches for new drugs in South American rain forests. Shaman's ethnobotanists rely on native healers and folklore to pinpoint plants with antifungal potential. The company then employs modern methods to isolate compounds from the plants. Lilly is making a $4-million investment in Shaman and commencing a four-year agreement in which Lilly will investigate any intriguing compounds Shaman discovers, then market the ones that prove effective.
Shaman CEO: Lisa Conte
Phone: (415) 837-1800

Synaptic Pharmaceutical Corp. is a start-up pharmaceutical company currently doing work to develop serotonin for the treatment of anxiety, depression, and other ills. Eli Lilly has invested $12 million in Synaptic to be used to develop serotonin treatments.
Synaptic CEO: Kathleen Mullinix
Phone: (201) 261-1331

Esaote Biomedica S.p.A
Via Siffredi, 58
16153 Genoa, Italy
Phone: 011-39-010-60091
Fax: 011-39-010-6009-275

Contact: Fabrizio Landi, Managing Director

Annual Revenues (mill $): N/A

Annual Net Income (mill $): N/A

Description of Business: Manufacturer of medical devices.

CPAs: N/A

Advisors and Gatekeepers: N/A

Strategic Alliances: **Endosonics Corporation** develops, manufactures, and markets combined angioplasty imaging catheters, diagnostic imaging catheters, and Cathscanner ultrasound imaging systems for the diagnosis and treatment of coronary and peripheral vascular disease. Endosonics and Esaote entered into an agreement in which Esatoe has exclusive distribution rights through January 31, 1998 to distribute Endosonics cardiovascular products in France, Italy, and the Soviet Union. Under this agreement Esaote purchased Endosonics preferred stock convertible into a 3.92-percent interest at an effective price of $8.60 per share.
Endosonics CEO: David H. Rammler
Phone: (510) 734-0464

Ford Motor Company
The American Road
PO Box 1899
Dearborn, MI 48121
Phone: (313) 322-3790
Fax: (313) 323-0816

Contact: Roger E. Maugh

Annual Revenues (mill $):

Annual Net Income (mill $):

Description of Business: Ford is the world's fourth-largest industrial corporation and the second-largest producer of cars and trucks.

CPAs: Coopers & Lybrand

Advisors and Gatekeepers:

- Colby H. Chandler, retired CEO Eastman Kodak Company
- Michael D. Dingman, Chairman The Henley Group, Inc.
- Roberto C. Goizueta, CEO Coca-Cola Company
- Irvine O. Hockaday, Jr., CEO Hallmark Cards
- Drew Lewis, CEO Union Pacific
- Ellen R. Marram, CEO Nabisco Biscuit Company
- Carl E. Reichardt, CEO Wells Fargo & Company
- Clifton R. Wharton, Jr., CEO Teachers Insurance and Annuity Association—College Retirement Equities Fund

Strategic Alliances: **Excel Industries, Inc.,** formed in 1928, is the leading independent designer, manufacturer, and supplier of window systems to automotive, van, and truck industries. In 1986, Ford and Excel entered into a strategic, long-term relationship. Ford purchased 40 percent of Excel's common shares, paid the company $19.3 million in cash, transferred its modular window manufacturing subsidiary to Excel, and agreed to purchase from Excel 70 percent of its modular window requirements through 1998.
President: James J. Lohman
Phone: (219) 264-2131

Genentech, Inc.
460 Point San Bruno Boulevard
South San Francisco, CA 94080
Phone: (415) 266-1000
Fax: (415) 225-2501

Contact: Gary Lyons, Vice President Business Development

Annual Revenues (mill $): $515.9

Annual Net Income (mill $): $44.3

Description of Business: Genentech is a leading biotechnology company that discovers, develops, manufactures, and markets human pharmaceuticals for significant medical needs. The company makes all its marketed products available free to needy, uninsured patients.

CPAs: Ernst & Young

Advisors and Gatekeepers:

- Herbert W. Boyer, retired Professor of Biochemistry & Biophysics, University of California
- James C. Morgan, CEO Applied Materials, Inc.
- Richard Munro, CEO Time-Warner, Inc.
- Donald L. Murfin, General Partner Chemicals & Materials Enterprise Associates
- David Packard, Chairman Hewlett-Packard Company
- Thomas J. Perkins, General Partner Kleiner, Perkins, Caulfied & Byers
- David S. Tappan, Jr., Director Fluor Corporation

Strategic Alliances: **Glycomed** is a leader in the discovery and development of a new class of pharmaceuticals based on complex carbohydrates, which represent the last major class of naturally occurring molecule to be explored for use in new therapeutics and which the company believes will address a broad range of diseases. In December 1990 Glycomed and Genentech entered into an agreement to collaborate on development of small molecule inhibitors of inflammation. Pursuant to the agreement, Genentech provides program funding for three years with an option for two additional. In return Genentech

retains the rights to make, sell, and use compounds developed in the project worldwide, excluding the Far East. Concurrent with this agreement, Genentech purchased preferred stock of Glycomed which converted to 441,919 shares of common stock as well as warrants for an additional 88,384 shares of common stock at $9 per share.
Glycomed CEO: Alan R. Timms
Phone: (510) 523-5555

Liposome Technology, Inc. (LTI) is engaged in the development of proprietary liposome and lipid-based products to treat life-threatening illnesses. LTI is collaborating with Genentech, Inc. to evaluate a stealth liposome formulation of an antiviral agent to inhibit the ability of HIV to infect human cells. Genentech provides a supply of drugs to LTI, and LTI is responsible for developing stealth liposome formulations and performing preclinical testing of these formulations in laboratory models.
LTI CEO: Nicolaos V. Arvanitidis
Phone: (415) 323-9011

In September 1991, the company and **Xenova Limited** extended an existing research collaboration, the goal of which is to discover and develop small-molecule pharmaceutical agents from natural biological sources to treat a variety of clinical indications. The agreement includes up to $10 million of research support over five years, and a multistage equity investment of up to $10 million by the company to Xenova. Genentech will obtain the rights to market products developed from this collaboration in certain territories, including North America. Genentech will pay royalties based on product sales.
Xenova CEO: Louis J. Nisbet
Phone: 011-44-753-692-229

Incyte Pharmaceuticals and Genentech entered into an agreement for a collaboration to develop and commercialize a human protein called BPI. This molecule offers potential as treatment for gram-negative septic shock and related conditions. Under the terms of the agreement, Incyte will receive up to $11 million for both research and support for an initial three-year period and milestone-based payments. The agreement also includes a two-stage equity investment of up to $3 million by the company in Incyte. The company will have exclusive rights to market BPI worldwide, except in Japan and the Far East. Genentech will pay royalties based on product sales.

Incyte Contact: Roy Whitfield
Phone: (415) 855-0555

Telios Pharmaceuticals and Genentech have entered into a research collaboration to develop and commercialize an injectable drug to help prevent the formation of bloodclots. Under the agreement, Genentech will pay Telios up to $15 million for research support for up to three years and for milestone-based payments. The companies will collaborate to codevelop a drug based on Telios' proprietary matrix-peptide technology and Genentech's expertise in peptide design and recombinant-receptor assay screening. In return, Genentech will have the right to market the drug worldwide, except in Japan and the Far East. Genentech will pay royalties based on product sales.
Telios CEO: Robert J. Erickson
Phone: (619) 622-2600

Univax Biologics, Inc. is focused on the development of proprietary vaccines and immunotherapeutic products for the prevention and treatment of serious infectious diseases. Univax and Genentech have reached an agreement to jointly develop a hyperimmune immunoglobulin product for the treatment of AIDS. Genentech will supply Univax with its gp120 vaccine, which will be used by Univax to produce the hyperimmune immunoglobulin product, which will then be evaluated by Univax. Genentech will market the product.
Univax CEO: Joseph Edelman
Phone: (212) 214-2170

General Motors Corporation
3044 W. Grand Boulevard
Detroit, MI 48202-3091
Phone: (313) 556-5000
Fax: (313) 974-5168

Contact: Robert O'Connell, CFO

Annual Revenues (mill $): $123,056

Annual Net Income (mill $): $4452.8

Description of Business: General Motors is the largest automobile manufacturer in the World.

CPAs: Deloitte & Touche

Advisors and Gatekeepers:

- Anne L. Armstrong, Chairman Center for Strategic and International Studies
- Thomas Everhart, President CIT
- Charles T. Fischer, President NBD Bancorp, Inc.
- Marvin Goldberger, President Emeritis CIT
- Willard Marriot, CEO Marriot Corp.
- Edmund Pratt, Chairman Pfizer, Inc.
- John G. Smale, Chairman Proctor & Gamble
- Leon Sullivan, Pastor Emeritus Zion Baptist Church of Philadelphia
- Dennis Weatherstone, Chairman J.P. Morgan & Co.
- Thomas Wyman, former Chairman of the Board CBS, Inc.

Strategic Alliances: **Valence Technology, Inc.** is engaged in research and development to produce advanced rechargeable batteries based on lithium and polymer technologies. The company believes that its lithium polymer batteries, when commercially introduced, will offer a number of performance characteristics superior to those of batteries currently in commercial use. In 1991, Valence entered into a research and development agreement with Delco (division of GM) to develop lithium polymer batteries for the land, marine, and air vehicle and load leveling markets. Under the agreement, Valence obtained a multiyear funding commitment of up to $20 million and, if its batteries are successfully commercialized by Delco, will receive ongoing royalties.

Valence CEO: Lev Dawson
Phone: (408) 365-6125

4th Dimension Software Ltd. develops, markets, and supports the CONTROL family of integrated system software products, which automate many key functions of data centers of large organizations. On November 15, 1991 the Company entered into a worldwide master software license agreement with EDS, a subsidiary of General Motors and the largest third-party data processing provider in the world. Under this agreement the company agreed to supply EDS with its products, maintenance, and support services at specified discounts from list price. In conjunction with the technical cooperation agreement, EDS purchased an aggregate of 183,333 ordinary shares representing a 2.53-percent interest in 4th Dimension.

4th Dimension CEO: Yossie Hollander
Phone: (972) 3-491211

Glaxo Holdings, p.l.c
Lansdowne House
Berkeley Square
London, WIX 6BP
Phone: 071-493-4060
Fax: 071-408-0228

Contact: Dr. Richard Sykes

Annual Revenues (mill $): $1409

Annual Net Income (mill $): $120

Description of Business: Manufacturer of pharmaceuticals.

CPAs: Coopers & Lybrand

Advisors and Gatekeepers:

- Anne Armstrong, former U.S. Ambassador to the United Kingdom
- John Cuckney, Chairman Royal Insurance Holdings
- James Ferguson, CEO General Foods Corp.
- Professor Richard Southwood, Vice Chancellor Oxford University

Strategic Alliances: **Gilead** is engaged in the discovery and development of a new class of pharmaceuticals based on nucleotides, the building blocks of DNA and RNA, which are a versatile class of molecules that can be chemically modified to inhibit the production or activity of disease-causing proteins. In July 1990, Gilead entered into a research and development agreement with Glaxo. The agreement calls for a five-year program for Gilead to conduct research with the goal of identifying antisense and triple helix compounds with potential application in the diagnosis, prevention, or treatment of cancer. Gilead granted Glaxo an exclusive, worldwide license to such compounds and any derivative products within the field. Gilead retains worldwide rights to all noncancer applications and will receive an annual research fee at the outset of each research year, benchmark payments upon the achievement of mutually agreed-upon goals, and royalties on sales of any products licensed to Glaxo. Concurrent with the signing of the agreement, Glaxo made an $8-million equity investment in Gilead which translated to a 6.2-percent interest.

Gilead CEO: Michael Riordan
Phone: (415) 574-3000

Amylin Pharmaceuticals, Inc. and Glaxo entered into a strategic alliance in October 1991 to develop and commercialize Amylin's blockade therapy which is intended to block the production, secretion, or action of a pancreatic hormone to provide a treatment for adult onset diabetes. Glaxo agreed to pay Amylin $1 million and loan Amylin _ million plus future royalty payments and to commit up to 35 scientists. It also agreed to invest approximately $200,000 in Amylin's common stock.
Amylin CEO: Howard E. Greene
Phone: (619) 552-2200

Gujarat State Fertilizers Company Ltd. (Gujarat)
T.O. Fertilizernagar
391750 Dist. Baroda
Gujarat, India
Phone: 011-91265-72451
Fax: 011-91265-72966

Contact: Dr. M. H. Mehta

Annual Revenues (mill $): N/A

Annual Net Income (mill $): N/A

Description of Business: Agricultural products and technology.

CPAs: N/A

Advisors and Gatekeepers: N/A

Strategic Alliances: **Ecogen** develops and markets biological pesticides derived from naturally occurring or genetically modified microorganisms for use in controlling insects, diseases, and weeds that affect agricultural crop production and forestry. In May 1989, Ecogen entered into a three-year agreement with Gujarat for the joint development of Bt-based bioinsecticides for specific target insects in India and of pseudomonas-based biofungicides. Ecogen has received research and development funding from Gujarat, and Gujarat will retain rights to the jointly-developed products in India while Ecogen will retain marketing rights outside of India to these same products.
Ecogen CEO: John Davies
Phone: (215) 757-1590

Hoffman-LaRoche, Inc.
340 Kingsland Street
Nutley, NJ 07110-1199
Phone: (201) 235-5000
Fax: (201) 235-2906

Contact: Elizabeth Czerepak

Annual Revenues (mill SF): SF 10,800

Annual Net Income (mill SF): SF 1,050

Description of Business: Hoffman-LaRoche is the U.S. subsidiary of Roche Group, Basel Switzerland, one of the world's leading pharmaceutical companies.

CPAs: Ernst & Young

Advisors and Gatekeepers:

- Fritz Gerber, CEO Roche
- Dr. Lukas Hoffman, Vice Chairman Roche
- Dr. Andres Leuenberger, Vice Chairman Roche
- Dr. Armin M. Kessler, Board Member Roche
- Dr. Jakob Oeri, Board Member Roche

Strategic Alliances: **Protein Design Labs, Inc. (PDL)** is involved in the computer-aided design of antibodies and other proteins to treat specific conditions including autoimmune diseases, cancer, and various viral infection infections. Currently PDL has ten compounds under development. Hoffman-LaRoche has agreed to collaborate on the research and development of SMART antibodies affecting the IL-2 receptor. In return, Roche USA has exclusive worldwide rights to manufacture, market, and sell these antibodies. Roche USA invested $5.2 million in PDL for preferred stock convertible into 10.3-percent of the company's equity.
PDL CEO: Lawrence Jay Korn
Phone: (415) 903-3700

Hormel & Company
501 16th Avenue
Austin, MN 55912
Phone: (507) 437-5611
Fax: (507) 437-5117
Contact: Forrest Dryden
Annual Revenues (mill $): $2681
Annual Net Income (mill $): $77
Description of Business: One of the largest food companies in the nation.
CPAs: Ernst & Young
Advisors and Gatekeepers:
- Clarence G. Adamy, former President National Association of Food Chains
- John Allen, Professor Food Industry Institute, Michigan State University
- Sherwood Berg, President South Dakota State University
- Eugene Mayberry, Chairman Board of Development Mayo Foundation
- Earl Olson, Chairman Jennie-O Foods, Inc.

Strategic Alliances: **United States Filter Corporation** obtained a license to manufacture and market the Lyco Rotating Biological Contactor which was developed by Hormel, in consideration for the payment of a 3-percent sales royalty to Hormel. U.S. Filter Corporation designs, develops, and produces wastewater treatment systems used in industrial production processes and by municipal water treatment facilities.
President: Richard J. Heckmann
Phone: (619) 340-0098

IBM Corporation
Old Orchard Rd.
Armonk, NY 10504
Phone: (914) 765-1900
Fax: (914) 765-4537

Contact: Michael Zeoli

Annual Revenues (mill $): $64,792

Annual Net Income (mill $): ($2827)

Description of Business: IBM is in the business of helping people solve problems through the use of advanced information technologies. IBM creates value by offering products and services that help customers succeed. These offerings include services, software systems, products, and various other technologies.

CPAs: Price Waterhouse

Advisors and Gatekeepers:

- Stephen Bechtel, Chairman Emeritus Bechtel Group
- Harold Brown, Chairman Foreign Policy Institute, Johns Hopkins University
- James E. Burke, retired Chairman Johnson & Johnson
- Thomas F. Frist, CEO Hospital Corp. of America
- Nannerl O. Keohane, President Wellesley College
- Richard W. Lyman, President Emeritus Stanford University
- J. Richard Munro, CEO Time Warner, Inc.
- Thomas S. Murphy, Chairman Capital Cities/ABC, Inc.

Strategic Alliances: **Zenith Data Systems** and IBM entered into an agreement calling for Zenith to produce notebook-sized computers for IBM. Zenith's computers are able to access networks where IBM has an installed base.
Zenith Data Systems CEO:
Phone: (708) 808-5000

Sapiens International Corporation N.V., incorporated in the Netherlands in 1990, develops, markets, and supports a software development tool used for building and maintaining a wide range of business applications. IBM and Sapiens entered into a software development

assistance agreement, pursuant to which IBM will provide certain technical assistance and documentation to the company. In May 1992, IBM purchased 179,212 shares and a warrant to purchase an additional 89,606 shares of Sapiens common stock (less than 2 percent) for $2 million.
Sapiens CEO: Shaul Shoni
Phone: 599-9-613277

Marcam Corp. is a small, fast growing software company with a current emphasis on software for process manufacturers. IBM and Marcam have entered into an agreement in which IBM will acquire a 16-percent stake in Marcam and Marcam will acquire worldwide marketing rights to IBM's Mapics integrated manufacturing software. IBM may receive additional payments from Marcam based on future sales of the software.
Marcam President: Paul Margolis
Phone: (617) 965-0220

Policy Management Systems Corporation is a provider of automation, administration support, and information solutions to meet the business needs of the global insurance industry. In August 1989, IBM acquired directly from PMSC a 19.8-percent interest in the company's outstanding voting stock for $116 million. IBM is entitled to increase its ownership interest up to a maximum of 30-percent by purchasing the company's common stock in the open market. IBM's ownership interest was 16.5 percent at December 31, 1991. IBM and PMSC work closely together to develop and market automation solutions for the insurance industry.
PMSC CEO: Larry Wilson
Phone: (803) 735-4000

Intel Corporation
2200 Mission College Blvd.
PO Box 58119
Santa Clara, CA 95052-8119
Phone: (408) 765-8080
Fax: (408) 765-1399
Contact: Leslie Vadasz, Director Business Development
Annual Revenues (mill $): $4778
Annual Net Income (mill $): $818
Description of Business: Intel Corporation and its subsidiaries operated in a dominant industry segment and are engaged primarily in the business of designing, developing, manufacturing, and marketing advanced microcomputer components and related products at various levels of integration.
CPAs: Ernst & Young
Advisors and Gatekeepers:

- D. James Guzy, Chairman NTX
- Richard Hodgson, Industrialist
- Max Palevsky, Industrialist
- Arthur Rock, Chairman Arthur Rock and Company
- David B. Yoffie, Professor of Business Administration, Harvard Business School
- Charles Young, Chancellor of the University of California at Los Angeles

Strategic Alliance: **Microtest, Inc.** is a leading worldwide supplier of diagnostic and certification tools for local area network (LAN) cabling. Microtest recently sold its printer connection technology and related customer license agreements to Intel Corporation, its principal licensee of this technology. In consideration for the technology, Intel paid Microtest $6 million at closing and agreed to pay an additional $1.5 million contingent upon the receipt of consents to the transfer by other licensees of the technology. Intel currently holds an 8.4-percent interest in Microtest.
CEO: Steve Richter
Phone: (413) 786-1680

The Japan Steel Works, Ltd.

Hibiya Mitsui Bldg.,
1-2, Yraku-cho 1-chome,
Chiyoda-ku, Tokyo, Japan
Phone: 011-813-3501-6111
Fax: 011-813-3595-4631

Contact: Keizo Ohnishi, Director R&D

Annual Revenues (mill $): $1116

Annual Net Income (mill $): $161

Description of Business: The Japan Steel Works is active in a wide range of areas. They include large-sized steel castings and forgings, heavy machinery and steel structures, steel plates, plastics machinery, industrial machinery, equipment related to petroleum, gas, chemical, and petrochemical industries.

CPAs: Ernst & Young International

Advisors and Gatekeepers:

- Hiroyuki Tokushige, Senior Managing Director Strategic Commodities Control.
- Yoshitaka Yoshida, Senior Managing Director in charge of Corporate planning
- Yukimasa Morishima, Senior Managing Director Machinery Business Headquarters

Strategic Alliances: **Research Frontiers, Inc.**, a development-stage company, develops devices that control the flow of light. Such devices, known as *light valves*, use the fluid suspension of microscopic particles that are enclosed between two plates, at least one of which is transparent. When an electrical voltage is applied to the suspension, the microscopic particles align, enabling the operator to vary and control the amount of light transmittted through or reflected from the device.

In 1989, the company granted The Japan Steel Works and Central Glass Works, Ltd. the rights to manufacture and sell variable light transmission windows for Japan plus other territories. In consideration, the company will receive a 3-percent running royalty on sales. Japan Steel Works paid the company $225,000 upon the grant of the

license and in January 1991 an additional $90,000 as deferred revenue. The license agreement has a term of 10 years.
Research Frontiers CEO: Robert Saxe
Phone: (516) 364-1902

Jia Non Enterprise Company Ltd.
46 Liu Tzu Nan
Nan Ai Lii
Hsinchun City, Taiwan
Republic of China
Phone: 011-886-3576-2122
Fax: 011-886-4523-9980

Contact: J. S. Hsieh, President

Annual Revenues (mill $): N/A

Annual Net Income (mill $): N/A

Description of Business: Pharmaceutical distributor.

CPAs: N/A

Advisors and Gatekeepers: N/A

Strategic Alliances: **Ecogen** develops and markets biological pesticides derived from naturally occurring or genetically modified microorganisms for use in controlling insects, diseases and weeds that affect agricultural crop production and forestry. In March, 1990, Ecogen and Jia Non entered into a seven-year agreement whereby Jia Non became Ecogen's exclusive distributor for most of its product line in Taiwan. Under this agreement Jia Non is required to pay Ecogen a fee of $300,000 as well as royalties based upon sales of such products. In connection with this transaction, Ecogen sold Jia Non 150,457 shares of common stock for $500,000 and shortly thereafter 199,156 shares for another $500,000.
Ecogen CEO: John Davies
Phone: (215) 757-1590

Johnson & Johnson
One Johnson & Johnson Plaza
New Brunswick, NJ 08933
Phone: (908) 524-0400
Fax: (908) 828-4107

Contact: James R. Utaski

Annual Revenues (mill $): $12,447

Annual Net Income (mill $): $1461

Description of Business: Johnson & Johnson is the world's largest and most comprehensive manufacturer of health care products serving the consumer, pharmaceutical, and professional markets.

CPAs: Coopers & Lybrand

Advisors and Gatekeepers:

- James Black, Professor of Analytical Pharmacology, Rayne Institute, King's College School of Medicine
- Joan Cooney, CEO Children's Television Workshop
- Clifton C. Garvin, retired CEO Exxon Corporation
- Philip M. Hawley, CEO Carter Hawley Hale Stores, Inc.
- Arnold G. Langbo, CEO Kellogg Company
- John Mayo, President AT&T Bell Labs
- Thomas S. Murphy, Chairman Capital Cities/ABC, Inc.
- Maxine F. Singer, President Carnegie Institution of Washington

Strategic Alliance: **Gene Shears Pty. Ltd.** is an Australian company working to develop commercial uses for technology that would regulate the action of genes. The technology opens the possibility of creating drugs to treat genetic diseases, viral infections, and other conditions. Johnson & Johnson has recently acquired an equity interest in Gene Shears and also has an exclusive worldwide license to this technology for selected applications.
Gene Shears CEO: Alain Maiore
Phone: 001-612-906-6363

Kubota Corp.
2-47, Shikitsuhigashi 1-chome
Naniwa-ku, Osaka 556, Japan
Phone: 001-816-648-2111
Fax: 001-816-648-3862
Contact: Shigekazu Mino, President
Annual Revenues (mill $): $6836
Annual Net Income (mill $): $31
Description of Business: Kubota Corporation is Japan's top manufacturer of farm equipment, ductile iron pipe, and cement roofing materials.
CPAs: Deloitte & Touche Tohmatsu
Advisors and Gatekeepers:
- Shigekazu Mino, President
- Kazutaka Iseki, Vice President
- Eiji Nakaya, Vice President
- Kouhei Mitsui, Vice President

Strategic Alliances: **Mycogen** develops, manufactures, and markets biopesticides as alternatives to chemical pesticides for the control of a variety of insects, weeds, and other pests. In October 1987 Mycogen and Kubota Corp. entered into a three-year collaborative agreement to develop and market certain microbial bioinsecticides for use against selected insects found in Far East Asia. Kubota has paid $6 million to Mycogen for research and development, but Mycogen no longer receives funding from Kubota. Under the terms of a future joint venture, Kubota and Mycogen will jointly own the rights to commercialize microbial bioinsecticides for agricultural applications in Far East Asia. Mycogen will retain exclusive rights throughout the rest of the world.
Mycogen CEO: Jerry D. Caulder
Phone: (619) 453-8030

Litton Industries, Inc.
360 North Crescent Drive
Beverly Hills, CA 90210-4867
Phone: (310) 859-5000
Fax: (310) 859-5940

Contact: Joseph T. Casey

Annual Revenues (mill $): $5693

Annual Net Income (mill $): $174

Description of Business: Litton is a multiindustry global corporation participating in resource exploration, industrial automation systems, advanced electronics, and marine engineering and production.

CPAs: Deloitte & Touche

Advisors and Gatekeepers:

- Paul Bancroft, retired President and CEO Bessemer Securities Corp.
- Wallace Booth, former Executive Ford Motor Company, Rockwell International
- Thomas Hayward, retired Admiral U.S. Navy
- Steven Sample, President University of Southern California
- Jayne B. Spain, former Executive Gulf Oil Corp.
- C.B. Thornton, President Thornton Corporation

Strategic Alliances: **Research Frontiers Inc.**, a development stage company, develops devices that control the flow of light. Such devices, known as "light valves," use fluid suspension of microscopic particles that are enclosed between two plates, at least one of which is transparent. When an electrical voltage is applied to the suspension, the microscopic particles align, enabling the operator to vary and control the amount of light transmittted through or reflected from the device.

In 1986, the company granted to Litton the exclusive worldwide rights for window display and eyewear products to be used in military and avionics applications. The company will receive a royalty of 5 to 6 percent of sales plus $2 per square inch for display products.

Minimum annual royalties range from $60,000 to $120,000, dependent on the application.
Research Frontiers CEO: Robert Saxe
Phone: (516) 364-1902

Marion Merrell Dow, Inc.
9300 Ward Parkway
Kansas City, MO 64114-0480
Phone: (816) 966-4000
Fax: (816) 966-3804

Contact: Malcolm Barbour

Annual Revenues (mill $): $2851

Annual Net Income (mill $): $585

Description of Business: Marion Merrell Dow is a global pharmaceutical organization involved in the discovery, development, manufacture, and sale of prescription and over-the-counter products.

CPAs: Deloitte & Touche

Advisors and Gatekeepers:

- John Biles, Dean School of Pharmacy USC
- Enrique Falla, CFO Dow Chemical
- James Gardner, Professor of Business, University of Utah
- Frank P. Popoff, CEO Dow Chemical
- James Wyngaarden, MD, Foreign Secretary National Academy of Sciences

Strategic Alliances: **Immulogic Pharmaceutical Corporation (Immulogic)** is a biopharmaceutical company developing products to treat allergies and autoimmune diseases. Marion Merrell Dow (MMD) and Immulogic will jointly develop, manufacture, and market Immulogic's ALLERVAX products in the United States with Immulogic retaining 50.1 percent of profits. MMD will develop and market the products outside the United States retaining 55.1 percent of the profits, with the balance going to Immulogic. MMD will make a $7-million initial payment to Immulogic as well as further license payments according to performance. In addition, MMD purchased a 10.3-percent stake in Immulogic for $19.1 million.
Immulogic CEO: Richard Bagley
Phone: (617) 494-0060

Gensia Pharmaceuticals is a fully integrated biopharmaceutical company focused on the discovery and development of innovative pharmaceutical products for the acute care hospital market. In

January 1990, Gensia and MMD entered into an agreement in which Gensia has agreed to use its best efforts to discover and investigate as many purine or pyrimidine compounds as Gensia deems feasible for activity in cardiovascular and cerebrovascular indications. MMD has the right through January 1995 to an exclusive license in North America, Europe, and certain other countries for any of the aforementioned compounds developed by Gensia. For any compound it licenses under the MMD agreement, MMD will make significant license and milestone payments to Gensia and will pay Gensia a royalty on net sales when any licensed products are marketed. Gensia also retains the rights to manufacture 75 percent of the final formulation of the nonoral form of any licensed compound as well as exclusive distribution rights to any parenteral-only products. Concurrent with this agreement, MMD purchased $15 million of Gensia common stock at a price of $8.40 per share. In October 1991, MMD purchased an additional $5 million of Gensia common stock. MMD total ownership in Gensia now stands at approximately 12.2 percent.
Gensia CEO: David Hale
Phone: (619) 546-8300

Cortech, Inc. is a biopharmaceutical company focused on the design and development of two novel classes of drugs to treat a broad range of inflammatory disorders. In June 1987, Cortech entered into research and license agreements with MMD, under which Cortech granted to MMD worldwide rights to develop, manufacture, and market any products resulting from Cortech's neutrophil elastase inhibitor program. Under the research agreement, MMD has paid a total of $7.9 million to Cortech in research funding through September 30, 1992. The company and MMD have extended the research agreement until December 31, 1993. Under the terms of the extension, MMD is expected to pay an additional $800,000 to Cortech in research and development funding in 1992 and $1.3 million in 1993. MMD may cancel the agreement at any time on 60 days' notice.
Cortech CEO: David Crossen
Phone: (303) 650-1200

Masco Industries, Inc.
21001 Van Born Rd.
Taylor, MI 48180
Phone: (313) 274-7405
Fax: (313) 374-6135

Contact: Frank Hennessey

Annual Revenues (mill $): $3141

Annual Net Income (mill $): $44

Description of Business: Masco Industries, Inc. is one of the country's largest manufacturers of brand name consumer products for the home and family.

CPAs: Coopers & Lybrand

Advisors and Gatekeepers:

- Erwin Koning, retired Vice President National Bank of Detroit
- John Morgan, Partner Morgan Lewis Githens & Ahn.
- Arman Simone, President Simone Corporation

Strategic Alliances: **Trimas Corporation** was founded in 1988, via an acquisition of 15 operating businesses from Masco Industries, Inc., including the manufacturing of industrial container closures, pressurized gas cylinders, towing systems products, specialty fasteners, and precision cutting tools. Masco Industries retained a 51 percent ownership interest, diluted to 36 percent following the company's initial public offering. Under a corporate services agreement, Masco provides the company with the use of its data processing equipment, research and development services, corporate administrative staff, and legal services for an annual base fee of 0.8 percent of the company's annual sales.

President: Brian P. Campbell
Phone: (313) 747-7025

Matsushita Communications Industrial, Ltd.
50 Meadowland Parkway
Secaucus, NJ 07094
Phone: (201) 348-7710
Fax: (201) 348-7016

Contact: Akiya Imura

Annual Revenues (mill $): $56,015

Annual Net Income (mill $): $999

Description of Business: Matsushita Electric Industrial Co., Ltd. is a world leader in the electronics industry.

CPAs: KPMG Peat Marwick

Advisors and Gatekeepers:

- Sohei Nakayama
- Kyonsuke Ibe
- Masahiko Hirata
- Akiya Imura
- Mikio Higashi
- Shiro Horiuchi

Strategic Alliances: **Fleet Call, Inc.** founded in 1987, is the leading provider of specialized mobile radio wireless communications services in six large U.S. metropolitan markets. In consideration for its being selected by Fleet Call, Inc. to supply a substantial number of two-way radio and cellular telephones to Fleet Call, subject to price competitiveness over eight years, Matsushita agreed to buy $45 million worth of Fleet Call's common stock, or 6 percent of the outstanding shares at $15 per share.
Fleet Call CEO: Brian D. McAuley
Phone: (201) 438-1400

Creative Technology Ltd. (CTL) develops, manufactures, and markets a family of sound and video multimedia products for IBM-compatible PCs. The company and Matsushita have entered an agreement in which the two companies are producing CD-ROM drives to meet MPC specifications.
CTL CEO: Sim Wong Hoo
Phone: (408) 428-6600

MedRad Inc.
271 Kappa Dr.
Pittsburgh, PA 15238
Phone: (800) 633-7231
Fax: (412) 967-9028

Contact: Thomas Witmer, CEO

Annual Revenues (mill $): $57

Annual Net Income (mill $): $3.5

Description of Business: MedRad is a leading developer, manufacturer, and marketer of equipment and disposable products that enhance the clarity of medical images of the human body.

CPAs: Deloitte & Touche

Advisors and Gatekeepers: N/A

Strategic Alliance: **Digivision** is a medical electronics company with $3 million in sales. It has developed a $25,000 device that enhances X-ray images used in cardiac surgery and other procedures. MedRad and Digivision have entered into an agreement in which MedRad will function as a marketing and service arm for Digivision's Fluoro-Vision video enhancer.
Digivision CEO: John Cambon
Phone: (619) 458-1111

Medtronics

7000 Central Avenue NE
Minneapolis, MN 55432
Phone: (612) 574-4000
Fax: (612) 574-4879

Contact: William Chorske, Senior Vice President

Annual Revenues (mill $): $1176

Annual Net Income (mill $): $161

Description of Business: Medtronic, Inc. is a leading therapeutic medical device company, focusing on improving the cardiovascular and neurological health of patients worldwide.

CPAs: Price Waterhouse

Advisors and Gatekeepers:
- Caleb Blodgett, retired Vice Chairman General Mills
- Antonio Gotto, Chairman Baylor College of Medicine
- Thomas Holloran, Professor School of Business St. Thomas
- Jack Schuler, Chairman Stericycle, Inc.
- Gerald Simonson, CEO Omnetics
- Gordon Sprenger, CEO and President Lifespan, Inc.

Strategic Alliances: **Spectranetics** develops, manufactures, and markets a proprietary excimer laser, the CVX-300 and proprietary disposable fiberoptic catheters to treat atherosclerosis in coronary arteries, the primary cause of heart attack. Medtronics has agreed to hold at least a 5-percent equity stake in Spectranetics, as well as purchase a minimum amount of products from Spectranetics to be agreed upon by the parties each year. In return, Medtronics has a right of first refusal on marketing agreements within particular geographic areas. Medtronics also obtains exclusive distribution rights of the companies current and future products in Europe, the Middle East, and Africa.

Spectranetics CEO: Robert Depasqua
Phone: (719) 633-8333

Merck & Co. Inc.
126 East Lincoln Avenue
Rahway, NJ 07065-0909
Phone: (908) 594-4000
Fax: (908) 594-5039

Contact: Jerry Jackson, Senior Vice President

Annual Revenues (mill $): $8602.7

Annual Net Income (mill $): $2121.7

Description of Business: Merck is one of the largest pharmaceutical companies in America.

CPAs: Arthur Andersen & Co.

Advisors and Gatekeepers:

- Brewster Atwater, CEO General Mills
- William Bowen, President Mellon Foundation
- Carolyne K. Davis, International Health Care Consultant, Ernst & Young
- Lloyd C. Elam, MD Professor Psychiatry, Meharry Medical College
- Richard Ross, MD Dean Emeritus Medical Faculty Johns Hopkins University
- Dennis Weatherstone, Chairman J.P. Morgan & Co.

Strategic Alliances: **Immulogic Pharmaceutical Corporation (Immulogic)** is a biopharmaceutical company developing products to treat allergies and autoimmune diseases. Immulogic's agreement with Merck provides Merck with exclusive rights to commercialize certain products for the prevention or treatment of type diabetes, rheumatoid arthritis, and organ transplant rejection. In return Merck is funding a research program at Immulogic over an initial three-year term. Merck has invested $10.3 million in Immulogic through purchases of equity and $6.1 million in funding.
Immulogic CEO: Richard Bagley
Phone: (617) 494-0060

ImClone Systems, Inc. is a biopharmaceutical company engaged primarily in the research and development of therapeutic products for the treatment of selected cancers, disorders of the hematopoietic

system, and inflammatory diseases. ImClone has entered into an agreement with Merck that provides Merck the exclusive license to manufacture, sell, and distribute in Europe, Australia, and New Zealand, if developed, ImClone's BEC-2 antiidotypic monoclonal antibody and recombinant gp75 antigen for all indications (licensed products). ImClone was paid a fixed fee for entering into the agreement and is entitled to receive research funding for a three-year period. ImClone is also entitled to a royalty on all sales of the licensed products by Merck.
Imclone CEO: Samuel Waksal
Phone: (212) 645-1405

Merrill Lynch & Co., Inc.
World Financial Center
North Tower
New York, NY 10281-1332
Phone: (212) 449-1000
Fax: (212) 449-0842

Contact: Jerome Kenney, Vice President Corporate Strategy

Annual Revenues (mill $): $12,362

Annual Net Income (mill $): $ 7256

Description of Business: Merrill Lynch & Co. is a holding company that, through its subsidiaries and affiliates, provides investment, financing, insurance, and related services.

CPAs: Deloitte & Touche

Advisors and Gatekeepers:

- William Bourke, CEO Reynolds Metals
- John Burlingame, retired Executive Officer of General Electric
- Jill Conway, Visiting Scholar MIT, President Smith College 1975-85
- William Crowe, retired Admiral U.S. Navy
- Robert Hanson, retired Chairman Deere & Company
- Earle Harbison, CEO Monsanto
- James Lorie, Professor Business Administration, the University of Chicago School of Business
- Robert Luciano, CEO Schering-Plough Corporation

Strategic Alliances: **IDEXX Laboratories, Inc.** develops, manufactures, and sells biotechnology based detection systems that use specialized immunoasssay, biochemical, or DNA probe technologies. In 1987 Merrill Lynch Technology Ventures (MLTV) and IDEXX entered into a series of agreements in which IDEXX issued MLTV a seven-year warrant to purchase 425,000 shares of series D preferred stock at a price of $7.50 per share. In return, MLTV made payments to IDEXX for defined research and development. During 1989 and 1990, IDEXX recognized over $3 million as revenue under this agreement.
IDEXX CEO: David Shaw
Phone: (207) 856-0300

Mitsui & Company, Ltd.
2-1, Ohtemachi 1-Chome,
Chiyoda-Ku, Tokyo 100, Japan
Phone: 001-813-3285-1111
Fax: 001-813-3285-9800

Contact: Naohiko Kumagai, President

Annual Revenues (mill $): $133,970

Annual Net Income (mill $): $202

Description of Business: Mitsui commands a worldwide network of information sources and operates global on-line data transmission facilities linking offices in over 200 cities around the world. Mitsui provides or arranges full land, sea, and air transportation services. Mitsui arranges all the details of financing for business agreements and industrial projects.

CPAs: Deloitte & Touche Tohmatsu

Advisors and Gatekeepers:
- Koichiro Ejiri, Chairman
- Kazao Horino, Vice Chairman
- Naohiko Kumagai, President
- Kazutami Ishiguri, Vice President
- Akira Utsumi, GM Osaka Office

Strategic Alliances: **Metricom** is a leader in digital wireless data communications networking technology. The company develops, manufactures, and markets proprietary products that permit installation and operation of private, license-free, regional data communications networks. Metricom has entered into a marketing partnership with Mitsui & Company, Ltd. in which Mitsui has obtained worldwide rights to market Metricom's products. Mitsui has made a $2-million equity investment in Metricom.
Metricom CEO: Robert Dilworth
Phone: (408) 399-8200

Monsanto Company
800 North Lindbergh Boulevard
St. Louis, Missouri 63167
Phone: (314) 694-1000
Fax: (314) 694-3011
Contact: Francis Stroble, CFO
Annual Revenues (mill $): $8864
Annual Net Income (mill $): $296
Description of Business: Monsanto Company makes and markets high-value agricultural products; chemical products, including plastics and manufactured fibers; pharmaceuticals; food products, process control equipment and other performance materials.
CPAs: Deloitte & Touche
Advisors and Gatekeepers:

- Joan T. Bok, Chairman New England Electric System
- Robert M. Heyssel, MD, CEO The Johns Hopkins Hospital
- Philip Leder, MD, Chairman Department of Genetics, Harvard Medical School
- Howard Love, retired CEO National Intergroup, Inc.
- Frank Metz, CFO IBM
- John Reed, Chairman CitiCorp
- William D. Ruckelshaus, CEO Browning-Ferris Industries, Inc.
- John Slaughter, PhD, President Occidental College
- Stansfied Turner, retired Admiral U.S. Navy

Strategic Alliances: **Mycogen** develops, manufactures, and markets biopesticides as alternatives to chemical pesticides for the control of a variety of insects, weeds, and other pests. In June 1990, Mycogen entered into an agreement with Monsanto Company to collaborate on the development of plants genetically improved to resist certain plant parasitic nematodes. Mycogen has received $1.2 million in funding from Monsanto to support research efforts and is entitled to receive additional benchmark payments and royalties on plants commercialized utilizing Mycogen's technology.
Mycogen CEO: Jerry D. Caulder
Phone: (619) 453-8030

Motorola, Inc.
1303 E. Algonquin Rd.
Schaumburg, IL 60196
Phone: (708) 576-5000
Fax: (708) 576-4768

Contact: Carl Koenemann, CFO

Annual Revenues (mill $): $11,341

Annual Net Income (mill $): $454

Description of Business: Motorola is one of the world's leading providers of electronic equipment, systems, components, and services for worldwide markets.

CPAs: KPMG Peat Marwick

Advisors and Gatekeepers:

- Erich Bloch, formerly Director National Science Foundation
- David Clare, retired President Johnson & Johnson
- Wallace Doud, retired Vice President IBM
- Lawrence Howe, Executive Director Civic Committee of the Commercial Club of Chicago
- Anne Jones, Partner Sutherland, Asbill & Brennan law firm
- Thomas Murrin, Dean Duquesne University Business School
- William G. Salatich, retired President Gillette
- Gardiner Tucker, Vice President Science and Technology International Paper Company
- Kenneth West, Chairman of the Board and CEO Harris Bankcorp, Inc.

Strategic Alliances: **StrataCom, Inc.** designs, manufactures, markets, and services IPX FastPacket cell switching systems for private wide area networks and public carrier high-speed data service offerings. Between April 1987 and January 1988, StrataCom sold 755,906 shares of series D preferred stock to Motorola Codex at a price of $3.70 per share. In connection with its equity investment, Motorola Codex entered into a reseller agreement with StrataCom, under which StrataCom agreed to sell its IPX systems to Motorola Codex for resale under Codex's label.

StrataCom CEO: Richard Moley
Phone: (408) 294-7600

Network Computing Devices, Inc. (NCD) designs, manufactures, and markets a family of terminal systems, which provide graphical user interface, windowing, and networking capabilities and enable users to access multiple applications simultaneously across a network. In May 1990, Motorola purchased 1.25 million shares of series C preferred stock for $10 million. Concurrently with this purchase of equity, the company entered into a one-year purchase agreement with Motorola under which Motorola agreed to use the company as its exclusive supplier for Motorola's terminal requirements.
NCD CEO: William Carrico
Phone: (415) 694-0650

Nestle S.A.
U.S. Corporate Offices
800 North Brand Boulevard
Glendale, CA 91203
Phone: (818) 549-6000
Fax: 4121 921 1885

Contact: Helmut Maucher, CEO

Annual Revenues (mill SF): 50,486 (Swiss francs)

Annual Net Income (mill SF): 2470 (Swiss francs)

Description of Business: Nestles is one of the largest food manufacturers in the world.

CPAs: KPMG Peat Marwick

Advisors and Gatekeepers:

- Helmut Maucher, CEO
- Rainer Gut, Vice Chairman
- Fritz Leutwiler, Vice Chairman
- Carl Angst
- Bruno de Kalbermatten
- Hans Strasser

Strategic Alliances: **VISX, Inc.** is engaged in the development and manufacture of excimer refractive surgical systems designed to recontour the front surface of the cornea of the human eye. Since 1986, VISX has been party to an agreement that grants Alcon U.S. (wholly-owned subsidiary of Nestle) the exclusive license to market and sell the Excimer system in the United States and, to Alcon International, the rights outside the United States. Under the agreement, Alcon advanced a total of $2.5 million to VISX in 1988 which was spent on developing the Excimer system.
VISX CEO: Charles R. Munnerlyn
Phone: (408) 732-9880

Nippon Steel U.S.A., Inc.
10 East 50th Street, 29th floor
New York, NY 10022
Phone: (212) 486-7150
Fax: (212) 593-3049

Contact: Takashi Imai

Annual Revenues (mill $): $19,792

Annual Net Income (mill $): $630

Description of Business: Nippon Steel is a world-leading steelmaker and highly involved in many high-technology ventures.

CPAs: Chuo Shinko Audit Corporation

Advisors and Gatekeepers:

- Akira Miki, CEO Nippon Steel
- Hiroshi Saito, Director and President
- Takashi Imai, Corporate Planning
- Hajime Nakagawa, Project Administration
- Takao Katsumata, Computer and Communication Systems

Strategic Alliances: **Simtek Corporation**, a development-stage company founded in 1986, develops and produces nonvolatile static random access memories (NVSCRAM). These memory products have greater capacity and faster data-access speeds, and they retain their information when power is interrupted. Nippon Steel, in 1988 obtained nonexclusive, worldwide marketing rights to Simtek NVSCRAM, the right to manufacture NVSCRAM, and the right to use Simtek's manufacturing process technologies for payments of approximately $5 million, a portion of which may be converted into Simtek common stock. Nippon Steel purchased 633,000 shares or 10.7 percent of Simtek common stock for $2 million.
Simtek CEO: Richard L. Petritz
Phone: (719) 531-9444

Norsk Hydro, A.S.
Bygdoy Alle 2
N-0257, Oslo 2, Norway
Phone: 01147-2-432-100
Fax: 01147-2-432-574

Contact: Egil Mykelbust

Annual Revenues (mill $): $61,423

Annual Net Income (mill $): ($498)

Description of Business: Norsk Hydro is an industrial group based on the processing of natural resources to meet needs for food, energy, and materials.

CPAs: Forum Touche Ross Ans

Advisors and Gatekeepers:

- Leif Haraldseth, Buskerud County Governor
- Einar Kloster, President Philips Lighting Holding B.V.
- Benedicte Berg Schilbred, Board Chairman of Odd Berg Group.
- Denis Schneiter, Director Banque Paribas
- Hans G.O. Torre, Information officer Porsgrunn, Employee Representative
- Per Wold, Trade Union Chairman, Employee Representative

Strategic Alliances: **Telios Pharmaceuticals, Inc.** was founded in 1987 to develop a new class of therapeutic products. Norsk Hydro purchased the right to develop the products of Telios Pharmaceuticals, Inc. in Europe, for which it has agreed to make milestone payments. Norsk Hydro purchased $7.5 million of the company's preferred stock and obtained one board seat.
Telios CEO: Robert J. Erickson
Phone: (619) 622-2600

OMNI Insurance Co.
1000 Parkwood Circle
Ste. 1000
Atlanta, GA 30339
Phone: (404) 952-4500
Fax: (404) 933-8285

Contact: Lowell Sims

Annual Revenues (mill $): N/A

Annual Net Income (mill $): N/A

Description of Business: Involved in South Eastern Insurance Industry.

CPAs: N/A

Advisors and Gatekeepers: N/A

Strategic Alliances: **Dateq Information Network, Inc.** provides information for use in the underwriting activities of insurance companies. Through its centralized information network, Dateq provides automobile insurers with motor vehicle reports on policy applicants. OMNI purchased 168,889 shares, equal to 4.8 percent of the common stock of Dateq.
Dateq CEO: Robert L. Stanley
Phone: (404) 446-8282

ONO Pharmaceutical Company, Ltd.
1-5 Dosomachi 2-Chrome
Chuo-ku, Osaka 541 Japan
Phone: 01181-6-222-5551
Fax: 01181-6-222-5706

Contact: Kazuo Sano

Annual Revenues (mill $): N/A

Annual Net Income (mill $): N/A

Description of Business: One of the largest pharmaceutical companies in Japan.

CPAs: N/A

Advisors and Gatekeepers: N/A

Strategic Alliances: **Telios Pharmaceuticals, Inc.** was founded in 1987 to develop a new class of therapeutic products. ONO purchased a right of first refusal to commercialize all of the products of Telios Pharmaceuticals, Inc. in the Far East, for which it has agreed to make milestone payments of up to $7.5 million. Ono will also financially support the development of ophthalmic and fibrotic disease products.
Telios CEO: Robert J. Erickson
Phone: (619) 622-2600

Pfizer
235 East 42nd Street
New York, NY 10017-5755
Phone: (212) 573-2323
Fax: (212) 573-2641

Contact: Barry Bloom

Annual Revenues (mill $): $6950

Annual Net Income (mill $): $722

Description of Business: Pfizer is one of the world's largest pharmaceutical companies.

CPAs: KPMG Peat Marwick

Advisors and Gatekeepers:

- Edward Bessey, President U.S. Pharmaceuticals Group
- Anthony Burns, CEO Ryder System, Inc.
- Barber Conable, former President The World Bank
- William Crowe, former Chairman Joint Chiefs of Staff
- Grace Fippinger, former Vice President Nynex Corp.
- Stanley Ikenberry, President University of Illinois
- Howard Kauffmann, former President Exxon
- Paul Marks, MD, CEO Memorial Sloan-Kettering Cancer Center

Strategic Alliances: **Opta Food Ingredients, Inc. (OPTA)** develops and markets proprietary new food ingredients which enable consumer food companies to improve the nutritional content, healthfulness, or taste of foods. Under the agreement with OPTA, Pfizer has purchased the equivalent of 13.5 percent of OPTA's common stock for $3 million. In exchange, Pfizer has exercised rights to commercialize the LITA, OPTEX, and EverFresh OPTA products. OPTA is entitled to payments from Pfizer upon certain sales milestones for these products.
OPTA CFO/Treasurer: Mark Skaletsky
Phone: (617) 252-0005

Phillips Medical Systems Nederland B.V. (Phillips)
Groenewoudseweg 1
5621 BA Eindhoven
The Netherlands
Phone: 011-31-40-786022
Fax: 011-31-40-785486

Contact: H. Van Bree, Chairman Phillips Medical Systems

Annual Revenues (mill $): $56,986 (gilders)

Annual Net Income (mill $): $1150 (gilders)

Description of Business: Phillips is one of the largest manufacturers and marketers of electronics products in the world.

CPAs: KPMG Klynveld

Advisors and Gatekeepers:

- W. Huisman, Chairman Phillips Communications Division
- H. Bodt, Chairman Phillips Consumer Electronics
- J.C. Tollenaar, Chairman Phillips Domestic Appliances
- F.A. de Bruijne, Chairman Phillips Industrial Electronics
- H. Van Bree, Chairman Phillips Medical Systems

Strategic Alliances: **ISG Technologies Inc., (ISG)** designs, manufactures, markets, and services computer-based visual data processing systems used by radiologists and surgeons to display, manipulate, and analyze two-dimensional and three-dimensional images of a patient's internal anatomy. Since 1987, ISG has worked on various projects to adapt its visual data processing technology to the MRI product line of Phillips. Phillips has funded such efforts largely by paying ISG's development personnel costs. Although the term of the agreement expired on October 31, 1991, the agreement has been extended for successive one-month periods since then while the parties negotiate a replacement agreement.

ISG CEO: Michael Greenburg, MD
Phone: (416) 672-2100

Policy Management Systems Corp.
One PMS Center
Blythewood, SC 29016
Phone: (803) 735-4000
Fax: (803) 735-6499

Contact: Robert L. Gresham

Annual Revenues (mill $): $415

Annual Net Income (mill $): $47.6

Description of Business: PMSC provides a complete spectrum of automation, administration support, and information solutions to meet the business needs of the global insurance industry.

CPAs: Ernst & Young

Advisors and Gatekeepers:
- Sterling Beale, CEO Seibels Bruce Group, Inc.
- Donald Feddersen, Charles River Ventures
- Lutz Hahne, Vice President Technology
- John Palms, President University of South Carolina
- Joseph Sargent, Chairman Conning & Company
- John Seibels, investor
- Richard Trub, Vice President Connecticut National Bank

Strategic Alliance: **FAI Insurances Limited** and PMSC entered into a ten-year agreement, effective September 1991, to provide complete systems management and data processing services to FAI Insurances Limited of Sydney, Australia. Pursuant to this agreement, PMSC acquired the majority of data processing assets and operations of FAI for an aggregate consideration of $12 million in cash and an interest-bearing promissory note.
FAI CEO: Rodney Adler
Phone: 011-612-430-1000

Procordia
Frosundaviks alle 15
S-17197 Stockholm, Sweden
Phone: 001-468-624-5000
Fax: 001-468-655-8010

Contact: Soren Gyll, CEO

Annual Revenues (mill $): $38,354

Annual Net Income (mill $): $3308

Description of Business: Procordia is a holding company for international operations in healthcare, food, and other services.

CPAs: Hans Karlsson, APA
Goran Tidstrom, APA

Advisors and Gatekeepers:
- Pehr Gyllenhammar, Board Chairman AB Volvo
- Stig Malm, Chairman Swedish Trade Union Confederation
- Soren Mannheimer, President GBCUM Bank
- Gustav Von Hertzen, President Helsinki Science Park
- Krister Hertzen, President SPP Insurance Company
- Anita Modin, Member of Parliament

Strategic Alliance: **Luther Medical Products, Inc.** develops stickless catheters, which reduce the possibility of accidental transmission of infection. Luther and Pharmacia Deltec, Inc., a subsidiary of Procordia, have entered into an agreement in which fees and debentures of up to $2 million are to be paid to Luther subject to completion of various development milestones. This agreement provides worldwide rights to Pharmacia for various Luther Medical products and triggers Pharmacia's "irrevocable" order for a minimum number of catheter units to be delivered within the next one year, totaling $780,000 in new revenues. These purchase minimums double by the third year of the contract.

Luther Medical Products: Tate Scott
Phone: (714) 544-3002

The Procter & Gamble Company

One Procter & Gamble Plaza
Cincinnati, OH 45202
Phone: (513) 983-1100
Fax: (513) 983-6891

Contact: Gordon Brunner, Senior Vice President R&D

Annual Revenues (mill $): $29,362

Annual Net Income (mill $): $1872

Description of Business: Procter & Gamble makes and markets a wide range of products worldwide for consumers and industry.
CPAs: Deloitte & Touche

Advisors and Gatekeepers:

- Norman R. Augustine, CEO Martin Marietta Corporation
- Theodore F. Brophy, retired Chairman GTE Corporation
- Robert Hanson, retired CEO Deere & Company
- Jerry Junkins, CEO Texas Instruments, Inc.
- Joshua Lederburg, Professor and President Emeritus, The Rockefeller University
- Walter Light, retired Chairman Northern Telecom Limited
- David Roderick, retired Chairman USX Corp.

Strategic Alliances: **Calgene** is a biotechnology company that is developing a portfolio of genetically engineered plants and plant products for the seed, food, and oleochemical industries. Calgene is developing three genetically engineered oils on behalf of Procter & Gamble. Under this collaborative agreement Calgene is funded by Procter & Gamble. If commercially viable products are developed, Calgene will have an opportunity to supply such products to Procter & Gamble or to receive royalties on Procter & Gamble's purchase of such products from others.
Calgene CEO: Roger Salquist
Phone: (916) 753-6313

Rhone-Poulenc Rorer Inc.
500 Arcola Road
Collegeville, PA 19426
Phone: (215) 454-8000
Fax: (215) 454-8028

Contact: Gilles D. Brisson

Annual Revenues (mill $): $3824

Annual Net Income (mill $): $326

Description of Business: Rhone-Poulenc Rorer, Inc. is one of the leading pharmaceutical companies in America.

CPAs: Coopers & Lybrand

Advisors and Gatekeepers:

- Charles-Henri Filippi, President Finley S.A.
- Michael H. Jordan, CEO Pepsico International Food & Beverage Division
- James S. Riepe, Managing Director T. Rowe Price Associates
- Edward Stemmler, MD Executive Vice President Association of American Medical Colleges

Strategic Alliances: **ISIS Pharmaceuticals** is a leader in the discovery and development of a new class of drugs, antisense oligonucleotides, which may form the basis for therapeutic drugs with greatly increased selectivity and additional advantages over existing drugs. Rhone-Poulenc and ISIS have entered into a collaborative research agreement in which ISIS receives financial support to investigate antisense compounds active against a specific target. ISIS has granted Rhone-Poulenc the option to obtain an exclusive license in all countries except the United States to make and sell any compounds discovered in the research program. ISIS has received an initial commitment fee and will receive milestone payments and royalties on sales of any products licensed to Rhone-Poulenc. ISIS has the right to codevelop and comarket in the United States all products discovered in the research program.
ISIS CEO: Stanley Crooke, MD
Phone: (619) 931-9200

The Immune Response Corporation (IRC), where Dr. Jonas Salk is chief scientific advisor, was engaged in experimentation with a "therapeutic immunogen" which had shown potential as a treatment for AIDS. In 1988, RPR entered into an agreement with IRC in which Rhone-Poulenc would provide research funding and or facilities while retaining North American marketing rights. Phase II and III placebo-controlled trials were scheduled for completion in late 1992. IRC CEO: James Glavin
Phone: (619) 431-7080

Roussel UCLAF
35, Boulevard des Invalides
75007 Paris
Phone: 011-331-4062-4062
Fax: N/A

Contact: Daniel Camus, Controller

Annual Revenues (mill $): $7781

Annual Net Income (mill $): $141.1

Description of Business: Roussel is one of the largest pharmaceutical/chemical companies in the world.

CPAs: Burnard Montagne

Advisors and Gatekeepers:
- Kurt Lanz, Honorary Chairman
- Jacques Machizaud, Chairman
- Jean Planet, Vice Chairman
- Pierre Joly
- Dr. Edouard Sakiz
- Jean-Pierre Godard

Strategic Alliances: **Ecogen** develops and markets biological pesticides derived from naturally occurring or genetically modified microorganisms for use in controlling insects, diseases, and weeds that affect agricultural crop production and forestry. Under the terms of the agreement between Roussel and Ecogen, Ecogen will undertake, over a four-year period, to develop improved or new bioinsecticides, based on its current Bt-based product line. In exchange for Ecogen's product development and distribution rights in Europe, Roussel has agreed to pay $12.725 million to Ecogen over this four-year period. Ecogen CEO: John Davies
Phone: (215) 757-1590

Sandoz Pharmaceuticals, Ltd. (Sandoz)
Corporate Communications
4002 Basle, Switzerland
Phone: 061-324-90-01
Fax: Undisclosed

Contact: Dr. Rolf Schweizer

Annual Revenues (mill SF): 13,444

Annual Net Income (mill SF): 1,114

Description of Business: Sandoz is one of the largest pharmaceutical companies in the world.

CPAs: Coopers & Lybrand

Advisors and Gatekeepers:

- Prof. Dr. Hans Letsch
- Dr. h.c. Pierre Languetin
- Dr. Nicolas Gossweiler
- Pierre Landolt
- Heinz Schoffler
- Dr. Jean Wander

Strategic Alliances: **Genetic Therapy, Inc. (GTI)** is a leader in the development of delivery systems for human gene therapy. GTI and Sandoz have entered into an agreement by which Sandoz will provide up to $13.5 million over three years to fund up to three projects in the designated disease areas, to which GTI is required to contribute $1 million per project. In addition, Sandoz will purchase equity in GTI amounting to $10 million as well as make milestone payments/royalty payments to GTI upon the occurrence of certain events.
GTI CEO: James Barrett
Phone: (301) 590-2626

Gensia Pharmaceuticals is a fully integrated biopharmaceutical company focused on the discovery and development of innovative pharmaceutical products for the acute care hospital market. In January 1992, Gensia and Sandoz entered into an agreement in which Sandoz will fund basic research at Gensia directed toward the

discovery of drugs for type II diabetes. Gensia will receive milestone payments as drugs are developed. The overall value of the research and development agreement to Gensia is expected to be approximately $22 million if one drug is developed. Additional milestone payments would be paid to Gensia if more than one drug is developed and marketed.
Gensia CEO: David Hale
Phone: (619) 546-8300

Systemix, Inc., based in Palo Alto, California, is a company with a promising research portfolio focusing on the characterization, isolation, and purification of stem cells from human bone marrow. Sandoz has purchased a substantial interest in Systemix, Inc. in order to solidify its position in immunological research worldwide and will be highly involved with Systemix's future research, development, and marketing.
Systemix CEO: Sue Gilbert
Phone: (415) 856-4901

SciMed
6655 Wedgewood Rd.
Maple Grove, MN 55369-7503
Phone: (612) 420-0700
Fax: (612) 494-1550

Contact: Thomas Hektner

Annual Revenues (mill $): $183

Annual Net Income (mill $): $34

Description of Business: SciMed is a global leader in the coronary angioplasty catheter industry, and produces a variety of other surgical products.

CPAs: Deloitte & Touche

Advisors and Gatekeepers:

- Randall Bellows, retired Vice President Cobe Labs, Inc.
- Richard Emmitt, Managing Director The Vertical Group
- Lawrence Horsch, Chairman 3E Management & Financial Corp.

Strategic Alliances: **Cardiovascular Imaging Systems, Inc. (CVIS)** develops, manufactures, and markets intravascular ultrasound imaging catheters and systems to aid in the diagnosis and treatment of cardiovascular disease. In March 1992, CVIS entered into a development agreement with SciMed, pursuant to which CVIS and SciMed will jointly develop an ultrasound imaging guidewire product for coronary and peripheral intravascular applications. Under the terms of the agreement, SciMed has the exclusive right to manufacture and sell the imaging guidewire product for intravascular applications, and CVIS has the exclusive right to manufacture and sell the guidewire product for other minimally invasive applications, each subject to the payment of royalties on such sales. As part of the agreement, SciMed has agreed to purchase 285,715 shares of common stock offered hereby for an aggregate purchase price of $2 million.

CVIS CEO: Richard M. Ferrari
Phone: (408) 749-9088

SmithKline Beecham (SKB)
One Franklin Plaza
Philadelphia, PA 19101
Phone: (215) 751-4000
Fax: (215) 270-5166

Contact: George Poste

Annual Revenues (mill $): $4685 (Swiss francs)

Annual Net Income (mill $): $638

Description of Business: SmithKline Beecham is one of the largest pharmaceutical companies in the world.

CPAs: Price Waterhouse
Coopers & Lybrand Deloitte

Advisors and Gatekeepers:

- Birgit Breuel, President Vorstand Treuhandanstalt
- Andrew Buxton, Managing Director Barclays PLC.
- William Grant, President Galen Associates
- Francis Lucier, retired CEO Black and Decker
- Ralph Pfeiffer, former CEO IBM World Trade Corp.
- Peter Walters, Chairman Midland Bank PLC and Blue Circle Industries

Strategic Alliances: **T-Cell Sciences** is a leading biotechnology company using proprietary T-cell and complement receptor technology to develop therapeutic products for the treatment of heart attacks, inflammatory diseases, cancer, and other diseases. SKB has been funding pre-clinical studies of the compound TP10HD and has assumed full responsibility for funding human clinical trials. In return, if the compound is successfully developed, SKB will receive exclusive worldwide marketing rights with the exception of the United States and Canada where, under specified conditions, T-Cell has copromotion rights, and Japan, where a separate agreement among T-Cell, SKB and YPC provides that Japanese comarketing rights will be shared by SKB and YPC.
T-Cell Sciences CEO: James D. Grant
Phone: (617) 621-1400

Zynaxis is an early-stage biotechnology company developing a variety of cell linker molecules for the delivery and retention of therapeutic drugs and radio-pharmaceuticals to disease sites and cellular diagnostic systems for the measurement of cell types found in blood. S.R. One, Ltd., a wholly owned subsidiary of SmithKline Beecham, invested approximately $1.8 million to buy 210,866 shares equal to 5 percent of Zynaxis, Inc. common stock and provided $106,000 in bridge loans.
Zynaxis CEO: Tom Cekoric
Phone: (215) 889-2200

Affinity Biotech, Inc. applies its proprietary microemulsion technology to the development of drug delivery systems. The company is focusing on the oral delivery of therapeutic proteins, such as calcitonin and insulin, that presently require administration by injection. Affinity and SmithKline Beecham entered into an agreement for the development and licensing of a formulation of Affinity's oral delivery system to be used for one of SKBs' therapeutic proteins. Under the terms of this agreement Affinity will receive $360,000 for research and is entitled to milestone payments from SKB up to an aggregate of $3 million. S.R. One, a subsidiary of SKB, also made an additional $1-million equity investment in Affinity. In return, Affinity has licensed to SKB any microemulsion system formulation developed in connection with such therapeutic proteins.
Affinity CEO: Alan Dickason
Phone: (215) 497-0500

In 1991, SKB also concluded collaborative agreements with **Scotgen Ltd.**, to develop and market a monoclonal antibody therapy for respiratory syncytial virus infection in children, and with **Bone Care International** to develop and market a product for treating osteoporosis.

Sony
7-35 Kitashinagawa 6-chome
Shinagawa-ku, Tokyo 141
Japan
Phone: 011-813-3448-2111
Fax: 011-813-3448-2244
Contact: Ken Iwaki
Annual Revenues (mill $): $28,733
Annual Net Income (mill $): $903
Description of Business: Sony Corporation is one of the world's leading manufacturers of video and audio equipment, televisions, displays, semiconductors, computers, and information-related products.
CPAs: Price Waterhouse
Advisors and Gatekeepers:
- Masaru Ibuka, Honorary Chairman
- Akio Morita, Chairman and Director
- Norio Ohga, President
- Masaaki Morita, Representative Director
- Nobuo Kanoi, Representative Director
- Tsunao Hashimoto, Deputy President and Director

Strategic Alliances: **Showscan** owns a proprietary, patented motion picture filming and projection process called Showscan®. Motion pictures filmed and projected in Showscan create a visual effect of depth, clarity, and realism that the company believes is superior to conventional films. The company acquired all the rights to the Showscan process from Paramount Pictures Corporation. Paramount now owns 216,666 shares of Showscan, a 4.8-percent interest, and is entitled to royalties associated with the future exploitation of the Showscan process.
Showscan CEO: Roy Aaron
Phone: (213) 553-2364

Southern California Edison (SCE)
2244 Walnut Grove Avenue
Rosemead, CA 91770
Phone: (818) 302-1212
Fax: (818) 302-4737

Contact: Alan Fohrer, CFO

Annual Revenues (mill $): $7502

Annual Net Income (mill $): $702

Description of Business: SCE is a 105-year-old regulated utility that provides electric service to 4.1 million customers in Central and Southern California.

CPAs: Arthur Andersen & Co.

Advisors and Gatekeepers:

- Roy Anderson, Chairman Lockheed Corp.
- Charles Miller, CEO Avery Dennison Corporation
- James Rosser, President California State University
- Walter Gerken, Chairman Executive Committee Pacific Mutual Life Insurance Company
- Joan Hanley, General Partner Miramonte Vineyards
- Carl Huntsinger, General Partner, DAE Limited Partnership Ltd.
- E.L. Shannon, Chairman of the Board Santa Fe International Corporation
- Edward Zapanta, MD physician and neurosurgeon

Strategic Alliances: **Metricom** is a leader in digital wireless data communications networking technology. The company develops, manufactures, and markets proprietary products that permit installation and operation of private, license-free, regional data communications networks. Through December 1991, Metricom has received from certain electric utility partners, principally Southern California Edison, approximately $26.2 million for the development of UtiliNet, a data communications network designed for the electric utility industry.
Metricom CEO: Robert Dilworth
Phone: (408) 399-8200

Sumitomo Corporation
2-2, Hitotsubashi 1-chome,
Chiyoda-ku, Tokyo 100,
Japan
Phone: 011-813-3217-5000
Fax: 011-813-3636-7220

Contact: Mutsumi Hashimoto, Vice President Metals

Annual Revenues (mill $): $149,900

Annual Net Income (mill $): $275

Description of Business: Sumitomo Corporation is one of the world's leading traders and distributors of a wide range of commodities, industrial goods, and consumer goods.

CPAs: Ernst & Young International

Advisors and Gatekeepers:
- Tadashi Itoh, Chairman
- Tomiichi Akiyama, President
- Akitoshi Oshima, Vice President Treasury and Accounting
- Eiichi Miyoshi, Vice President Iron & Steel Group
- Hiroshi Matsushita, Vice President Living related group
- Mutsumi Hashimoto, Vice President Metals, Chemicals

Strategic Alliances: **Biomagnetic Technologies, Inc. (BTi)** is the leader in the emerging medical diagnostic technology of biomagnetic imaging. Based on this technology, BTi developed the first commercial biomagnetometer and currently manufactures the third generation of this breakthrough medical diagnostic device, the Magnes system. In January 1990, BTi and Sumitomo Metal Industries entered into a series of agreements, in which BTi granted Sumitomo exclusive distribution rights for the biomagnetometer product line in certain portions of Asia, Australia, and New Zealand. Also included were rights to manufacture the technology in Japan and a new magnetically shielded room. In exchange for these rights, BTi received $1 million of funding. Sumitomo also acquired 818,000 shares of BTi's common stock at $11.
BTi CEO: Stephen James
Phone: (619) 453-6300

Syntro Corporation
9669 Lackman Rd.
Lenexa, KS 66219
Phone: (913) 888-8876
Fax: (913) 894-9373
Contact: William Davies
Annual Revenues (mill $): $4.4
Annual Net Income (mill $): $0.9
Description of Business: Syntro Corporation is a biotechnology company engaged in the research, development, manufacturing, and marketing of innovative vaccines for the animal health market.
CPAs: Ernst & Young
Advisors and Gatekeepers:

- Stephen E. O'Neill, Chairman of the Board Attorney and Private Investor
- Patrick Owen Burns, Vice President R&D Funding Corp.
- Russell T. Stern, Jr., private investor
- James Bittle, Member Department of Molecular Biology Research Institute of Scripps Clinic
- H. Lowell Thomas, Consultant HLT & Associates

Strategic Alliances: **Protein Polymer Technologies, Inc. (PPT)** designs protein "building blocks" and then, using synthetic genes, genetically assembles these blocks in a repetitive polymeric form. Through this process PPT creates unique protein polymers having specific physical, biological, and chemical properties without the limitations inherent in synthetic polymers and natural proteins. Syntro and PPT have entered into several agreements, pursuant to which PPT has acquired licensing to use certain confidential and proprietary information relating to the design and development of protein polymers. As part of their partnership PPT and Syntro entered into a loan and security agreement in which Syntro provided PPT with a nonrevolving line of credit in the sum of $430,000. Syntro subsequently exercised a warrant to acquire 14 percent of PPT, thereby canceling the previous indebtedness.
PPT CEO: Thomas Parmeter
Phone: (619) 558-6064

3A S.R.L. Parco Technologies Agroalinentare
Frazione Pantalla
Jodi, Italy
Phone: 011-39-7589-44006
Fax: 011-39-7588-8149

Contact: Dr. Gianfranc Formica, President
Annual Revenues (mill $): N/A
Annual Net Income (mill $): N/A
Description of Business: Agritechnology
CPAs: N/A
Advisors and Gatekeepers:
- Dr. Dorio Mutti

Strategic Alliances: **Ecogen** develops and markets biological pesticides derived from naturally occurring or genetically modified microorganisms for use in controlling insects, diseases and weeds that affect agricultural crop production and forestry. On January 25, 1991, Ecogen entered into a long-term research and development assistance contract with 3A S.R.L, a not-for-profit Italian organization, backed by the Umbria regional government, which is developing an agricultural technology park in the Umbria region of Italy. Under the terms of this agreement, Ecogen has issued 150,000 unregistered shares of common stock to 3A and will assist 3A in establishing an agricultural biotechnology research and development facility. Ecogen will also perform certain research activities in exchange for $2.1 million to be funded over the next three years.
Ecogen CEO: John Davies
Phone: (215) 757-1590

Tanabe Seiyaku Co., Ltd.
2-10 Dosho-machi 3-chome
Chuo-ku, Osaka 541, Japan
Phone: 011-81-6-205-5085
Fax: 011-81-6-205-5028

Contact: Ichiro Chibada

Annual Revenues (mill $): $1910

Annual Net Income (mill $): $42

Description of Business: Tanabe Seiyaku Co., Ltd., is one of Japan's largest pharmaceutical companies.

CPAs: Asahi Shinwa & Co.

Advisors and Gatekeepers:
- Jyunichiro Tanabe
- Mikio Takeda, PhD
- Tetsuya Tosa, PhD
- Masahiro Sato
- Ichizo Inoue, PhD
- Takeshi Fujita

Strategic Alliances: **Dura Pharmaceuticals, Inc.** is an early-stage pharmaceutical company focused on developing and marketing prescription pharmaceuticals for the treatment of asthma, hayfever, and the common cold. Tanabe invested $2.5 million in Dura while acquiring Dura as a vehicle for its products.
Dura CEO: Cam L. Garner
Phone: (619) 457-2553

Tandem Computers, Inc.

19333 Vallco Pkwy.
Cupertino, CA 95014-2599
Phone: (408) 725-6000
Fax: Call first

Contact: Gerald D. Held, Vice President Strategy and Corporate Development

Annual Revenues (mill $): $1922

Annual Net Income (mill $): $35

Description of Business: Tandem Computers, Inc. is a leading supplier of fault-tolerant computer systems and networking products for critical information processing requirements.

CPAs: Ernst & Young

Advisors and Gatekeepers:

- Thomas Perkins, Chairman of the Board, Kleiner Perkins Caufield & Byers
- Jack Bennett, retired Senior Vice President and Director Exxon Corporation
- Franklin Johnson, General Partner Asset Management Partners
- Robert Stone, Chairman of the Board Kirby Corporation
- Ralph Ungermann, President and CEO Ungermann-Bass, Inc.
- Thomas Unterberg, Managing Director, Unterberg Harris

Strategic Alliance: **Net Worth, Inc.** is a leading developer, manufacturer, and supplier of NetWare-optimized intelligent hubs and related products for local area networks. In November 1991, Net Worth and Ungerman-Bass, a wholly owned subsidiary of Tandem Computers, entered into an agreement in which Ungerman-Bass purchased a 50.4-percent equity interest in Net Worth, Inc. As a result of this relationship, Net Worth obtains access to the Ungermann-Bass worldwide sales and support capabilities, as well as certain key technologies. The two companies have also commenced joint product development.

Net Worth CEO: John McHale
Phone: (214) 929-1700

Tele-Communications, Inc.
Regency Plaza One
4643 South Ulster Street
Denver, CO 80237
Phone: (303) 267-5500
Fax: (303) 448-3220

Contact: Robert J. Lewis, Vice President Development

Annual Revenues (mill $): $3625

Annual Net Income (mill $): $287

Description of Business: TCI is one of the largest providers of cable television in the nation.

CPAs: KPMG Peat Marwick

Advisors and Gatekeepers:

- John W. Gallivan
- Kim Magness
- Robert Naify
- Paul O'Brien

Strategic Alliance: **Faroudja Research Enterprises** has developed and successfully tested, both over the air and on cable, a method for Enhanced Definition Television telecasting, which closely approaches the quality of 35 mm. TCI has invested a large sum of money in Faroudja in the hope that such technology can be used on its networks.
Faroudja CEO: Not available
Phone: (408) 735-1492

Eidak Corporation has developed and is field testing an alternative process that will prevent the successful taping of motion pictures or other programming shown on cable television systems. TCI has invested heavily in Eidak with the hope that, if successful and if accepted by producers of motion pictures, such technology could result in many more motion pictures becoming available to cable programmers earlier in the product life. This is in addition to the other obvious advantages to the cable industry.
Eidak CEO: Richard Leghorn
Phone: (617) 876-9000

Tele-Communications, Inc. was one of the founding members of **Cable Television Labs**, a nonprofit research and development corporation that is endeavoring to initiate the first high-definition television broadcasts on a regularly scheduled basis.
Cable Labs CEO: Dick Green
Phone: (303) 939-8500

The Tribune Company
435 N. Michigan Avenue
Chicago, IL 60611
Phone: (312) 222-3232
Fax: (312) 321-0688

Contact: Scott Smith

Annual Revenues (mill $): $2035

Annual Net Income (mill $): $141

Description of Business: The Tribune Company is a leading information and entertainment company, with media operations in 12 of the nation's largest metropolitan markets.

CPAs: Price Waterhouse

Advisors and Gatekeepers:

- Andrew McKenna, CEO Schwarz Paper Co.
- James O'Connor, CEO Commonwealth Edison
- Arnold Webber, President Northwestern University
- Diego Hernandez, Senior Vice President Wright Associates
- James Cowles, Inland Empire Paper Company

Strategic Alliances: In 1991, **America Online, Inc.** entered into an agreement with the Tribune Company by which the parties agreed to produce "local editions" in Illinois and Florida of *America Online,* a subscription news information service provided for online personal computer users. Material for *America Online* is taken, in part, from the Tribune Company's primary newspaper, *The Chicago Tribune* and its television station WGN. In consideration, Tribune Company invested $2 million in *America Online's* preferred stock, subsequently converted into 511,921 shares or 9.5 percent of its common stock.

Tribune Company CEO: James Kinsey
Phone: (703) 448-8700

Unisys
PO Box 500
Blue Bell, PA 19424-0001
Phone: (215) 986-4011
Fax: (215) 986-6352
Contact: Reta Braun
Annual Revenues (mill $): $8696
Annual Net Income (mill $): ($578.9)
Description of Business: Unisys Corporation makes and markets computer-based networked information systems, software, and related services on a worldwide basis.
CPAs: Ernst & Young
Advisors and Gatekeepers:

- Dr. James J. Duderstadt, President University of Michigan
- Melvin R. Goodes, Chairman Warner-Lambert Company
- Curtis Hessler, Senior Vice President Times Mirror Company
- Kenneth A. Macke, Chairman Dayton Hudson Corporation
- Robert McClements, Chairman Sun Company, Inc.
- William G. Milliken, former Governor, State of Michigan
- Donald Seibert, retired Chairman J.C. Penney Company

Strategic Alliances: **EMC Corporation** and its subsidiaries design, manufacture, market, and support high-performance storage products and provide related services for selected mainframe and midrange computer systems. In January 1992, EMC entered into a two-year OEM agreement for the sale of Unisys-compatible Symmetrix products to Unisys. This agreement gives Unisys exclusive worldwide marketing rights to these products. This agreement requires Unisys to purchase at least $21 million of such products in 1992 and at least $32 million of such products in 1993. Unisys is required to take delivery of certain quantities of products in accordance with a specified quarterly schedule, as well as annually, or it will be liable for the unpurchased amounts.
EMC Corp. CEO: James Conway
Phone: (508) 435-1000

United States Postmaster General
475 L'Enfant Plaza West SW
Washington, D.C. 20260
Phone: (202) 268-2000
Fax: N/A

Contact: Marvin Runyon, Postmaster General

Annual Revenues (mill $): N/A

Annual Net Income (mill $): N/A

Description of Business: Postal service provider.

CPAs: N/A

Advisors and Gatekeepers: N/A

Strategic Alliance: **Transitions Research Corp. (TRC)** is involved with the development and manufacture of service robots. TRC received $425,000 from the United States Postal Service to be used toward the development of Scrubmate, a robot that cleans bathrooms. The USPS is very interested in such robots to perform such undesirable chores.
TRC CEO: Joseph Engelberger
Phone: (203) 798-8988

VLSI Technology, Inc.
1109 McKay Drive
San Jose, CA 95131
Phone: (408) 434-3100
Fax: (408) 263-2511

Contact: Larry Carter, CFO

Annual Revenues (mill $): $413

Annual Net Income (mill $): $9

Description of Business: VLSI Technology, Inc. is a leading worldwide supplier of complex application-specific integrated circuits, application-specific standard products, and computer-aided engineering software.

CPAs: Ernst & Young

Advisors and Gatekeepers:

- Pierre Bonelli, CEO Sema-Metra
- Robert Dilworth, CEO Metricom In.
- James Kim, CEO AMKOR Electronics

Strategic Alliances: **Photronics, Inc.** founded in 1969, is a manufacturer of photomasks, which are ultrahigh-precision photographic glass plates containing microscopic images of electronic circuits. Photomasks are a key element in the manufacture of semiconductors, specificallly for the transfer of circuit patterns onto semiconductor wafers. In 1987, VLSI agreed to purchase the greater of $2 million of photomasks per year, or 50 percent of its annual photomask requirements. Sales of photomasks to VLSI are at discount prices. In consideration, Photronics issued to VLSI warrants to purchase 120,000 shares or approximately 2.7 percent of its common stock at $6.80 per share.
Photronics CEO: Constantine S. Macricostas
Phone: (203) 775-9000

Wal-Mart Stores, Inc.
(Insert Street Address)
Bentonville, Arkansas 72716
Phone: (501) 273-4000
Fax: (501) 273-1969

Contact: Paul Carter

Annual Revenues (mill $): $43,886

Annual Net Income (mill $): $ 1608

Description of Business: Wal-Mart is one of the largest retailers in the world.

CPAs: Ernst & Young

Advisors and Gatekeepers:

- David Banks, CEO Beverly Enterprises
- John Cooper, Chairman Cooper Communities
- Robert Dedman, Chairman Club Corporation International
- Kenneth Iverson, CEO Nucor Corp.
- Robert Kahn, President, Kahn and Associates

Strategic Alliances: **National Vision Associates, Ltd.** operates retail optical vision centers in 74 Wal-Mart stores in 22 states under the name "Wal-Mart Vision Center." Under this agreement, Wal-Mart currently gives the company the right to open and operate a total of 173 vision centers typically in newly opened Wal-Mart stores. In addition to certain maintenance fees, the company is required to pay to Wal-Mart annual license fees based on the gross sales of its vision centers, subject to certain minimum requirements.
NVA CEO: Edward Weiner
Phone: (404) 955-8500

American Studios, Inc. currently provides portrait photography services in over 1450 Wal-Mart stores in 32 states in the United States and Puerto Rico. Under the Wal-Mart Agreement, the company pays to Wal-Mart on a weekly basis a commission of 15 percent of the company's gross sales in exchange for the right to provide portrait photography services in Wal-Mart stores.
American Studios CEO: Randy Bates
Phone: (704) 588-4351

Yamaha Corp. of America

6600 Orange Thorpe Ave.
Buena Park, CA 90620
Phone: (714) 522-9011
Fax: N/A

Contact: Masahiko Arimoto

Annual Revenues (mill $): N/A (privately held)

Annual Net Income (mill $): N/A

Description of Business: Yamaha is one of the largest privately held producers of electronics in the world.

CPAs: N/A

Advisors and Gatekeepers: N/A

Strategic Alliances: **Creative Technology Ltd. (CTL)** develops, manufactures, and markets a family of sound and video multimedia products for IBM-compatible PCs. Yamaha and CTL have entered into an agreement in which the two companies are working to enhance the functionality and reduce the cost of a chip set used by CTL. CTL will be required to purchase approximately $11 million of the new chip sets over a two-year period.
CTL CEO: Sim Wong Hoo
Phone: (408) 428-6600

Index

Abbott Laboratories, 73-74, 141-42
ActMedia, 68, 100-101
Adelson, Sheldon, 98
Adobe Systems, Inc., 142, 152
Advanced Magnetics, Inc., 160, 176
Advent International, 3
Affinity Biotech, Inc., 234
Agouron Pharmaceuticals, Inc., 179
Alliance Pharmaceutical Corp., 153
Alpha tests, 114
Alpha Therapeutic Corp. (ATC), 144
A. Menarini SRL, 54-55, 147
American Cyanamid Company, 3, 145
American Home Products Corp. (AHP), 3, 53-54, 148
American Research & Development Corporation (AR&D), 68
American Studios, Inc., 248
American Telephone & Telegraph, 145-46
America Online, Inc., 81, 244
Ameritech Development Corp, 3, 150
Amgen Inc., 91, 151
Amway Corporation, 83
Amylin Pharmaceuticals, Inc., 15, 190
Analog Devices, Inc., 57-58
Annual reports, 118, 125
Apple Computer, Inc., 18, 39-40, 68, 105, 152
Applied Immune Sciences, Inc. (AIS), 153-54
Arthur Murray Dance Studios, 85, 100
ASK Computer Systems, Inc., 43-44
Associational thinking, 4-6, 75-76
Athena Neurosciences, Inc., 148, 180
Avon Products, 100

Bausch & Lomb, 3
Baxter International, Inc., 153-54
BCE, 155
Bentley Laboratories, 73
Berlinni's Oven Baked Pizza chain, 68

Beta tests, 115-16
Biomagnetic Technologies, Inc. (BTi), 237
Blockbuster Entertainment, 60
BMC West Corporation, 158-59
Boehringer Ingelheim, Inc. (BII), 157
Boise Cascade Corp., 158-59
Book-of-the-Month Club, Inc., 93
Boots Company PLC, 54
Boyer, Herbert W., 48-51
Branson, Richard, 52
Bristol-Meyers Squibb, 54, 160-61
Burlington Industries, Inc., 162
Business plan:
   components of, 109-15
   fixed costs, 114-15
   revenue, 109-13
   variable costs, 113-14
   writing, 103-21
   See also Launch plan

Cable News Network (CNN), 94-96
Cable Television Labs, 243
Calgene, 226
Capital equipment SDM, 93-96, 108
Cardiovascular Imaging Systems, Inc. (CVIS), 232
Carlson, Chester, 105, 123-24
Celebrity-endorsed consumer products, 85-89, 108
Centocor, Inc., 163
Centripetal/centrifugal project, 123
Century 21 Real Estate, 100
Cetus Corporation, 31, 105
Chemlawn Corporation, 164
Chemtrak Incorporated, 53-55, 144, 148-49, 160-61
   corporate partners, 53-55
   licensee money, 55-56
   licensing opportunities, developing, 56-57
   mission statement, 53

CIBA-GEIGY Corporation, 5-6, 165-66
Citicorp, 71
Citizens Utility (Portland, Ore.), 74
CLEAR Communications Ltd., 155-56
Closing, 121-32
   clarity at, 124-25
   data collection, 124-26
   DEP Factor, finding, 122-24
   gatekeepers, finding/going around, 126-28
   leveraging, 129-30
   questions for, 130-31
   third-party endorsements, 131-32
CMP Communications, 100
Cobe Laboratories, 73
Commerce Clearing House Corporation, 93
Com Net S.p.A., 167
ComputerLand Corporation, 100
Confidential disclosure agreement, 131
   sample of, 133-35
Consumer products start-up, 84-85, 108
Control Data Corporation, 68
Cookie cutter SDM, 91-92, 108
Cooperation, 13-14
   at exit stage, 58
   at growth stage, 57-58
   at marketing stage, 51-57
   at production stage, 34-51
   at research and development stage, 15-34
Coors, 31
Coppola, Francis Ford, 24, 45
Corning, Inc., 168
Corporate venture capital investments, 59-74
   adding new products to distribution channels, 61
   capital gains, generating with, 67-68
   and competition, 71-72
   and cost of acquistions reductions, 59-60
   and encouragement to local entrepreneurs, 74
   as form of R&D, 62
   as group therapy for senior management, 69-70
   as income generators, 69
   as investigative tool, 68-69
   ITEK reason for, 73-74
   as junior management training, 63-64
   meshing department activities with, 66-67
   middle management exposure to entrepreneurship, 62-63
   for new market exposure, 60-61
   and plant space/time/people utilization, 64-66
   as public relations tools, 70-71

Cortech, Inc., 205
COR Therapeutics, Inc., 179
Corvas International, Inc., 163
C. R. Bard, Inc., 169
Creative Technology Ltd. (CTL), 207, 249
Crop Genetics International Corp. (CGI), 175
Cummins Engine Corporation, 68
Cytogen Corp., 179

Dateq Information Network, Inc., 220
Davis, Tommy, 105
Debugging, 116
Defense Software & Systems, 170
DEJ Factor Test, 76-80
   DEJ, definition of, 76
   existence of competent sellers (DEJ 4), 78
   existence of qualified buyers (DEJ 1), 78
   "Hey, it really works!" (DEJ 6), 79
   homogeneity of buyers (DEJ 2), 78
   invisibility of new company (DEJ 7), 79
   lack of institutional barriers to entry (DEJ 5), 78-79
   large number of buyers (DEJ 3), 78
   Majority DEJs, 77
   optimum cost/price relationship (DEJ 8), 79
   Super DEJs, 76-77
   "unlikely" ventures, 77
DEP (Demonstrable Economic Proposition) Factor, finding, 122-4
Digital Equipment Corporation, 68, 171-72
Digivision, 209
Directory of Strategic Partners, 141-249
Discovery Toys, 83
Dow Chemical Company, 173-74
Dow Jones, 3
Downside planning, 109
Dun & Bradstreet, 3
Dura Pharmceuticals, Inc., 241

Ecogen, 164, 173, 179-80, 191, 199, 229, 239
Eidak Corporation, 242
E. I. du Pont de Nemours and Company, 175
Eiken Chemical Company, Ltd., 176
Eisai Company, 177
Electric LightWave, 74
Electronics for Imaging, Inc. (EFI), 142
Eli Lilly and Company, 3, 51, 121, 178-81
EMC Corporation, 245
Endosonics Corporation, 182

Index   **253**

Entrepreneurs:
  characteristics of, 16-21
  emotional background, effects of, 21-25
  personal guilt, 25-27
  problem-solving approach, 29-34
  and security, 63
  and spouses, 28-29
Esaote Biomedica S.p.A., 182
Esprit, 100
EST, 100
Evelyn Wood Reading Dynamics, 100
Excel Industries, 35, 183
Exit stage, 58
Express Scripts, Inc., 34-35
Exxon Corporation, 67-68

Facilities management, 81, 82, 108
FAI Insurances Limited, 224
Failing, Bruce, 100-101
Farley, Peter, 105
Faroudja Research Enterprises, 242
Federal Express, 68, 71, 104, 123, 126-27
Fees collected, as revenue, 112
Financial investors:
  questions of, 103-6
  raison d'etre, 105-6
First National Bank of Chicago, 71
Fixed costs, components of, 114-15
Fleet Call, 207
Ford Motor Company, 31, 35, 183
4th Dimension Software Ltd., 188
Franchise on OPA (other people's money), 100-101, 108
Franchising, 81, 82-83, 108
Franklin Mint, 93
Frist, Dr. Thomas F. Sr., 91-92

Galey & Lord, Inc., 162
Gatekeepers, 126-27, 129
Gates, Bill, 77, 97
Genentech, Inc., 31, 91, 184-86
General Dynamics Corporation, 104-5, 126-27
General Motors Corporation, 187-88
Gene Shears Pty. Ltd., 201
Genetic Therapy, Inc. (GTI), 231
Geneva Pharmaceuticals, Inc., 6
Gensia Pharmaceuticals, 205-6, 231-32
Gilder, George, 47-48
Gilread, 190-91
Glaxo Holdings, p.l.c., 15, 189-90

Glycomed, Inc., 178, 184-85
Goren, Charles, 85-86
Gould, Jay, 24
Growth stage strategic alliances, 57-58
Guilt, of entrepreneurs, 25-27
Gujarat State Fertilizers Company Ltd., 191

Hankuk Glass Industries, 4
Harry & David, 93
Heinze, Walter, 97-98
Hewlett-Packard, 104
High-technology start-up, 89-91, 108
Highway tollgate SDM, 96-98
Hoffman-LaRoche, Inc., 3, 192
Home marketing, *See* Party plan SDM
Honda Motor Company, 124-25
Hormel & Company, 193
Hospital Corp. of America, 91-92
Hewlett-Packard, 104
Hwang, K. Philip, 37-38
Hybritech, 68

IBM Corporation, 1-2, 97, 194-95
IDEXX Laboratories, Inc., 212
ImClone Systems, Inc., 143, 210-11
Immulogic Pharmaceutical Corporation, 204
Immune Response Corporation (IRC), 228
Incyte Pharaceuticals, 185-86
Information Partners, L.P., 3
Information prototypes, 115
Intel Corporation, 68, 105, 196
Interactive Images, Inc., 1
International Water Savings Systems, Inc. (IWSS), 97-98
Intromed, 169
ISG Technologies Inc. (ISG), 223
ISIS Pharmaceuticals, 165, 177, 227
ITEK, 73-74

Japan Steel Works, Ltd., 4, 197-98
Jeffrey Norton Publishers, Inc., 93
Jia Non Enterprise Company Ltd., 199
Jobs, Steve, 18-19, 38-40
Johnson & Johnson, 200
Johnson, David M., 84-85
J.R. Simplot Corporation, 46-48

Kelly, Tom, 24
Klein, Raphael, 41-42

Kroc, Raymond A., 42-43, 48
Kubota Corporation, 201
Kurtzig, Sandra, 43-44

Launch plan, 106-19
  beta tests, 115-16
  corporate achiever, hiring, 117-18
  debugging/modifications, 116
  formulating, 107
  PERT chart, creating, 108-9
  problem solution, developing, 107-8
  production system, putting into operation, 117
  prototype, creating/protecting, 115
  roll-out, 118-19
  SDM, selecting, 108
  strategic partner, raising capital from, 118
Leveraging, 64-66, 129-30
Licensing, 55-57, 61
Licensing agreement, sample of, 137-39
Liposome Technology, Inc. (LTI), 185
Litton Industries, 202-3
Lucasfilms, Inc., 44-46
Lucas, George, 44-46
Luther Medical Products, Inc., 225

McCaw Cellular Communications, Inc., 91, 123-24, 145-46
McCaw, Craig, 123-24
McDonald's, 42-43, 48
Majority DEJs, 77
Marcam Corporation, 195
Marion Merrell Dow, Inc. (MMD), 204-5
Marketing-oriented strategic alliances, 51 57
Markulla, Mike, 105
Marsam Pharmaceuticals, Inc., 5-6, 165-66
Mary Kay Cosmetics, 83, 100
Masco Industries, 82
Masco Industries, Inc., 206
Matsushita Communications Industrial, Ltd., 207
Maxicare, 100
MCI Telecommunications, 31-32
MedRad Inc., 208
Medtronics, 209
Merck & Co., Inc., 3, 210-11
Merrill Lynch & Co., Inc., 212
Meter income, as revenue, 112
Metricom, 213, 236
Microsoft Corporation, 68, 77, 97
Microtest, Inc., 196

Millimeter Wave Technology (MWT), 170
Mitsui & Company, Ltd., 213
Modified business plan, 116
Monsanto Company, 3, 60, 214
Morgan, J. Pierpont, 24
Motorola, Inc., 38-40, 215-16
Multiple strategic alliances, 3-4
Mycogen, 201, 214

National Vision Associates, Ltd., 248
Neditch, Jean, 77
Nestle S.A., 217
Network Computing Devices, Inc., 216
Net Worth, Inc., 241
Newsletter/seminar launch, 98-100, 108
New York Times, The, 31
Nippon Steel U.S.A., Inc., 89-90, 218
Norsk Hydro, A.S., 219
North American Biologicals, 142

OMNI Insurance Co., 220
ONO Pharmaceutical Company, Ltd., 221
Opta Food Ingredients, Inc. (OPTA), 222
Organo-genesis, Inc., 180

Park, Roy C., 86-89
Party plan SDM, 83-84, 108
Patents, 115
Paulucci, Gino, 24
Peripheral sales, as revenue, 112
PERT chart, 108-9
Pfizer, 222
Philips Electronics N.V., 60
Phillips Medical Systems Nederland B.V., 223
Photronics, Inc., 89, 247
Pinnacle Publishing, 84-85
Policy Management Systems Corporation, 195, 224
Polo Ralph Lauren, 57
Polycon, 173-74
Positioning your company, 7-8
Prepaid subscription method, 92-92, 108
Price Company, 77, 93
Price, Sol, 77, 93
Pritikin, Nathan, 86
Procordia, 225
Procter & Gamble Company, 226
Production-oriented strategic alliances, 34-51
Product prototypes, 115

Index

Program evaluation and research tool, *See* PERT chart
Protein Design Labs, Inc. (PDL), 192
Protein Polymer Technologies, Inc. (PPT), 238
Prototype, creating/protecting, 115

Regeneron Pharmaceuticals, Inc., 151
Renovators Supply, 100
Rentals, as revenue, 109
Research and development stage, 15-34
Research Frontiers, Inc., 3-4, 197-98, 202-3
Revenue, components of, 109-13
Revson, Charles, 24
Rhone-Poulenc Rorer Inc., 227-28
Risk aversion, 105-106
Rock, Arthur, 105
Roll-out, 118-19
Ross Systems, Inc., 171
Rouse Co., 32
Roussel UCLAF, 229
Royalties, as revenue, 112

Sales, as revenue, 109
Sales and merchandising plan, 110-12
Sandoz Pharmaceuticals, Ltd., 230-31
Sapiens International Corporation N.V., 1-2, 194-95
Satellite Technology, 167
Schiff, Jacob H., 24
Schoen, Dr. Leonard, 105
SciMed, 232
SDMs, *See* Solution Delivery Methods (SDMs)
Sears, Roebuck & Co., 35, 68
Security, and entrepreneurs, 63
Service income, as revenue, 112
Service industry, 99-100
Service prototypes, 115
Shaklee Corporation, 83, 100
Shaman Pharmaceuticals, Inc., 180-81
Showscan, 235
Simplot, Jack R., 46-48
Simtek Corporation, 89-90, 218
Smith, Frederick W., 104, 126
Smith-Kline Beecham (SKB), 233-34
Solution Delivery Methods (SDMs), 80-101
  capital equipment, 93-96
  celebrity-endorsed consumer products, 85-89
  consumer products start-up, 84-85

Cookie Cutter SDM, 91-92
facilities management, 81, 82
franchise on OPA, 100-101
franchising, 81, 82-83
high-technology start-up, 89-91
highway tollgate, 96-98
newsletter/seminar launch, 98-100
party plan, 83-84
prepaid subscription method, 92-92
selecting, 108
Sony Corporation, 235
Southern California Edison (SCE), 236
Spectranetics, 209
Spirit of Enterprise, The (Gilder), 47-48
SPS Transaction Services, Inc., 35
Start-up, stages of, 14
Stata, Raymond, 57-58
Stone, W. Clement, 22-23
StrataCom, Inc., 171-72, 215-16
Strategic partnering:
  DEJ Factor Test, 76-80
  elements of, 13-58
    cooperation, 13-14
    exit stage, 58
    growth stage, 57-58
    marketing stage, 51-57
    points of alliance, 14-15
    production stage, 34-51
    research and development stage, 15-34
  reasons for, 6-7
  Solution Delivery Methods (SDMs), 80-101
Strategic partners:
  closing, 121-39
  financial investors compared to, 2
  multiple, 3-4
Sumitomo Corporation, 237
Super Clubs, 60
Super DEJs, 76-77
Swanson, Robert A., 48-51
Synaptic Pharmaceutical Corp., 181
Syntro Corporation, 238
Systemix, Inc., 231

Tanabe Seiyaku Co., Ltd., 240
Tandem Computers Inc., 241
T-Cell Sciences, 233
Tele-Communications, Inc., 242-43
Teledyne, 68
Telios Pharmaceuticals, Inc., 187, 220, 222
Thermo Electron Corporation, 35-36
Third-party endorsements, 131-32

3A S.R.L. Parco Technologies Agroalinentare, 239
Time Corporation, 100
Tollgates, 108, 126-27
Transart Industries, 83
Transitions Research Corporation (TRC), 246
Tribune Company, 3, 81, 244
Triconex, 150
Trimas Corporation, 82, 206
Tupperware Division of Dart-Kraft, 83
Turner, Robert Edward (Ted), 94-96

U-Haul Systems, 105
Unilab Corporation, 168
Unisys, 245
U.S. Copyright Office, 115
United States Filter Corporation, 193
U.S. Patent Office, 115
United States Postmaster General, 246
Univax Biologics, Inc., 144, 186
Universe of selling sites, 78

Valence Technology, Inc., 187-88
Valentine, Don, 105

Variable costs, components of, 113-14
Venture Capital Clubs, 99
Venture capitalists:
  corporations as, 59-74
  exit strategies, 9-11
Venture capital return, 8-11
Virgin Airlines, 52
VISX, Inc., 217
VLSI Technology, Inc., 247

Wal-Mart Stores, Inc., 91, 248
Weight Watchers International, 77, 100
Wilson, Kemmons H., 21-22
Wollum, Owen, 84
Wozniak, Steven, 38-40

Xicor, 41-42

Yamaha Corporation of America, 249

Zenith Data Systems, 194
Zynaxis, Inc., 234

About the Author

A. David Silver is president of ADS Financial Services, Inc., a Santa Fe, New Mexico–based investment banking and venture capital firm. Dubbed "the high priest of entrepreneurship" by *USA Today*, he has raised more venture capital for more entrepreneurs since 1970 than any other venture capitalist in the U.S.: *over $300 million for more than 175 corporations and individuals*. Mr. Silver has also served as an advisor to the U.S. Congress Committee on Technology and Innovation. He is the author of more than 20 books on entrepreneurship and venture capital, including *The Entrepreneurial Life, Venture Capital, Upfront Financing*, and *The Turnaround Survival Guide*.